College Belonging

Critical Issues in American Education

Lisa M. Nunn, Series Editor

Taking advantage of sociology's position as a leader in the social scientific study of education, this series is home to new empirical and applied bodies of work that combine social analysis, cultural critique, and historical perspectives across disciplinary lines and the usual methodological boundaries. Books in the series aim for topical and theoretical breadth. Anchored in sociological analysis, Critical Issues in American Education features carefully crafted empirical work that takes up the most pressing educational issues of our time, including federal education policy, gender and racial disparities in student achievement, access to higher education, labor market outcomes, teacher quality, and decision making within institutions.

Judson G. Everitt, *Lesson Plans: The Institutional Demands of Becoming a Teacher*

Megan M. Holland, *Divergent Paths to College: Race, Class, and Inequality in High Schools*

Laura Nichols, *The Journey before Us: First-Generation Pathways from Middle School to College*

Lisa M. Nunn, *College Belonging: How First-Year and First-Generation Students Navigate Campus Life*

Daisy Verduzco Reyes, *Learning to Be Latino: How Colleges Shape Identity Politics*

College Belonging

How First-Year and First-Generation
Students Navigate Campus Life

LISA M. NUNN

Rutgers University Press

New Brunswick, Camden, and Newark, New Jersey, and London

Library of Congress Cataloging-in-Publication Data

Names: Nunn, Lisa M., 1975—author.
Title: College belonging: how first-year and first-generation students navigate campus life /
    Lisa M. Nunn.
Description: New Brunswick, New Jersey: Rutgers University Press, 2021. | Series: Critical issues
    in American education | Includes bibliographical references and index.
Identifiers: LCCN 2020019284 | ISBN 9781978807655 (paperback) | ISBN 9781978807662
    (cloth) | ISBN 9781978807679 (epub) | ISBN 9781978809529 (mobi) | ISBN
    9781978809536 (pdf)
Subjects: LCSH: College freshmen—United States. | First-generation college students—United
    States. | Belonging (Social psychology) | College environment—United States. | College
    student orientation—United States. | Teacher-student relationships—United States.
Classification: LCC LB2343.32 .N863 2021 | DDC 378.1/98—dc23
LC record available at https://lccn.loc.gov/2020019284

A British Cataloging-in-Publication record for this book is available from the British Library.

www.rutgersuniversitypress.org

Manufactured in the United States of America

For Melissa, Manejé, Chlóe, Anne Marie, Aleta, Colleen, Amy, Josh, Josset, Laurelle, Tony, and Thomas, whose friendships were foundational cornerstones of belonging in my life as a young person.

Contents

College Belonging

Introduction

• • • • • • • • • • • • • • • • • • • •

In my interviews with college students, I ask them if their campus is a place where they feel like they belong. I then ask, "What does it mean to belong?"

> It just feels like home. You feel comfortable here. No judgment. That is what it means to belong. You feel safe, you feel comfortable, you just feel, "I belong here."
>
> Valentina, first-generation student, Public University[1]

> Just to have your place, to have like-minded people who share the ambitions or share the same goals, maybe share the mindset as you do. And just to have a support system if ever stuff goes awry.
>
> Cristian, continuing-generation student, Private University

> To me it means to be part of the community. Contributing to the community and giving it back and also gaining something from it, like a mutual relationship.
>
> Ling, first-generation student, Public University

> If I felt like I belonged, I would feel like this was meant to be and this was my right place. I was supposed to be here.
>
> Armanda, continuing-generation student, Public University

1

These quotes capture the most common sentiments that students in this study express. I often heard that belonging meant to feel "at home" or "comfortable"; that they were "meant to be there" or had "found their place"; that they felt "safe," "welcome," "happy," and free to "truly be yourself." Their responses are similar to what Annemarie Vaccaro and Barbara Newman (2016) found when they asked college students to define belonging.[2] Some students such as Cristian and Ling emphasize the community aspects of belonging. Students' descriptions of community tend to focus on not feeling "judged," not having to "worry" about what others think or say about them, and a sense that members of the community are "working together to make each other better," as Julianne, a continuing-generation student at Private University articulates it.

Belonging is positive. It provides a sense of security, which engenders emotional well-being. Often, research conceptualizes sense of belonging at college as students being "integrated" academically and socially into the campus community; that is, they are "connected" through their relationships with others, including participation in student organizations, teams, academic clubs, support programs, resource centers, and the like (Tinto 1993; Strayhorn 2012; Chambliss and Takacs 2014). Although scholarship has taken wide and varied approaches to measuring those connections and their effects on belonging, researchers like myself find it valuable to allow students themselves to define what belonging means to them and to describe their personal experiences at college that are part of their sense of whether they feel like they belong on their campuses (see also Chambliss and Takacs 2014; Vaccaro and Newman 2016; Means and Pyne 2017; Silver 2020).

Students describe belonging as a sense of feeling accepted for who they are and feeling valued by the larger community. They explain that belonging brings a kind of confidence, the liberty to let their guard down, to not feel self-conscious or worry about being judged. This in turn offers them the freedom to explore and thrive because they are unencumbered by doubt and insecurities about whether they are wanted. They describe belonging as feeling "comfortable" and "at home."

Research on Belonging

A sense of belonging is not mandatory for students to be successful. Indeed, some students in my study do not feel that they belong to their campus community, such as Armanda who was quoted in the opening of this chapter—but they are determined to stick it out, graduate college, and move on with their lives. However, existing research shows that feeling a sense of belonging has a positive impact on academic achievement and persistence (Freeman, Anderman, and Jensen 2007; Hausmann, Schofield, and Woods 2007; Zumbrunn et al. 2014). Whether it is called integration or engagement or belongingness, we know that students perform better if they have it (Levett-Jones and Lathlean 2008; Tinto 2012; Quaye and Harper 2015; McCabe 2016). Equally important, students *feel* better when they have it (Pittman and Richmond 2008; Van Ryzin, Gravely, and Roseth 2009; Stuber 2011; Strayhorn 2012; Chambliss and Takacs 2014). In that way, belonging is akin to what social psychologists call "mattering" (Schlossberg 1989; Elliott, Kao, and Grant 2004; Rayle and Chung 2007). This means that even if we only care about having high persistence and graduation rates, we should also care about student belonging. And if we care about student well-being in addition to graduation rates, then we absolutely need to care about belonging (Pascarella and Terenzini 2005; Kuh et al. 2010; Museus, Yi, and Saelua 2017).

In this book I argue that if we care about educational equity for first-generation college students, which means greater social and economic equity for our entire nation (Nunn 2019b), then we need to care about their sense of belonging. As Anthony Jack (2019, 189) articulates it,

> Too often we think about those youth who make it out of distressed communities and into college—especially elite colleges—as having already won. These young people, we assume, hold a golden ticket ... but graduation rates do not tell us of students' experiences in college, their trials or their triumphs. After all, it is one thing for students to graduate. It is another for them to do so whole and healthy, ready for whatever the next adventure brings.

This book offers insights into how belonging happens differently for different groups of college students and how universities seem to operate with a limited understanding of how belonging is created, which leads to programs and policies that have limited effectiveness for first-generation students and students of color who are in the minority on their campuses.

Belonging is not just important for college students but also is fundamental in all of our lives. Terrell Strayhorn (2012, 1) draws on Abraham Maslow's hierarchy of needs to remind us that "belongingness is a basic human motivation and all people share a strong need to belong." Strayhorn articulates a definition of belonging as it pertains to student life on college campuses: "sense of belonging refers to perceived social support on campus, a feeling or sensation of connectedness, the experience of mattering or feeling cared about, accepted, respected, valued by and important to the group (e.g. campus community) or others on campus (e.g. faculty, peers)" (3). He goes on to emphasize that sense of belonging happens through relationships that are mutual and reciprocal. Members benefit from being connected to the group, and the group benefits from the connection of each member. The quotes at the beginning of the chapter from the students in the two universities in my research study demonstrate that their everyday thinking about belonging centers on those same definitions.

Comparative Research Design: Public University and Private University

This book takes up the question of how students experience belonging at college through a comparative study of students' experiences at two very different types of residential four-year universities, which I call "Public University" and "Private University."[3] Public is a large, "most selective" institution, the highest classification in *U.S. News and World Report*'s five categories of selectivity. Private is a medium-sized, "more selective" institution (*U.S. News and World Report*'s second-highest category) with a religious affiliation. Both universities are located in California, and neither has a reputation as a party school. I systematically compare first-generation college students and continuing-generation college students within each campus context.[4] Definitions of who counts as a first-generation student vary (Toutkoushian, May-Trifiletti, and Clayton 2019). Some scholars and institutions limit the definition of first-generation to students whose parents have never attended college, whereas while others limit it to students whose parents have not completed a degree of any kind in higher education.[5] In my study, like many others that similarly focus on student's experiences on campus, I use a third definition of first-generation students: neither parent has earned a four-year degree. Thirty-five randomly selected first-generation college students (15 from Private and 20 from Public) and thirty-two randomly selected continuing-generation students (21 from Private and 11 from Public) participated, for a total of 67 participants. All participants were incoming first-year students in the fall of 2015. I followed them over their first two years of college, collecting data through one-on-one in-depth interviews at three points in time: near the start of their first term in college, near the end of their first year, and near the end of their second year in 2017. Fifty-six of the original sixty-seven participants remained in the study for the third and final round of interviews. A total of 186 interviews were conducted (see the "Methodological Appendix" for more details).

Throughout the study I paid close attention to race and generational status. In each of the three interviews I asked students to describe their ethnoracial identities in their own words, and throughout this book I allow space for those self-descriptions to stand on their own. I value the creative and complicated ways that students announced their heritage and identity and, as I wrote this book, could not bring myself to reduce them to categories we typically see on official forms. I agree with other scholars who argue that we risk misunderstanding individuals' ethnoracial identities when we do that (Johnston et al. 2014; Johnston-Guerrero and Renn 2016). Students' rich and nuanced identity descriptions help us better understand their college experiences, especially regarding racial dynamics. In the interviews, many White students fumbled awkwardly over how to articulate their racial identity. As a White person myself, I could reassure them that it was okay to name their Whiteness. For others, I could only listen appreciatively and honor their self-descriptions.

First-Generation College Students

First-generation students have been getting a lot of attention in recent years (Wildhagen 2015; Beattie 2018), and rightly so. Understanding first-generation students' experiences is important both because they have rapidly become the majority of students enrolled in higher education (Ward, Siegel, and Davenport 2012) and because they represent the promise of upward mobility in the United States through educational equity (Nunn 2019b). Although first-generation students participate in higher education in strong numbers, they attend highly selective colleges at one-third the rate of continuing-generation students (Redford and Hoyer 2017). They also have lower GPAs, persistence rates, and graduation rates in college (Araugo and Anastasiou 2009; Martinez et al. 2009; Soria and Stebleton 2012; Furquim et al. 2017). This is partly because many first-generation students' high school academic experiences underprepared them for the rigors of college curriculum, but certainly not all first-generation students had this experience (Hand and Payne 2008; Reid and Moore 2008; Duncheon 2018a).

First-generation students bring many strengths with them. They are eager learners, independent, resourceful, and highly motivated to succeed (Lundberg et al. 2007; Davis 2010; Azmitia et al. 2018; Duncheon 2018b). They are determined to make their families proud (Oldfield 2009; Clark 2017). Yet they face a host of obstacles in college, which makes both success (Collier and Morgan 2008; Bryan and Simmons 2009; Stuber 2011; DeRosa and Dolby 2014; A. Yee 2016), and belonging harder to come by (Stebleton, Soria, and Huesman 2014). Scholars like myself look for ways to understand first-generation students' experiences so that institutions of higher education can make transformational changes to better serve them and, by so doing, make higher education more democratic and equitable (Lundberg et al. 2007; Davis 2010; Jehangir 2010; Ward, Siegel, and Davenport 2012; Silver and Roksa 2017).

Universities' Limited Understanding of Belonging

The existing wisdom about sense of belonging on college campuses tends to neglect an important dynamic. Emile Durkheim (1858–1917), a foundational thinker in the discipline of sociology, gave us an understanding of how communities work that allows us to see belonging in a fundamentally sociological way: *belonging is something that communities provide for individuals; it is not something that individuals can garner for themselves.*

This insight about the nature of belonging is embedded in Durkheim's larger theory about social life. According to Durkheim, a healthy society both integrates its members and regulates its members. Integration and regulation are two interrelated dynamics. He writes about these dynamics in multiple ways in various works over his career (see Marks 1974; Besnard 1993; Acevedo 2005; see "Theoretical Appendix: Durkheim and Belonging" for an in-depth discussion of Durkheim's writings in connection to belonging).

First, regarding integration, a healthy society ensures that individuals feel that they are a part of the society, that they are emotionally and functionally connected to the larger community. Durkheim calls this "integration" in some places ([1897] 1951) and "attachment to social groups" in others ([1925] 1973). He explains that "when belonging to a group they love" individuals are able to transcend their "private interests"; they feel like they are part of something larger than themselves, a community whose "interests they put above their own" ([1897] 1951, 209–210). He theorizes that we benefit from prioritizing the well-being of our community over ourselves because doing so gives meaning and purpose to our lives. If our community does not integrate us, we feel alone, and we despair: "it is society that we consider the most important part of ourselves" ([1925] 1973, 71).

Durkheim's conception of social bonds is key to understanding the second feature of a healthy society: regulation. For Durkheim, social bonds are constructed out of shared norms and values. To be a member of a particular society means to believe in that society's shared moral code, to be willing to behave in accordance with that code and also to hold others accountable to it. That is, society must "regulate" its members ([1897] 1951) or, as he calls it elsewhere, instill "the spirit of discipline" in members ([1925] 1973). Shared beliefs and behaviors comprise the social bonds that bind members to the collective group, and those bonds are created and maintained through social interaction.

The importance of the idea that society performs the function of regulation cannot be overemphasized. Durkheim sees regulation as impossible for individuals to accomplish on their own: "Men would never consent to restrict their desires . . . they cannot assign themselves this law of justice. So they must receive it from an authority which they respect, to which they yield spontaneously . . . society alone can play this moderating role; for it is the only moral power superior to the individual, the authority of which he accepts" ([1897] 1951, 249).

Thus, society teaches us what is appropriate to aspire to in our lives through regulation, and society binds us to each other and to the group with social bonds that integrate us. We can do neither of these things for ourselves. This brings us to a decidedly sociological understanding of what a sense of belonging is and where it comes from. Durkheim's theory offers the insight that the feelings of belonging and attachment that we experience are due to a larger group's effect on us. Society (or community) is an entity that inspires feelings in each of us; it is an entity that motivates our behaviors, that teaches us what to value, and that shows us our place within the group. It comprises the individuals who are members, but in its collectivity, it takes on its own character as well. Durkheim explains, "Certainly society is greater than, and goes beyond, us, for it is infinitely more vast than our individual being; but at the same time it enters into every part of us. It is outside and envelops us but it is also in us and is everywhere an aspect of our nature. We are fused with it" ([1925] 1973, 71).

Clearly then, feelings of belonging are not forged by our own hand. Instead they are bestowed on us by the group itself. One person cannot simply decide that she is a member of a society or a social group—the group must extend such membership to her. The group must integrate and regulate her, which inspires a feeling of acceptance in her, a sense that she is valued and wanted, a sense that she belongs. Belonging must be given. It is a gift and only exists when a group collectively offers it to a member. Of course, a group can withhold belonging from an individual just as a group can make an individual feel accepted and valued in some moments or circumstances and unwanted in others. It is possible to experience partial belonging or no belonging at all. No matter how much we desire it or chase it down, it is not up to us whether we obtain it. It is up to the community.

We would do well to take this Durkheimian insight as a guiding principle. If universities want to generate a sense of belonging among their students, they must take institutional responsibility for integration and regulation at the community level. Currently, this is precisely where colleges are coming up short.

Sense of Belonging at College

Sociologists who study students' experiences in college emphasize the importance of belonging (Jack 2016; McCabe 2016; Warikoo 2016; Reyes 2018), yet many do not theorize belonging or operationalize it. Most of the current scholarship on college students' sense of belonging that theorizes, measures, or operationalizes it comes from education studies, psychology, and social psychology, each of which offers important definitions and explanations of how belonging works and how it affects students' experiences, including academic success, persistence, and graduation (Ostrove and Long 2007; Pittman and Richmond 2008; Langhout, Drake, and Rosselli 2009; Morrow and Ackermann 2012). Much of this scholarship does not focus on the community-level responsibility of universities, yet some who study retention do take such an approach, often explicitly drawing on Durkheim (Spady 1970; Pascarella, Terenzini, and Wolfle 1986; Chambliss and Takacs 2014; Kerby 2015). One highly influential researcher is Vincent Tinto (1975, 1993, 1997, 2012). In his 1993 book *Leaving College*, Tinto emphasizes the importance of institutional action: "if there is a secret to successful reten-tion, it lies in the willingness of institutions to involve themselves in the social and intellectual development of their students" (6). Tinto's call to action focuses on Durkheim's theory that lack of integration leaves individ-uals feeling adrift, isolated, and unanchored to the community. This moti-vates them to abandon the community altogether by transferring schools or dropping out.

Tinto pays attention to Durkheim's sociological premise (as did Spady [1970] before him) that, fundamentally, the mal-integration of individuals into the fabric of social life is the fault of the larger community, not the indi-viduals themselves; thus, it is the responsibility of the university as a whole to connect each member to the institution in meaningful ways. The solutions that come out of this premise are good ones. Socially oriented solutions create opportunities and spaces for students to connect with one another in smaller groups that provide them a sense of community and make them feel valued and part of the university's cultural life more broadly; these opportunities let students find their "niche" (Brower 1992). Academically focused solutions create structures that foster relationships between students and faculty (Halawah 2006; Vetter, Schreiner, and Jaworski 2019) and pro-vide opportunities for students to work on academic projects together and resources that foster academic success (Means and Pyne 2017). Other schol-ars have pointed out the limitations of these approaches (see Museus et al. 2017 for a review). What I offer in this book are nuanced, qualitative data that demonstrate how these solutions are incomplete in meeting the belong-ing needs of first-generation college students and minority students of color.

What Is Missing?

What Tinto and others are missing is the importance of feeling that one belongs to the wider campus community beyond the smaller groups that one joins and the academic integration one experiences. Students in my study, such as Brandon, illustrate this dynamic. Brandon is a first-generation stu-dent at Private who ethnoracially identifies as "African American for sure." He told me, "I did not like it in the beginning because it was just so differ-ent from what I'm used to. I knew I belonged in certain communities. I can belong at Associated Black Students. I can belong in my soccer club. I can belong at work, and at the sports center. I can belong at Student Support

Resources." Yet, Brandon was hesitant to say that he belonged at Private more generally. He said, "It's a weird way. Yeah. Even though the community is totally different."

My study is not the first to identify the more complicated belonging experiences of first-generation and ethnoracial-minority students, particularly those who attend predominately White campuses (Hurtado and Carter 1997; Nuñez 2009; Stuber 2011; Walton and Cohen 2011; Padgett, Johnson, and Pascarella 2012; Harper 2013; DeRosa and Dolby 2014; Vaccaro and Newman 2016). However my study does offer new insights that expand our understanding of belonging, allowing us to envision more complex strategies for fostering it for our students. By allowing students to define belonging on their own and also to talk open-endedly about their academic and social experiences, my study reveals that belonging happens in multiple realms for college students.

In their interviews with me, students describe social belonging as distinct from academic belonging and I find that neither of those realms is a substitute for campus-community belonging, which they describe as a third arena of belonging. Grayson, a continuing-generation student at Private, who ethnoracially identifies as "Latino and White,"[6] illustrates this well when I ask him what it means to belong. He responds, "Being comfortable in different settings around campus. Being comfortable in my classes, feeling like the difficulty is the right level for me. And that my peers aren't outsmarting me in every area and I'm falling behind or something like that. And also having a group of friends who is accepting of you, how you are, and enjoys hanging out with you genuinely." Grayson thus gives back-to-back responses that cover all three realms of belonging. He starts with campus community belonging: "being comfortable in different settings around campus." Next he articulates academic belonging: feeling competent and "comfortable in my classes." Third comes social belonging: an "accepting" friend group that "enjoys hanging out with you genuinely."

My data reveal how striking the differences are among the three realms. As table 1 shows, students do not experience them equally. The data in table 1 come from the students' first interview with me, near the start of their college experience. As the rest of this book demonstrates, belonging shifts over time according to students' experiences, so these percentages move up and down across the three interviews. Additionally, first-generation students and continuing-generation students have different belonging opportunities and obstacles to navigate.

Table 1
Percentage of Students Who Experience Belonging in Each Realm at First Interview

	N	Campus-Community Belonging	Social Belonging	Academic Belonging
Interview 1				
Public	31	45.7%	41.9%	29.0%
Private	36	75.0%	58.3%	61.1%

Existing scholarship does not distinguish these three realms of belonging clearly or consistently, and this oversight has led to misguided efforts to foster belonging for students. No matter how well we do as a university in linking students to resource centers, student organizations, sports teams, academic clubs, friendships, academic mentorships, and so on, we cannot count ourselves successful until we are also offering the gift of belonging to our students at the campus-community level at the same time. Of course, this is a much more difficult task than creating a space or program in which particular students where can feel supported, valued, and "at home." It requires shifts in the broader campus culture.

This book explains how first-generation and students of color have distinct experiences navigating campus life in their first year and distinct belonging experiences compared to continuing-generation and ethnoracial-majority students. Our efforts to help students develop a sense of belonging can be effective, but my study reveals two problems. First, existing organizational programs and structures put the onus of responsibility on students for finding organizations and spaces where they feel comfortable and happy. Certainly, universities do the work of providing programming and campus structures to facilitate both safe spaces and opportunities for students to get involved; however, they ultimately view it as the task of the individual student to "get out there" and cultivate her own sense of belonging. That is fundamentally at odds with a Durkheimian understanding of how belonging works. The insights from Durkheim that I outline here allow us to identify this important blind spot in our approach to fostering student belonging. As I demonstrate in chapter 1, the current approach is a reasonable and effective one for helping continuing-generation and ethnoracial-majority students become attached to the campus community. However, it leaves first-generation and students of color to struggle and stumble as they search for groups that will extend belonging to them. It also leads students to believe that, if they fail to find a club or organization or friendship circle where they are offered belonging, that failure is their own fault.

The second problem my study reveals with our current approach to fostering student belonging is that there are limitations when one's belonging needs are only met by small, subcommunities on campus. The experiences of first-generation and minority students of color in my study, like Brandon, illustrate how students can feel out of place as they navigate college life outside the pockets on campus where they feel "at home." As I describe students' experiences throughout this book, I draw on the extensive research on the cultural dynamics of higher education that helps us understand why continuing-generation and ethnoracial-majority students experience a greater sense of ease, acceptance, and comfort on college campuses. I discuss in greater detail in chapter 2 how their life experiences, family histories, and cultural sensibilities are reflected by the university (Bourdieu and Passeron 1977; Feagin, Vera, and Imani 1996; Stuber 2011; E. Yee 2016; Warikoo 2016; Byrd 2017; Jack 2019). It signals that the campus values people like them; it is a gesture from the community, at both the institutional and organizational levels, that they belong there. In contrast, first-generation students who are becoming acquainted with university norms and taken-for-granted expectations for the first time experience feelings of alienation instead (Davis 2010; Jehangir 2010; DeRosa and Dolby 2014). They feel out of place. Everything from the cafeteria food to the landscaping to office hours to syllabi requirements can feel new and foreign. For some in my study this discomfort fades over time, for some it never goes away, and for others it waxes and wanes in ways we might not predict.

My study reveals that understanding this second problem requires us to recognize that there are three distinct realms of belonging for students: academic belonging, social belonging, and campus-community belonging. Experiencing belonging in one of these realms does not directly translate to belonging in any other realm.

Universities Shape Belonging Opportunities

Applying Durkheim's theory requires us to hold a view of belonging that is centered on the community that offers it, while recognizing that multiple communities coexist in our lives and smaller communities can be nested within larger ones without necessarily being aligned with one another. To comprehensively understand college belonging, we need to look carefully not just at students' experiences but also at the organizational structures that shape those experiences.

Chapter 1 explains the differences between social belonging and campus-community belonging and how one does not directly translate to the other. I demonstrate that social belonging shifts over time, increasing for some and decreasing for others. My data show that Private has greater success than Public in offering social belonging and that continuing-generation students at Public have greater access to it; however, at neither Public nor Private do an overwhelming majority of students experience social belonging, be they first- or continuing-generation. I further discuss the limitations of a current practice that universities commonly use to foster belonging in first-year students: encouraging them to join student organizations and groups to "find their place." This strategy falls short of meeting the belonging needs of first-generation students because they do not have access to easy or automatic campus-community belonging the way many continuing-generation students do.

Chapter 2 explains how the organizational structures on each campus, such as first-year housing programs, curriculum policies, and the like, contribute to distinct campus cultures at each school while at the same time offering or withholding campus-community belonging to individual students. Public has a culture that prioritizes academics above all else, whereas Private's culture prioritizes relationships with other members of the campus community. These dynamics yield stronger rates of campus-community belonging at Private, including multiple instances where first-generation students have higher levels than continuing-generation students. The same cannot be said for Public.

Chapters 3 and 4 focus on academic belonging, an essential element of which is feeling academically competent in courses. Chapter 3 provides a detailed description of first-generation students to explain both why they face more academic challenges than continuing-generation students do and how their strengths such as resilience and self-reliance play out in both their academic success and belonging experiences. My data reveal that students at Public have dramatically lower rates of academic belonging at the start of college than do students at Private. Over time at Public, academic belonging improves abundantly for continuing-generation students and hardly at all for first-generation students. Chapter 4 demonstrates how the academic community—including faculty, TAs, fellow students, and athletic coaches—offers academic belonging. I highlight organizational structures that help explain the higher rates of academic belonging at Private. Students illustrate how validating it is for them when they receive academic belonging and how lost and alone they feel when it is withheld from them. Chapter 4 concludes by highlighting first-generation academic success stories at each school and discussing the complex nature of belonging, given students' complex identities and complex lives.

Chapters 5 and 6 focus on the ethnoracial dynamics of belonging. Chapter 5 discusses the tensions on campus around the small numbers of ethnoracial-minority students, tensions in cross-ethnoracial roommate relationships, and tensions related to the national political climate during the Black Lives Matter movement and the 2016 presidential campaign and election of Donald Trump. Further tensions exist on campus because ethnoracial-minority students are negatively perceived as self-segregating when they join student organizations that are connected to their ethnoracial identities. All of these tensions constrain campus-community belonging and social belonging for minority students.

Chapter 6 discusses ethnoracial-majority students' perceptions of diversity on their campuses. Drawing on Natasha Warikoo's "diversity frames" and Angelina Castagno's theory of "niceness" as fundamental to Whiteness, I argue that ethnoracial-majority students desire "nice diversity" on their campuses; that is, diversity in which everyone gets along harmoniously and brings interesting, positive elements to the greater community from their diverse backgrounds, but only in nonconfrontational ways that "gloss over" the injustices and inequities of today and the past. Minority students of color, meanwhile, desire diversity that is not so "nice."

I conclude the book with a list of nine suggestions in chapter 7, ways that universities can make targeted changes to improve how well they are meeting the belonging needs of our first-generation students, minority students of color, and first-year students across the board. Anchoring our understanding of student belonging to Durkheim's theory allows us to see belonging as an outcome of successful integration and regulation by the university. It is not up to our students to find it. It is up to us to give it.

1

Social Belonging versus Campus-Community Belonging

• • • • • • • • • • • • • • • • • • • •

Of the three realms of belonging, social belonging is perhaps the most straightforward to understand, particularly in terms of the Durkheimian insight that belonging is a gift that is offered by a community to individual members. If you feel like you belong in a social group such as a friendship circle or a soccer team or a hiking club, it is because the members of that group make you feel like you are a part of it. Belonging is a feeling that you matter to the group, that you are valued for who you are and what you bring. Katie sums it up well in her first semester when she describes her new college friends: "I love hanging out with them. I feel like they want me to hang out with them. Like I'm not just there. And it just makes me happier to know that I have friends that want me there, that make me feel like I belong." Katie is a continuing-generation student at Private who describes her ethnoracial identity as "I am Vietnamese, but if I were to describe myself, I would say Asian American." For the most part, Katie is poised and a bit formal in our interview, but when she starts talking about her college friends, she softens, and her eyes light up. She unmistakably experiences social belonging: she feels wanted.

Like Katie, students at both universities generally describe social belonging as finding friends whom they enjoy. Social belonging often includes participating in student organizations, sports teams, clubs, performance troupes, religious groups, and the like where students meet new people and strengthen friendships through shared experiences and shared interests. Dormitory life is also a common source of friendships for first-year students. Even students who do not get along well with their assigned roommates often find friends among their fellow floor-mates.

Immediate Social Belonging

Some students experience a sense of social belonging right away. Madison at Private is an example. She is a continuing-generation student who ethnoracially identifies as "White." In her first interview with me she is exuberant, her long blond hair tied stylishly over one shoulder, accenting the wide scoop neck of her t-shirt: "It's weird only being here for five weeks, but I do feel like I belong here and I know that I'll be here for the next four years. I can't see myself being anywhere else. I feel like part of the community." Madison was full of smiles as she elaborated:

> I just feel like going to class, you automatically are part of the community. Just meeting people in class and your professor and just walking around. Just friends and going to class . . . After classes we always go to Campus Café and get eggs afterward, and then do our homework there sometimes. We do that two or three times a week. We have been getting our nails done, shopping, going to the beach, going to the pool, studying, eating, like us all eat together, going to parties together.

Madison seems to have found friends quite effortlessly, including "just meeting people in class," which other students did not find easy to do. In her response in her first interview, she also includes all three realms of belonging as parts of a whole: friends, classes, and community. After "only being here for five weeks," she already experiences belonging in all three realms.

Joining student organizations or simply being open to building friendships in the dorm created strong social belonging for many students. Spencer offers a description of both. He is a continuing-generation student at Private who describes his ethnoracial identity as "I can't really identify as anything other than White." In our first interview, Spencer tells me, "I think for me the best thing about Private would be probably just the solidarity in the community. I think I've said it a lot, but just so far the fact that I honestly felt like these places are like home. Not just a temporary living space for students. I guess it's more in the organizations I've been a part of." Spencer is soft-spoken but not shy. His quiet voice and strong eye contact hold my attention as he thoughtfully tells me about his experiences. We are sitting in the breezy outdoors at a table near a campus coffee shop. He talks about the differences he sees between high school and college:

> I've found much more community here. I found that everything's so united. You live with the same people you consider your friends, so you don't have to worry so much about the social anxiety of who you go out with and all that kind of thing. It's just a very much more supportive community, I believe. There's thousands of student organizations where you can easily make friends. You don't have to be invited to go out as it was in high school. I think that most of the social barriers that create social classes just disappear in college.

In general, students at both schools sound a lot alike when they describe social belonging. Easton is a continuing-generation student at Public who identifies as "I would say White. My dad is fully Swedish. I call myself Western European." Social belonging was immediate for Easton, as it was for Madison over at Private. "I found my initial group of friends on Visiting Day," which is a day for accepted students to come to campus while they are still in high school. "The people that I met there were unbelievably friendly," he shares with me. Easton's voice and demeanor exude confidence, and so I was not surprised to hear that friendships come easily to him. Apparently he became fast friends that Visiting Day afternoon with a fellow prospective student who had also just been accepted. Easton laughs heartily as he describes the scene: "He brought a microphone with him, and there was a giant Jenga table with the bricks; he was just screaming, 'Friendship and Jenga!' I thought he was someone that was [already enrolled] here. But nope, it was one just like us."

The two of them were still close friends, along with other "Visiting Day buddies," as Easton calls them, when we had our third interview at the end of his second year. Easton is one of the 28.0 percent of Public students who had steady social belonging at all three interviews. He had also joined a fraternity, and he said he maintains his "two sets of friends" quite easily. He

Table 2
Percentage of Students Who Experience Social Belonging

	Public		Private	
	N	Social Belonging	*N*	Social Belonging
Interview 1				
All students	31	41.9%	36	58.3%
Continuing-gen	11	54.4%	21	52.4%
First-gen	20	35.0%	15	66.7%
Interview 2				
All students	29	48.3%	34	58.8%
Continuing-gen	10	60.0%	19	63.2%
First-gen	19	42.1%	15	53.3%
Interview 3				
All students	25	64.0%	31	61.3%
Continuing-gen	9	77.8%	18	61.1%
First-gen	16	56.3%	13	61.5%

explains, "Everyone coexists well together. I don't think there's much division between people at Public." In this regard, Easton sounds similar to Spencer at Private, who commented, "I think that most of the social barriers that create social classes just disappear in college."

At the same time, important differences exist between Public and Private, and differences also exist between continuing-generation and first-generation students at both schools. Students in my study, like Easton at Public, experience social belonging at a higher rate in their first semester than do first-generation students (see table 2). In contrast, at Private first-generation students claim it at a higher rate than do continuing-generation students. Despite that finding, I highlight three continuing-generation Private students here—Katie, Madison, and Spencer—because in their first interviews, continuing-generation students more commonly described their social belonging as occurring immediately and being complete, whereas first-generation students rarely experienced it that way.

Social Belonging Shifts over Time: At Private

Certainly not everyone has "automatic" access to social belonging, as Madison calls it. At Private 58.3 percent (21 of 36) of my sample describe experiencing social belonging in their first interview, near the start of their first semester.[1] Yet that means more than 40 percent experienced only partial social belonging or no social belonging early in their first semester.[2] Of course, belonging is not static. It is dynamic, just as communities themselves are dynamic. Belonging shifts over time for many students, waxing for some, waning for others, and for a few in my study it is a roller coaster of ups and downs.

Karla is a typical example of how social belonging can build slowly over time. She is a first-generation student who identifies ethnoracially as "I don't limit myself to one of my ethnicities. I'm Puerto Rican, African American and Ecuadorian. I'm very proud of all those." In her second interview with me at the end of her first year, she is sitting across from me, leaning comfortably back in her chair. Her long, dark curly hair is pulled back, and she is dressed simply but neatly in a t-shirt and flannel. She excitedly shares, "I just rushed to join a sorority. So now I'm a part of a sorority, so I feel like now I'm a part of the Private community for real now." Karla is not unusual in this way. I heard from multiple students at both Private and Public that joining Greek life offered a profound sense of social belonging by providing a large number of welcoming new friends and a never-ending stream of events to be a part of.

On many campuses, sororities and fraternities play a central role in the social scene, particularly at universities with a "party school" reputation (Armstrong and Hamilton 2013). Although the Greek system is often critiqued as solidifying socioeconomic class inequalities among students, scholarship also emphasizes the benefits of the social networks that students access through fraternities and sororities (Delgado-Guerrero, Cherniak, and Gloria 2014; Stuber 2015; Walker, Martin, and Hussey 2015; Thiele and Robinson 2019). It seems that, even at schools like the two in my study, which do not have "party school" reputations, Greek letter organizations are perceived as central to campus life.

Like others, Karla expressed a sense of relief that Greek life met her social belonging needs so easily. She said that, at Private, her sense of belonging, which she defined strictly as social belonging, was "iffy at first." Her voice seemed sincere; she did not cover her vulnerability with laughter or distracted fidgeting. When I asked what she had struggled with the most as she was adjusting to college during her first semester, she answered, "Finding where I belong." She continued, "Just figuring out that one group of people or those multiple groups of people that I really

Table 3
Social Belonging Shifts over Time

	N	Consistent Social Belonging	Improved Social Belonging	Consistent Partial Social Belonging	Declined Social Belonging	Consistent Absent Social Belonging	Up & Down Social Belonging
Public							
All students		28.0%	32.0%	8.0%	20.0%	4.0%	12.0%
Continuing-gen	9	44.4%	22.2%	11.1%	11.1%	0%	11.1%
First-gen	16	18.8%	37.5%	6.3%	25.0%	6.3%	12.5%
Private							
All students	31	45.2%	16.1%	16.1%	12.9%	0%	9.7%
Continuing-gen	18	50.0%	16.7%	11.1%	11.1%	0%	11.1%
First-gen	13	38.5%	15.4%	23.1%	15.4%	0%	7.7%

can be myself around and go to for things. Because for a long time it was just me and my best friend, the RA. It was just us and we'd go from group to group and be like, 'Okay, we've found our place.' And then we'd be like, 'Oh wait, we don't really like these people. You don't want to hang around these people!'"

At Private, 61.3 percent (19 of 31) of students experienced social belonging at their third interview at the end of their second year, which is a slight increase from the 58.3 percent (20 of 34) at the first interview (see table 2). Karla was part of that uptick. However, only 45.2 percent (14 of 31) experienced social belonging consistently over their first two years; 12.9 percent (4 of 31) declined in social belonging, whereas 16.1 percent (5 of 31) increased over time, including Karla (see table 3).

Importantly, first-generation students and continuing-generation students do not have parallel access to social belonging at Private. As table 2 shows, a larger share of first-generation students experienced social belonging at the first interview (66.7%, or 10 of 15) compared to 52.4 percent (11 of 21) of continuing-generation students. The pattern flip-flops at the end of the students' first year, with 10 percent more continuing-generation than first-generation students experiencing social belonging. By the end of the third year, they are at parity, at approximately 61 percent in each group. However, as table 3 shows, the 45.2 percent who experienced steady social belonging represent 50.0 percent (9 of 18) of continuing-generation students and only 38.5 percent (5 of 13) of first-generation students. These numbers illustrate that first-generation students are somewhat more likely to have ups and downs with social belonging at Private.

However, being a continuing-generation student does not ensure strong belonging by any stretch. Whereas Spencer was one of the 45.2 percent with steady belonging, Madison was not. In fact, she transferred to a new university in the middle of her second year, despite telling me five weeks into her first semester that "I do feel like I belong here and I know that I'll be here for the next four years. I can't see myself being anywhere else."

In a phone interview from her new campus on the East Coast, Madison explains how she made the decision to leave:

> I was evaluating who I was acting like at Private and it was so different from who I am when I am around my friends at home. Was I trying to be someone I'm not? . . . Things like always wearing makeup to class, I found myself doing that at Private even though I had never been like that, caring about how I look for class. I was evaluating: Do I want to be friends with these people? I just wasn't loving it anymore.

Social belonging was clearly a critical part of Madison's decision to leave. Her experience helps us see an important distinction between belonging and "fitting in." As social psychologist and popular author Brené Brown (2010) articulates it, fitting in is about knowing what you have to do to make yourself acceptable to a particular crowd, but belonging is being accepted and valued for who you are, for your authentic self. Madison seems to have realized that what had felt like belonging at first turned out to be merely fitting in, and it drove her to find a new university to call home.

Blake Silver (2020) demonstrates how ubiquitous it is for college students to reshape their identities to fit in. In his research at a large public university, he shows that students follow patterned ways of presenting themselves in interest-based student organizations such as the "Cardio Club" running group and "Volunteer Community" service organization. Students often get trapped into "cookie-cutter selves," which he describes as two-dimensional identities that constrain how individual students are able to behave and express themselves. The group dynamics seem to cement very quickly around initial presentations of self, and then students' "cookie-cutter selves" are policed and reinforced in microlevel interactions with surprising consistency. In interviews with Silver, many students expressed dissatisfaction because the group they joined did not make room for them to be more dynamic, complex, authentic versions of themselves. Silver rightly critiques the university for not better equipping first-year students with the tools to engage in campus social spaces as equals. Many students were "liminal figures" and struggled to feel a sense of belonging because they did not feel valued or recognized by the group. Silver's study underscores the important role that peer relationships through student organizations can play in social belonging. His findings also reinforce the understanding held by the students in my study that being able to be their "true self" is at the heart of what it means to experience social belonging. For students like Madison, not having it is enough to make transferring schools a viable solution.

Social Belonging Shifts over Time: At Public

Although students define social belonging in the same ways at both schools, at Public, it is experienced at lower rates: in their first interview near the start of their first year in college, 41.9 percent (13 of 31) of my sample experienced social belonging at Public compared to 58.3 percent at Private. In the next chapter I suggest that an explanation for Private's higher rate of belonging is that their organizational structures and campus culture prioritize relationships. By the third interview 64.0 percent (16 of 25) of the sample at Public experienced social belonging, which is just above the level at Private of 61.3 percent. Thus, accessing increased social belonging over time is fairly common at Public: 32 percent (8 out of 25) experienced this. However, another 20.0% (5 of 25) saw decreased social belonging, so experiences ranged widely.

Additionally, differences exist at Public in how social belonging is offered to continuing-generation versus first-generation students. As table 2 shows, at Public, there is a steady pattern of continuing-generation students consistently having their social belonging needs met at higher rates than do first-generation students. It is a difference of approximately 20 percent at each of the three interviews. Adding another layer of complexity to these dynamics, 44.4 percent of continuing-generation students at Public experience steady social belonging across their first two years, compared to 18.8 percent (3 of 16) of first-generation students (see table 3). Higher numbers of first-generation students see their social belonging improve over time (37.5% compared to 22.2% of continuing-generation students), but higher numbers also see their social belonging decline over time (25.0% compared to 11.1%

of continuing-generation students). Clearly, social belonging is neither steadfast nor easy to come by at Public.

Skylar is a good example of a student who has experienced increased social belonging over time, which happens for 32.0 percent of my sample at Public. She is a continuing-generation student who ethnoracially identifies as "just White." By the time of our first interview, Skylar was already an active member of a performance art team but "was looking for something more," so she joined a sorority and also got involved in student government. In her first interview with me, she seems reserved; she sits a bit drooped over the table between us, which is noticeable because she has such a petite, trim frame that she nearly disappears behind the table. Her brown hair is down around her shoulders, and she is wearing a delicate gold necklace and earrings. She shares, "I'm in some activities on campus, which I like, but I wouldn't necessarily say I found my place. So I wouldn't really say I belong . . . maybe later, but I wouldn't say that right now."

Indeed, by the end of her second year, social belonging had improved for Skylar: "I have my very, very, very, very close friends, so, it's definitely gotten better. But it has taken a long time I think to find those people." She described herself as shy (which had been my impression of her too) and said that in her first year she had often felt lonely and sad: "I would just kind of go off by myself and maybe just stay in my room and not really talk to anyone." She strikes me as much more confident in this third interview, striding cheerily across the crowded café patio to my table. Her hair is back in a ponytail, and she is wearing a sweatshirt with her sorority's logo on it.

Becoming involved in student organizations helped meet Skylar's social belonging needs, as it did for other students. She said she found that joining orgs and taking leadership positions had benefited her because "they force me to be more involved and force me to talk to more people about more things." Skylar's example is instructive for understanding the dynamics of belonging. I have been emphasizing the communal nature of belonging, that it must be offered to an individual and cannot be garnered or demanded by the student. Skylar reminds us that for belonging to be given, an individual must also make some effort to join the community. Shutting oneself up in a dorm room will not lead to belonging.

Skylar's experience of improved social belonging over the first two years similarly occurred for 22.2 percent (2 of 9) of continuing-generation students and 37.5 percent (6 of 16) of first-generation students. This indicates that things improved more often for first-generation students, even though their social belonging consistently lagged behind their continuing-generation counterparts.

Another similarity is that students at both schools were often offered social belonging by their dorm floor-mates. As Karla at Private noted earlier, the one friend she was close to was also the RA on her floor. Patrick is a first-generation student at Public who identifies as "I'm an Asian-American. I still hold close ties to my Asian culture because that's what I grew up with, but I've deviated from it. That's why I feel like I'm an Asian American." Patrick is bubbly in our interviews, sometimes with excitement and other times with anxiety. He wears wire-rimmed glasses that waggle around a bit when he scrunches up his nose, deep in thought. I found it touching the way Patrick lingers at the end of our interview, as though he were not quite ready to leave and have it end. Patrick happily told me that, in his first semester, the place where he found friends was "in my dormitory." He continues, "There's a lot of Asians there of course, but the point being we all like to hang out with each other, have fun and then we go places. And then we also interact with other buildings as well. So I feel like this is a second home I guess I would call it. I don't know, it's kind of—it's the new feeling of having a second home." First-year student housing helped meet many students' belonging needs, and this was particularly important for students like Karla and Patrick who did not find it easy to make other friends in their first year.

Although social belonging improves over time for Karla at Private, the opposite happens for Patrick at Public. Despite his initial delight in his dorm friends, Patrick's social belonging dwindles rapidly. At the end of his first year he tells me, "I feel like my circle of friends has gotten a lot smaller now." He no longer hangs out with the men in his dorm: "I actually have tried it. I just personally didn't like—there's people there, they hang out, it's just that their little circle didn't include me. When I went up there all I did was sit there listening to conversations, that was about it. I didn't really get to have any input in anything . . . so I just keep to myself a lot now." Patrick says he found "a friend in the dorm who is also basically a shutout like me," and they plan to room together in their second year. In this second interview, he seems both confused and disappointed by how things have turned out for him in the dorm: "If I tried to hang out with them, they don't interact with me either. So I'm kind of in a lose-lose situation. . . . And I guess it's uncomfortable for them because I'm like that person they never see but they are living with the same time. I guess maybe that's why they are uncomfortable. But they don't talk to me so I have no idea." Patrick's experience is a clear example of what it feels like when a community withholds belonging from an individual. Patrick is making an effort to join the group, but the group is not making him feel wanted, valued, or included. Things are not better a year later when I talk to Patrick again. He is getting along just fine with his friend, the fellow "shutout," who is now his roommate, but he tells me, "Other than him I haven't really made a whole lot of friends."

Thus, for some, belonging decreases over time, even though at Public, a more common experience is for social belonging to start out low and increase over students' first two years. Twenty-eight percent of students at Public and 45.2 percent at Private experienced steady social belonging, and only 4 percent (1 of 25) at Public and 0 percent at Private had an absence of social belonging consistently over the two years. This means that for most students, social belonging shifts over time. Belonging is dynamic, not static. It can be offered, rescinded, or withheld in any order at any moment. My data show that continuing-generation students overall have greater access to it at Public, but at neither school do an overwhelming majority of students experience it, be they continuing- generation or first-generation.

Social Belonging Does Not Equate to Campus-Community Belonging

An important insight derived from my analysis of students' open-ended descriptions of belonging is that having social belonging does not automatically equate to feeling like one belongs more broadly at the university. Dannisha is a good example. She is a continuing-generation student: "I identify as African-American because both my parents are immigrants from Africa but I grew up here." Dannisha spent a lot of time at the Black & African American Student Resource Center, known around campus as BAfA. In our first interview, when I ask Dannisha whether Public is a place where she feels like she belongs, she mentions BAfA right off the bat: "That's a place where I belong. But then, the university as a whole I don't really feel that's meant for people like me."

Dannisha is charismatic, with a gregarious smile that she flashes often. She is tall and in our first interview is wearing a long cardigan sweater that is bright yellow with large polka dots. Everything about her seems self-assured: her bold fashion, her graceful gait, and her easy sense of friendliness and openness. Her relaxed curls bounce around her chin as she talks.

I cannot help but find it improbable that someone like her would struggle with belonging. She continues, "I have BAfA and they reach out to us. So we know they are there for us. That's something that really helped me when I got here on campus. That's a family that I have now. But without that I would feel definitely like I'm just a number. I'm at the Student Union and I'm kind of alone. So I don't know." This sentiment of feeling well anchored to groups that offer social belonging, yet feeling adrift, out of place, or "alone" when navigating wider campus life, is shared by several students, particularly first-generation students or students like Dannisha, who is a continuing-generation student of color.

Another example of someone who has social but not campus-community belonging at Public is Javier. He is a first-generation student who identifies as "Latino—well, I'm American like everybody else here. But both my parents are from El Salvador. And keep in mind that Latino is very different from Chicano, because Latino is Latin America, anything in Central America. And Mexico is part of North America; a lot of people get that mixed up." During our first interview, soon after he started the first semester, he seems both weary and wary. He is wearing a hoodie and a beanie hat, and it takes a while for him to warm up to our conversation. He had just come out of a big exam, and I attributed his demeanor to that—but I was not entirely sure.

In our second interview, conducted at the end of his first year, Javier is sitting straight in his chair and making meaningful eye contact with me; he seems to me to be much happier and more confident than the first time we spoke. Javier is candid in all of our interviews. He does not shy away from referring to professors he perceives as offensive as "dicks" and "douches" (I tried my best not to cringe) or from criticizing the administration or fellow students with equally colorful cusswords. Yet he does not seem to be doing it for effect: he simply has an irreverent vernacular. He strikes me as sincere, and I respect him for it. He has a youthful growth of mustache and beard and wears dark-rimmed glasses.

By this end of his first year, Javier has cultivated strong friendships on campus. When I ask him in our second interview whether he has found true friends, he responds, "Yeah, to be honest. Because there's some that I met here, I met during Summer Bridge,[3] and we actually go home together. I slept over at a couple of friends' houses." Yet, when I ask Javier whether he belongs at Public, those strong friendships—including weekends and breaks spent with each other's families—do not seem to override his wider feeling of being out of place: "I want to say no. The dynamic of the school caters to different people."

Javier continues, describing the students to whom the university caters: "People who have had things that a lot of people I know have never . . . Like a good education in general, or a good background, or parents motivating them . . . Talking to a lot of the people here, they seem very—I don't want to say they seem extremely privileged, but I don't think they really get how blessed they are." Javier sees his fellow students' privilege as part and parcel of the cultural environment that the university is intentionally cultivating:

> The general attitude of the school, the students and the faculty. The school is meant to be a top-tier, extremely well known place of study, and it has hundreds of research stations. . . . For someone growing up like I did, that's incredible just getting there . . . the students, they don't realize that—they don't realize the privilege they hold. So, when they're talking to other people, about their successes and things and things they've had, they don't—it doesn't click that not everybody has had that.

For Javier, the problem extends beyond being able to relate to other students: "The faculty, I feel like they are here—I don't want to say for the paycheck. . . . They can see the privilege. . . . I'm pretty sure the professors can see it, but they are just like . . . they are not really concerned with it." I ask Javier whether he finds all this disappointing, and his answer reflects the determination and resiliency characteristic of first-generation students: "Well, there's nothing you can do about it. . . . Just because I don't belong here doesn't mean I can't succeed here. That applies to anyone."

This experience of having social belonging that is present in particular pockets on campus, while lacking a wider sense of campus-community belonging, occurs at Private too, but less often. At Public, 45.2 percent (14 of 31) of the sample experienced social belonging without campus-community belonging in at least one interview. For half of those (22.6%), campus-community belonging was absent, and the other half experienced partial campus-community belonging. By contrast at Private, only 13.9 percent (5 of 36) had social belonging without campus-community belonging, 8.3 percent experienced no campus-community belonging, and 5.5 percent had partial campus-community belonging in at least one interview. Violet is an example of a student who experienced social belonging without campus-community belonging. She is a first-generation student who identifies as "I'm Indian."

Violet has a soft, sweet voice that matches her sweet demeanor. Her abundant curly dark hair frames her face. She often takes long pauses in our interviews as she decides how to answer, thinking carefully. When I ask her in our second interview, at the end of her first year, whether Private is a place where she feels like she belongs, she responds, "I would say in my everyday relationships—everyday how I interact with all of my friends and with people, I would say yes. Because I feel comfortable with them and I know that people care about me on this campus and I care about them as well. So in that sense, yes. But to the institution of Private, I wouldn't say so." She does not experience campus-community belonging.

Like Javier at Public, Violet's example highlights the university's role in offering belonging to students, which I take up in detail in the next chapter. At this moment for Violet, her aid package is a driving factor: "I think that that has to do with my financial situation and stuff. I feel like—it's really hard to feel like you belong somewhere where they don't make it completely accessible or they don't—I know someone who left for the same reasons, financial reasons. So it's hard to feel valued if they have the ability to do something but they don't." Violet has just been informed that her family no longer qualifies for the same level of financial aid she received in her first year: "This [past] year I was considered low-income but my dad started working a lot more to cover expenses. So now we're not considered low-income, which is very challenging because earning more doesn't mean we can afford it." Violet feels abandoned by Private. She believes that the university could simply rework her financial aid package if it wanted to. Frustration is evident in her voice as she tells me, "If there weren't financial issues then I wouldn't have any doubts about returning. I don't know. I feel really disappointed, to be honest, just because I feel kind of trapped."

In the end, Violet did not return to Private, and we never had a third interview. Her case illustrates how money plays a role in shaping campus-community belonging. More affluent students whose families shoulder the costs of college (with and without loans) will never face the kind of rejection by the institution that Violet feels: "it's hard to feel valued if they have the ability to do something but they don't." It is especially salient considering that Violet says she "wouldn't have any doubts about returning" otherwise.

From these examples of Dannisha, Javier, and Violet, it is clear that social belonging does not automatically translate into more holistic belonging to the wider university. Yet the scholarship on college belonging often assumes that attachment to smaller groups can yield a sense of membership in the university community. That premise is not entirely wrong. Recall Karla who said, "Now I'm a part of a sorority, so I feel like now I'm a part of the Private community for real now." Likewise, several students answered my question about whether they feel like they belong with an immediate reference to the friendships they made and the organizations where they found a sense of "family": thus, some students' experiences of social belonging and campus-community belonging occur simultaneously. Yet, in my data, this tends to happen more often for continuing-generation and ethnoracial-majority students, and not as often for everyone else. This insight reveals a shortcoming in the strategies universities use to foster belonging in students.

"Find Your Place" Is Bad Advice for First-Generation Students

First-year students hear over and over again that, to get the most out of their college experience, they need to get involved on campus (Nathan 2005; Silver 2020). Universities are highly aware that this involvement fosters belonging, so campuses work hard to provide opportunities for students to participate in student organizations, athletic teams, affinity groups, resource centers that target particular (usually minoritized) identities, academic support centers, and research opportunities: the list goes on and on. At Private University, a favorite line used by the Admissions Office is, "There are more than a hundred student organizations, and if you can't find the right one for you, all you have to do is start it yourself." I heard students repeat this to me several times in interviews. Recall Spencer, who said, "There's thousands of student organizations where you can easily make friends." However, my data show that it is not as easy for many first-generation students to find social belonging in organizations as it was for Spencer. Brianna, a first-generation student at Private who identifies as "I'm White," is a good example. Brianna is very energetic, a fast talker whom I sometimes had a hard time keeping up with; she told me, "I think any campus community you can feel you belong once you make the effort to belong there.... Coming to college, you are thrown into a new environment. You don't know anyone, or you have a few friends, but you have got to put a lot in to create that belonging. You know, find that sorority or fraternity or whatever is on campus, it's a group of people that you like to be around every day."

Students at Public express similar ideas. One example is Tan, a first-generation student who identifies as "I just describe myself as: Queer. First-generation. Vietnamese American." Tan has a slight build but a large presence, zipping up to our third interview on a narrow foot scooter that she effortlessly collapsed and put under her chair before sitting down. She speaks openly; she is a genuine conversationalist with a clear, confident voice. Her shoulder-length hair is dyed blue (it had been dark brown in previous interviews). She says,

> A lot of the communities that I'm in now, you have to build it for yourself—with others. I don't know. It's a very big university and there aren't really any—I guess there *are* groups that you can just jump in and join, but for the most part it's not that way. There's a lot of: "if you want this, you have to go for it." . . . There are some people who I've met who say that this university doesn't feel like the place for them because they just can't find a community that they feel attached to.

Both comments by Brianna and Tan come from their third interviews with me at the end of their second year. Like others, both Brianna and Tan have relied primarily on organizational opportunities that the university provided for them, yet neither seems to give the university credit for it. Instead, they clearly view their experience as relying on their own individual efforts to "put a lot in and create that belonging," as Brianna phrased it. For her part, Tan has become an invested member of the community at the LGBTQ+ Center at Public, a place she enjoys so much she got a job working at the front desk. Meanwhile over at Private, Brianna is an active member of a business fraternity. She had joined a sorority during her first year, but dropped out "just because I didn't think it was that helpful." She has dabbled in several student clubs: "I like getting involved and stuff just as a way to get to know more people. It's just nice to do it and get your feet in the water and get to know the people in it, because I feel those organizations were helpful not really for the benefits of them but just meeting more people." Brianna decidedly sees her sense of social belonging as due to the "effort" she has expended in her quest for making Private a place she wants it to be. She even describes dormitory life the same way: "I think making your environment feel more comfortable is that you are doing a lot of the effort, putting in effort of having a relationship with your roommates and things like that."

When I ask her what it means to belong, Brianna centers on campus-community belonging. She talks about school pride, that a person who belongs would feel "happy" to say that they graduated from Private and would "definitely encourage other kids to attend Private too." She goes on to say, "In a place that you belong, you know the place in and out. The positives and negatives. What you have to do to make it work. Because not everything goes smoothly—that's not normal. For everything just to work out—it is never going to happen."

For Brianna and many others who struggle over both social belonging and campus-community belonging, this notion that the onus of responsibility is on their shoulders to "make it work" can be taxing. It can also be fraught with self-blame. David, a continuing-generation student at Private who identifies as "Black and Caribbean," recounts his experience:

> I know some friends who feel like—being Black—they don't belong. I feel like you've just got to suck it up, man. I was raised whether the odds are a million to one, or nine in ten, your task is still the same. So whether you feel like you were set up and you came here in a position where you're set up for failure, you're set up in a position where you won't fit in, your task is still to be here and meet the people you have to meet and have a good enough time here so that you can stay and function and, you know, do well and be a good student. So I feel like you've just got to suck it up. And me, ever since I took on that mentality—I had that defeatist attitude last year, you know, woe is me, I don't get along here, blah blah blah. But I just forced myself to accept where I was, and be happy with it and do well with it. And it's working. . . . You've got to really just hit the ground running and just go hard, 100 percent, and just make yourself. Do psychological warfare on yourself. Trick yourself into believing that you belong here and you'll start to belong here; you'll start to really feel like you belong here. So I think I'm good on that.

David connects part of his struggle for belonging to his racial identity, an important dynamic that I take up explicitly in chapters 5 and 6. As already mentioned, in my study, minority students of color who were continuing-generation students at both campuses had many similar kinds of experiences regarding belonging as did first-generation students. David's voice was light and teasing as he claimed to be doing "psychological warfare" on himself, which made me smile at his hyperbole. I noticed that many of the phrases he used throughout all three of his interviews sounded like they might be echoes of his ROTC training. He wore his uniform to one of our interviews. His speech is peppered with war metaphors and positive mindset mantras. Even with all that in mind, the attitude he expresses is rather extreme and is a vibrant example of how deeply responsible he feels for creating his own sense of belonging on campus, even if it means "tricking" himself into it.

Although important differences exist between Private and Public, this belief prevails at both schools. Alma, a first-generation student, identifies as "Chicana and Latina. Chicana because I was born here, but my family comes from Mexico, but I'm also from here, so it's the best of both worlds. And Latina too because I am from a Latin American country in the sense of my family and my ancestors, I'm proud to say." The first time I interviewed Alma she apologized for not wearing "professional attire." I assured her it was not that kind of interview, that her authentic college self was what I was interested in. To my eye, she was dressed well in her jeans and fashionable sweater. By contrast, I told her that one of my recent interviewees came in her pajamas because she was feeling a little under the weather, so Alma had nothing to apologize for. I took her comment as a mark of how important it seemed to her to be a part of a research study. She seemed to find it easy to open up in that first interview, speaking quite emotionally about her parents' recent divorce, the stroke that her father had when she was young, and the effect it had on her. Eventually we got around to the topic of belonging and her voice became tight with frustration:

LN Is Public a place where you feel you belong?

ALMA No.

LN Tell me more.

ALMA Actually, I take that back, it's like I had to make myself belong here. I don't feel it was a welcome flag showing, "Oh! You belong here!"—maybe like the first week. And then just, "Okay, you are on your own." I felt like I had to make myself belong here. I felt like I had to really put in the effort, which is understandable because when you are an adult, things aren't handed to you and that's understandable. But I was just—yeah, I really had to make myself belong here.

Alma's answer helps us see how Durkheim's insight that communities must offer belonging reveals the shortcomings of universities' typical approach. Encouraging students to embark on a search for the right friends, the right student organizations, athletic teams, academic clubs, and so on, where they feel comfortable puts a burden on first-generation and minority students of color. It can be a daunting task. To be sure, exploring various groups is an effective way to discover like-minded others and be welcomed into smaller communities (Chambliss and Takacs 2014; McCabe 2016). However, it is not as straightforward of a dynamic as much of the literature on student belonging assumes (Silver 2020). First-generation and students of color have more limited success in having their social belonging needs met this way (Museus 2008; Stuber 2015), as do students from lower-income backgrounds more generally (Armstrong and Hamilton 2013; E. Yee 2016; McClure and Ryder 2018). Consequently, these students are more likely to bear the burden of "creating your own belonging," as Brianna phrases it, in intense and potentially harmful ways.

Importantly, the failure to cultivate social belonging is experienced as personal failure. Students blame themselves, as David shows us, and invent new and creative ways to solve the problem on their own, like "doing psychological warfare on yourself." According to Durkheim, a healthy community integrates and regulates its members, which makes them feel valued and part of something larger than themselves—and not, as Alma describes it, to have "a welcome flag showing, 'Oh! You belong here!'—maybe like the first week. And then just, 'Okay, you are on your own.'"

"Find Your Place" Works for Continuing-Generation Students

Meanwhile, continuing-generation students who are in the ethnoracial majority on their campus often describe social and campus-community belonging as happening not only quickly but also nearly automatically; that is, as happening without any effort or concern on their part whatsoever. Recall the way Madison experienced campus-community belonging simultaneously with social belonging: "I just feel like going to class, you automatically are part of the community. Just meeting people in class and your professor and just walking around. Just friends and going to class." Another example is Shane. Campus-community belonging happened the moment he visited campus as a high school student, before he had even enrolled: "I went to another school first and I liked it. Then I came to Private and just fell in love. This is the school . . . Just walking around seeing kids in flip-flops and their board shorts and just t-shirts. That's me, clearly. It's a very relaxed feel, but you can still tell you're going to be academically challenged, which is kind of what I was looking for. . . . That's the main reason why I came here. I just got that feeling like I belonged here."

Shane is a continuing-generation student who identifies as "just White." He has a cool and easygoing demeanor, routinely brushing back his floppy, sandy brown hair that hangs a bit over his eyes. Shane's effortless community-campus belonging is not unique among continuing-generation students. Spencer, whom we already met in this chapter, expresses the same sentiment when I ask him in the first interview whether he feels like he belongs: "Yeah, absolutely. I think that I chose it for those reasons." This experience stands in sharp contrast to descriptions of intense effort, "making it work," and "tricking yourself" that we heard from Brianna, David, and others.

It is well established that universities reflect the cultural sensibilities of the dominant society, which in the United States is White and affluent (Bourdieu and Passeron 1977; Feagin, Vera, and Imani 1996; Gusa 2010; Harper 2013; Byrd 2017). Thus, it is not a great surprise that students such as Shane, Madison, and Spencer have a seamless experience entering Private and feeling that they belong to the campus community. Gavin, another continuing-generation student at Private, articulates it well: "just the culture . . . the people that I've met, and just like everything in general has been very similar to home. . . . yeah, I feel like I belong." Gavin ethnoracially identifies as "I would say White. Sometimes I throw in Hispanic—I think I'm like a quarter Hispanic or something, but I don't really culturally or racially identify as Hispanic." Although an automatic or effortless sense of campus-community belonging happens less often at Public, it is continuing-generation students who are more likely to feel optimistic that it will come in time. Skylar, whom we met earlier in this chapter, is a typical example. At the end of her second year, even though she has gained many valuable friendships that offer her social belonging, when I ask about belonging in general, she says: "Sometimes. And sometimes not." Skylar explains that campus-community belonging is what is missing for her: "It's feeling really comfortable. No matter where you are around the school or what you're doing. Whether you're with your friends or you're just walking around."

Just as Skylar and others have shown us that a student can have social belonging without experiencing campus-community belonging, the reverse is also true. Alejandro, a continuing-generation student at Private, is an example. He ethnoracially identifies as "I'm Hispanic and American Indian because I'm 100 percent Mexican. My dad tracked down our ancestry to a tribe in Guadalajara, which is where my dad's family is from and a certain family in Spain." In his first semester when I asked him if Private is a place where he feels like he belongs, his answer sounded a lot like Shane's. He said, "As soon as I stepped on campus on that tour back in the spring of junior year, yes." Alejandro is emphatic: "I was dead stoked on this school." I then asked him what it means to belong: "When I say, 'I belong here at Private,' the first thing in my mind is just looking around and just seeing everything. I don't know. I like to just take in everything at once. So I just look around at the buildings. Yeah, I still feel the sense of community here that I felt back on my trip. And when it comes to friends, I'll say that ranks second compared to that." Alejandro does not seem able to articulate exactly what it is that makes the campus feel so comfortable, but his comment that "just looking around" at the buildings gives him a sense of belonging echoes the same sentiment that Shane described, "Just seeing kids in board shorts and flip flops," and that Gavin said, "Just like everything in general has been similar to home."

At the same time, however, Alejandro does not experience social belonging. Although he joined a club lacrosse team, works on campus and met many people on a summer pre-enrollment camping trip run by Private, he has not made many friends: "Everyone knows me but I feel like—have you ever heard that saying, 'I don't have a lot of friends, I just know a lot of people?'" When I ask Alejandro what he means, he replies, "Like you are generally received, your name is well known but it's not connected with anything." Alejandro is tall and athletically built. In this first interview his black hair is tucked under a headband. He explained to me that he wore the headband everyday lately to manage his unruly hair, which he had not yet cut it in the nine weeks he had been at college. At some moments he was confident and expressive, but when he talked about personal struggles his body language deflated, and his voice became almost a whimper. It was during one of the latter moments that he spoke about his longing for social belonging: "I don't go out that often. I would like to. It would be very nice. Especially today. But I work on Fridays. . . . I do see them a lot when I'm in my dorm room. I just see them and say hi to them. Which is really nice. But usually every single time I eat I'm usually by myself and I'm always doing homework while I'm eating . . . usually I say, 'Well, I'll just bring homework with me so I can do homework and study so I don't feel totally depressed.'" Despite this, Alejandro was adamant: "I belong at Private."

Clearly, social belonging and campus-community belonging are not one and the same thing for students. At Private, 33.3 percent (12 of 36) of students experienced campus-community belonging without social belonging in at least one interview. That number includes 8.3 percent for whom social belonging is absent, like Alejandro, and 25.0 percent who experience partial social belonging. At Public, the overall percentage of students experiencing campus-community belonging without social belonging is similar: 32.3 percent, which includes 12.9 percent for whom social belonging is absent and 19.4 percent who had partial social belonging.

Part of the easier congruence for continuing-generation students has to do with money (Stuber 2011; E. Yee 2016; Hamilton, Roksa, and Nielsen 2018; Jack 2019). Marisol, for example, a first-generation student at Public who identifies as "I'm Mexican," grew up in a neighborhood that is nothing like the spacious, well-manicured aesthetics of Public's campus. I interviewed her for the first time over Thanksgiving break; we met at her family's home in South Central Los Angeles, an area famous for its crime, gangs, and rap musician superstars. The streets leading to her home showed signs of poverty and city neglect: there were cramped houses with roofs in disrepair, thinly patched asphalt roads, overgrown weeds in the medians between lanes, lopsided chain fencing around vacant lots, and full size couches on lawns and sidewalks, including one so far out in the street that I had to navigate my car carefully around it. These details are not a comment on Marisol herself, but on the neighborhood she calls home.

She welcomed me warmly into her house, proudly showing me the space at the end of a long, elegant dining room table that her family reserved for her books during all her years of high school. It was her private homework station in an otherwise bustling space. I felt honored to be invited in. What I want to underscore about Marisol's home and neighborhood is that, unlike Alejandro, Gavin and others, she cannot simply "look around" her spacious, aesthetically designed college campus and feel an automatic sense of familiarity and belonging. I doubt there is much about Public's campus that resembles home to Marisol. Students from backgrounds like hers describe feeling like a fish out of water around campus. They experience a sense of "otherness" (Havlik et al. 2020, 124); they feel like "outsiders" (Jack 2019, 38) and "strangers without codebooks" (Jehangir 2010, 29).

Fit versus Financial Package

Another dynamic that allows for greater access to automatic belonging among continuing-generation students is the process of applying to college and making the decision on where to attend. My first question in the first interview is "What made you decide to come to this school?" Over and over again, continuing-generation students described a process of applying to a range of schools, including reach schools and safety schools, just as the guide-books recommend. Once all the acceptance and rejection letters came in, they sat down with their families and evaluated their options, weighing which school was the best "fit" for their personality and interests (also just as the guidebooks recommend), while keeping an eye on tuition costs. First-generation students, in contrast, typically described applying to the maxi-mum number of schools allowed by the application-fee waiver available to low-income families, which in California can include four schools within the University of California (UC) system and four within the California State University (CSU) system, plus an additional four private schools through the SAT-linked College Board application fee waiver. Alma at Pub-lic is a typical example: "I liked to have options," she said: "12 schools: 4 Cal States, 4 UCs and 4 privates . . . I was taking advantage of my college fee waiver so I was like, 'why not?' To have, you know, opportunities."

First-generation students rarely described selecting where to apply or where to attend based on ideas about "fit." The main exception was first-generation students at Private who had attended private high schools; they tended to look for small class sizes or a religious environment similar to their high schools. Being a first-generation student means that neither parent has a four-year college degree, so by definition, such students do not have fami-lies with firsthand wisdom about the importance of "fit." Some first-generation students like Javier admitted, "I don't know why I picked Public." Javier also used the fee waiver, but decided not to apply to any private schools. He was accepted at three of the four UCs and two of the CSUs and waitlisted at the other two CSUs, so he had multiple choices. "I don't really know exactly or what," he continued, "I'll be honest. I just chose." Other first-generation students like Ilana felt similarly: "Isn't college just college?"

For the most part, first-generation students decided where to apply based on positive things they had heard that made it a "good school," including rankings, national reputation, and perhaps firsthand experience from current or former students whom they knew personally. However, making the final decision about where to attend was heavily weighted toward the financial package. Lucas at Private is a typical example: "It's a combination of being a first-year student and not knowing where to apply to college. I just kind of applied to a lot of really, really different schools. And then getting into here, combined with not being accepted other places, but combined with the financial aid package I got here—that was the biggest factor. This was the place where I got the most money to go." Lucas ethnoracially identifies as a "White Irish kid." He is eager about how much he likes Private: "I love it here!" So his decision turned out to be a good one. However, like Lucas, first-generation students in my study tended to choose either Public or Private because they offered the best financial support of all the schools that accepted them, not because they were confident that they would love it.

Financial aid is an important consideration as college debt is increasing nationally (Dwyer, McCloud, and Hodson 2012; Houle 2014). This strategy of choosing college based on the financial aid package works to first-generation students' benefit because they are much more likely to shoulder the cost of college on their own than continuing-generation students, whose families are more likely to contribute some or all of the costs (McCabe and Jackson 2016). Although debt is undeniably a burden that students would avoid if they could, research also points to the ways that indebtedness can foster a more serious approach to academic achievement than taken by students who receive ongoing financial support from their families during college (Hamilton 2013; Quadlin and Rudel 2015; Quadlin 2017). So, there is a way to see debt as not entirely negative. Yet for the first-generation students in my study, concerns over the cost of college were indeed very burdensome, and they loomed large over the decision of where to enroll. Eric, a first-generation student at Public, explains,

"For me cost is a big factor. Luckily I have my financial aid and everything, but let's say I didn't. Then I probably would've considered a community college. . . . The education is the same; it's just the name of the school campus. And everyone says "connections, connections," but I mean really, do you really even make connections your first two years? I think that comes later on . . . and anyone I meet is a connection. I don't have to necessarily find connections at Public my first two years.

Eric's dismissal of the idea that social and academic connections made in college are valuable for one's future is common among first-generation students. Continuing-generation students, on the contrary, are more likely to have parents who know firsthand how beneficial such college connections can be because they have reaped those benefits themselves. Yet even though Eric's decision centered on cost, the school's reputation was also a factor. Eric is boisterous and quick-witted. His humor is often self-deprecating, but at the same time he exhibits great curiosity about anything and everything, which adds to his easygoing friendliness. He has a laughing smile. Eric identifies as "I'm Chinese. Asian. Cantonese, specifically." He explained to me that he only applied to schools that his parents thought were "prestigious." His parents are immigrants from China: "I guess a lot of their information comes from the Chinese newspapers, you know, what the Asian community says." In the end, he was choosing between two schools that had offered him generous financial support and were equally prestigious in his parents' eyes. Like many other first-generation students, he chose the one closest to home (Davis 2010; Mullen 2010). Public is a two-hour drive from Eric's hometown, whereas the school he decided against was an eight-hour drive away.

Similarly, Lucia said: "Applying and stuff, I didn't really know what I was doing but I was just applying. Then once I started receiving acceptance letters, I figured before I started receiving them that it'd be a few and I'd just decide from there. But as I received, I was a little more confused on which one to choose. But like I said, it was the financial aid and the distance that ultimately did it for me." Lucia is a first-generation student who describes her ethnoracial identity as "I have African ancestors, I have Spanish ancestors, and indigenous Native American ancestors. So it's not as easy to just say, 'Oh I'm just this.' I'm all three. I'm both. I'm a Black Cuban, I'm an Afro-Latina." Where Eric's parents had strong opinions about which schools he should choose, Lucia's parents did not offer any input. Yet at the same time, her parents are an important part of Lucia's motivation to go to college and to graduate: "I feel like college is a big—it's a way to gain status." She explains.

My parents were teen parents and there is kind of a negative view on teen parents. And so other people might see them with a young child and say, "Those kids, they don't know what they are doing." Or just automatically have negative ideas. But I feel like my family now—me going to college and my other cousin too—automatically when they meet family friends or hang out, they are like, "Oh yeah, she's in college. She's doing so good." It's a way to gain more status. I think. Socially, to feel more accepted. Like, "Oh yeah, my family goes to college. We are at that level."

Although her parents did not have college knowledge to help Lucia with her application and decision process, she did have another adult in her life whom she could turn to for advice once she started receiving all those acceptance letters:

> It didn't really hit me how expensive college would be. . . . As far as the financial aid you receive and how it's broken down, it can be a little confusing to understand. . . . Once I narrowed it down to three schools, I printed out a copy of my financial aid and I went to my AVID advisor. He broke it down and told me, "Okay, you'll receive more from this school. Maybe if you save in this area, you can make it work with this school." So he narrowed it down and helped me ultimately choose, just because I really didn't have too much information about how it all worked.

Lucia was still basing her decision entirely on financial aid, but with the help of her AVID mentor, she did not do it alone.[4] From that first round of interviews, it seemed to me that many first-generation students did not have a clear idea about whether they would "fit" on that campus until they arrived the first day to move in. By contrast, many continuing-generation students had strategized carefully to try and guarantee an easy sense of belonging at the school they decided to attend. This was particularly common at Private, but it happened at Public too, as we saw with Easton who knew before enrolling that "Jenga and friendship" awaited him on campus.

Yet, that is not to say that first-generation students did not experience any campus-community belonging whatsoever before move-in day. In fact, many viewed their financial aid packages as evidence that the university wanted them. The aid was perceived as flattering, especially by those who saw their packages as generous. This is one way that universities can offer belonging to students. Of course, it is a rather precarious way to offer belonging. Recall Violet at Private, who felt abandoned by the university when her family was "no longer considered low income" and Private required her to pay more than her family could manage. Similarly, Alma at Public was upset in our third interview by an upcoming tuition increase: "Why am I having to pay so much for my education? For wanting to get ahead in life? . . . It just makes me really angry at the system, wanting to increase tuition. Why? Where is all the money going to? Last time I checked it's not really going to students. It's going to something else. Probably the administration's paycheck . . . They are just sitting there in the office typing away trying to make Public a brand." She sets her jaw hard and leans into the microphone that is recording our interview: "I hope they hear that. I want them to hear that!"

Remember that Alma also said, "I had to make myself belong here. I don't feel it was a welcome flag showing, 'Oh! You belong here!'—maybe like the first week. And then just, 'Okay, you are on your own.'" Durkheim's insight that belonging is offered by the community is central here. First-generation students generally do not receive the automatic validation and effortless acceptance that continuing-generation students often do—not in terms of campus-community belonging nor in terms of social belonging. Instead, they have to scramble for it.

2

Campus-Community
Belonging and
Organizational Structures

● ● ● ● ● ● ● ● ● ● ● ● ● ● ● ● ● ● ● ●

Each school has its own distinct campus culture (Stevens 2009; Khan 2010; Mullen 2010; Nunn 2014), yet most college campuses are places where continuing-generation and ethnoracial-majority students feel more at home because higher education institutions reflect the cultural sensibilities of the dominant class. Recall Gavin from the previous chapter, who feels that he belongs because "just the culture . . . the people that I've met, and just like everything in general has been very similar to home." Yet, even though colleges are similar in this way, the differences between them are also important if we want to understand how belonging works.

As we have seen, some students experience social belonging without simultaneously feeling campus-community belonging and vice versa. It is possible to have one without the other because they are distinct realms of belonging, and both are distinct from academic belonging, which I discuss in detail in the next chapter.

The particular campus environments and organizational structures at each school influence students' experiences of belonging, so to fully understand how campus-community belonging is offered, we need to get acquainted with each campus' culture. In the following sections I show that academics are front and center at Public, and this priority makes academic belonging a more salient concern for students than social belonging. At Private, the reverse is true. Relationships are prioritized; thus, social belonging is the principal concern for students. Certainly, both social and academic realms of belonging matter at both campuses, and neither translates directly into campus-community belonging. Even though all three realms of belonging are distinct, students' experiences of campus-community belonging are also related to and intertwined with the academic and social components of their college lives. Importantly, those components are shaped and influenced by the organizational structures that foster the particular culture of their campus (Armstrong and Hamilton 2013; Warikoo 2016; Reyes 2018).

Public University: Academic Belonging Is Salient

Students at Public describe their school as having an academically focused and often competitive environment. Isabella says, "We just know how to put academics first." Benjamin tells me about a heated argument that erupted between his two roommates over grades. Amy laughs about students who camp out at the library during finals and rolls her eyes about a friend of hers whose favorite refrain is, "We aren't done studying until we feel like dying." Mason says he was "informed several times" that students at Public will "claw people out of the way" and "step on everyone else to get to the top." Mason has not found this to be true exactly, but others have. Lucia laments that "everyone's competing to set the curve. It's like: 'Well, I'm not going to help you because I want to set the curve.'"

This unforgiving focus on academics pervades students' descriptions of Public's campus culture, and students are deeply affected by it. Only 29.0 percent of my sample experienced academic belonging at the time of their first interview. Concerns over academic performance come up at many different moments in our interviews: when I ask about their favorite and least favorite classes, when I ask them to describe a successful college student, when I ask them (in hindsight) what they struggled with the most as they were getting the hang of college, and even when I ask about the friends they have found in college. It also surfaces immediately for many students at Public when I ask about belonging.

Charlotte, a first-generation student at Public, tells me, "College isn't sup-posed to be this fun camp that you go to. I am here for a reason. The main goal is to learn. Not to sit here and relax and hang out with friends and just socialize all the time." Charlotte is tall and rather quiet. She identifies as "I normally describe myself as biracial and I say I'm half-Japanese, half-Caucasian. A lot of people are super surprised. They're like, 'Wow, you're half Japanese? I totally didn't know.'" Charlotte wore a different Public sweatshirt to each of our interviews. While she adamantly disavows college as a "fun camp," she also shares with genuine sadness that she wishes she had more friends on campus. It is our second interview at the end of her first year, and she talks about how happy she was to have been chosen as an orientation leader for the incoming first-year students in the fall because it is helping her get involved and meet new people.

At the same time, Charlotte is very proud of her grades—"Last semester I got one A-minus and the rest were either A's or A-pluses"—and that she puts schoolwork first. When I asked whether Public is a place where she feels like she belongs, she immediately zeroes in on academics: "It's kind of a mixed opinion. Part of me says yes because I feel like it is really challenging here. . . . Public has the perfect amount of that. Yes, it is hard and there have been stressful nights where you are studying all night long and you are wor-ried about how you are going to do. But, I think being challenged has pushed me. . . . I feel like I am a lot smarter than I give myself credit for some-times. In that aspect, this is where I'm supposed to be."

Even though she does not claim to fully belong, but rather has a "mixed opinion," she does not elaborate on anything beyond academics, which is the part of her that "says yes" that she belongs. I have to ask follow-up ques-tions to learn why belonging feels mixed: "A lot of people here I haven't really found a certain connection with—I am not even sure why. I have just never felt a certain connection with someone where I was like, 'I should ask them to hang out again soon' or 'I should give them my phone number so we can keep in touch.'" Clearly it is social belonging that is lagging for Charlotte; hence, her "mixed opinion."

A year later in our third interview, after she has become a seasoned ori-entation leader for new students, her response is similar, but this time she claims belonging, rather than a "mixed" feeling: "I would say so. I would say yes. Oh, I guess this reminds me of a question that a lot of parents or students will ask me when they first come here. They'll be like, 'Oh, what is this school like?' . . . What I always tell them is the school is challenging, but it challenges me in a good way." When I ask, "What does it mean to belong?" Charlotte tells me, "I feel like it's doing well here, but also most importantly, feeling comfortable here. . . . You don't have to have perfect grades in order to feel like you are doing well. But just feeling like you are being challenged. So, I feel like I'm learning a lot and I'm benefiting a lot from the experience, but also feeling comfortable in this environment. I would say that's what it means to me to belong here." Charlotte shows us how campus-community belonging, or "feeling comfortable in this environment," is something distinct from "doing well" (which is tied to academic belonging); yet, because we know that the environment at Public is academically ferocious, it makes sense that the two are intertwined for Charlotte.

Many students at Public seem to simply take it as an unquestioned fact that academics should be prized over all else. However, a few like Lucia, are critically aware of that dynamic: "I was thinking of transferring to maybe a school with a better social life. I think that academics are important, but I don't think that they should consume someone's life. I think that's unhealthy. And I feel like this school does that to some people, or some people allow this school to do that to them." We met Lucia in the previous chapter. She is a first-generation student who identifies as "I have African ancestors, I have Spanish ancestors, and indigenous Native American ancestors. So it's not as easy to just say, 'Oh I'm just this.' I'm all three. I'm both. I'm a Black Cuban; I'm an Afro-Latina." Lucia is vivacious in our interviews, full of thoughtful insights and expressive emotions. She wears her long dark curls loose, which complements her stylish thick-rimmed glasses. The first time we met she is wearing jeans with a long-sleeve button-up shirt which is open revealing a t-shirt with images of Africa. I find her to be mature, able to easily articulate her feelings and experiences. Lucia seems comfortable in her own skin. She continues,

> The climate in general—and just feeling like people don't really support each other, people don't really care about getting to know each other that much better. Yeah, within smaller groups, like certain spaces on campus or certain orgs or something, yeah, people are interested . . . but as a whole, everybody's just kind of doing their own thing in their own bubble: "I'm here to study and not socialize and not create bonds with people." And I like doing that. I like creating bonds and connections with folks. So, that was difficult.

Lucia's comment that students at Public hold an attitude of "I'm here to study and not to socialize" echoes a common refrain. Students clearly seem to perceive each other that way. For example, Regina knows all too well that Public's focus on academics is not just a matter of rumor and reputation. A first-generation student who identifies as "Mexican," Regina tells me, "When you want to make friends, they are like, 'No, I am only here for my grades.'" Charlotte shows us that the reality of individuals' experiences is more complicated. Although she does not prioritize socializing—she believes college should not be a "fun camp"—she also longs for meaningful friendships and connections. In my sample, only one student described Public as not being academic enough. Grace, a first-generation student who identifies as "Vietnamese and Chinese," told me, "Before I thought I was more of a social person. Now that I'm around all these people—sometimes they're not the brightest. I feel like I've been a little bit less social." She described herself as "pickier" about whom she wants to befriend and said that Public is "a good fit for me . . . like my own personality," because socializing is a lower priority.

Grace is a tough interview subject. She is kind and gracious, for example, offering to switch sides of the table so that the sun would not be in my eyes. Yet her facial expressions are somewhat stoic, and she is the opposite of long-winded. Her answers are not rude or abrupt, but they are—well— short-winded. Her long dark hair is immaculately styled each time we meet. She wears flashy pink glasses with green stripes on the earpieces. Although the overwhelming majority of students communicated to me that they enjoyed our interviews—some by hugging me hello or goodbye, some by calling it "fun," and some by expressing gratitude for the chance to reflect on their own experiences—Grace was the only one who made me wonder whether she thought our interviews were a waste of her time. I simply could not read her well. She continued saying yes to participating in all three interviews, so in the end I hope she got something out of the interviews too, more than the $10 gift cards I gave as participation incentives.

It might be tempting to assume that Public has a reputation for having cutthroat competition, and therefore it attracts students who are drawn to such a place, like Grace. Although there is some truth there, it is not the whole story. Public certainly seems to attract prospective students who are academically minded. The school is ranked "most selective," which is the highest of five selectivity categories of *U.S. News and World Report*'s college ranking system (by comparison, Private is ranked as "more selective," the second-highest category). Thus, when students choose Public they are signing up for an academically rigorous curriculum. My interview data suggest that it is only once they arrive that they discover that it is an academically competitive environment too, rather than one where students "support each other," as Lucia wishes it were. Students learn the cultural dynamics of their college only after they are part of its daily rhythms.

Even Charlotte, who appreciates the academic "challenges" that characterize Public, has had to learn about its culture the hard way. In our first interview Charlotte tells me, "I definitely think that I do belong here . . . because I've gotten into the swing of things and I understand what I'm supposed to do. . . . But I feel like part of the reason why I feel like I belong here now is also acceptance. Acceptance that it's hard. Acceptance that I may not have a bunch of close friends here. But it's one of those things where you have to do what you have to do." It seems that Charlotte was hoping for or expecting something else but has resigned herself to accepting the way things are at Public during her first semester. This means that the campus culture is not simply a reflection of the students it attracts. Instead, the campus culture shapes and changes students' own expectations and attitudes once they join campus life (Armstrong and Hamilton 2013; Binder and Wood 2013; Nunn 2014; Silver 2020).

Several students in my study found it a painful process to adjust to Public's culture. Regina, whom we met earlier, felt burned by this dynamic. "You can't avoid the competitive aspect," she tells me. Regina is shy, even a bit awkward in our first interview, although she is very considerate, asking me whether I had eaten and whether I would prefer to go to the food court and eat lunch during our interview. She tells me she is "too nervous" to be recorded, so I take handwritten notes as we talk. She sits across from me in a soft white sweater and a thin gold necklace with a small Cinderella pendant around her neck. She fiddles with Cinderella off and on as we talk.

At first Regina "really liked" how academically intense Public was because she had not been challenged by her high school. Yet, she soon discovered to her dismay that classmates "are not willing to make a relationship with you, but they will ask you for help on their homework." With emotion shaking her voice, she recounts how "a girl in math class" asked her for help. Regina spent time with her, carefully reviewing the homework problems, making sure that her classmate understood them. From the way she described it to me, Regina saw herself as doing a kindness, a generous act with high hopes that a friendship would develop. "But she doesn't even say hi to me now,"

Regina says, holding back tears. "She used me." Regina shrugs her shoulders: "You have to get used to it. It's like that." She is looking down, not making eye contact with me, when she continues, "I was disappointed. I thought we'd go and get hot chocolate and study together. But no."

Regina's experience highlights the interconnections between social belonging, academic belonging, and campus-community belonging. Ideally, students offer social belonging to fellow students, as Regina tried to do with her math classmate, and those social relationships might contribute to academic belonging as students "get hot chocolate and study together," which helps garner academic confidence and success. Yet a school's campus culture matters for how those social and academic realms operate; in Regina's case, Public's competitive culture thwarted friendship building. Regina's offer of social belonging was unreciprocated. Lucia very aptly describes this dynamic: "this school does that to some people, or some people allow this school to do that to them." Students are influenced and changed by the campus culture. To feel like they belong to the campus-community, they have to feel "comfortable" in the campus culture. Campus-community belonging is not simply the sum of social and academic belonging, nor it is entirely independent of them.

How Universities Offer Campus-Community Belonging

As this analysis is grounded in Durkheim's insight that belonging is given by a community to an individual member, we need to understand how exactly an institution like a university can offer belonging to its members. We know that college campuses, as well as many K–12 schools, feel familiar and comfortable to more affluent students; that is, members of the dominant class who tend to be continuing-generation and ethnoracial- majority students (Bourdieu and Passeron 1977; Lareau 2003; Stevens 2009; Khan 2010; Bastedo and Jaquette 2011; Carter 2012; Martin 2012; E. Yee 2016). Their life experiences and cultural sensibilities are reflected by the school.

How does cultural reflection work? The campus is familiar because such students have grown up in neighborhoods with pleasing architecture, expansive green spaces, well-organized roads, and walking paths through aesthetic landscaping. They are used to school libraries with abundant books and computers, they assume they can call police and get an immediate response, and they expect to have coffee shops and frozen yogurt spots conveniently located around the corner. All of these are standard features of universities like Public and Private. Such students have also grown up eating the same foods that they find in the campus cafeterias, working out on the same exercise equipment they find in the campus gym, drying their laundry in machines rather than clotheslines, and refilling their reusable water bottles with filtered water. They find the kinds of clothes they like to wear in the campus bookstore and hear music they enjoy listening to playing in campus cafes. Many have also grown up surrounded predominately by white bodies in their schools, parks, grocery stores, sports teams, and shopping malls. The list goes on and on. It is why Gavin describes it so generically as "just like everything in general has been very similar to home." He is right. Generally everything feels familiar to students like him. It is also why Javier, by contrast, perceives that his university "caters to different people" from himself, people with "privilege."

Of course, crafting a physical environment that is similar in aesthetics, style, and function to their students' upbringings is only part of how universities offer campus-community belonging. They also offer it through implementing programs and cultivating a campus culture that make students feel that they matter, that they are valued and wanted. This in turn allows students to feel "comfortable," which is one of the most common words they use to describe belonging.

Scholars use the term "cultural reproduction" to explain these dynamics, following the sociological theories of Pierre Bourdieu. Bourdieu argues that educational institutions are designed to maintain and legitimate the dominance of the ruling class through oppression, by committing "symbolic violence" on subordinated groups (Bourdieu 1977; Bourdieu and Passeron 1977). As education systems embody dominant culture, they simultaneously devalue nondominant language forms, histories, and cultural habits. Many first-generation students learn implicitly and explicitly that they are members of groups that do not matter as much through what education scholarship describes as the "hidden curriculum" (Rosenbaum 1976; Apple 1979; Weis, McCarthy, and Dimitriadis 2006). For the students at Public and Private, I analyze the way these implicit and explicit messages from the hidden curriculum surface in descriptions of their sense of belonging.

Further drawing on Bourdieu, scholarship shows that each school campus has its own "organizational habitus" that embodies and espouses its hidden curriculum in particular ways (McDonough 1997; Horvat and Antonio 1999; Stuber 2011; Armstrong and Hamilton 2013; Stuber 2015).

As we have just seen through the students' descriptions, Public's campus culture has a distinct character; later, I discuss the structural features that foster it. By contrasting it to the structures and resulting culture at Private, my analysis reveals each school's "organizational habitus." Using cultural reproduction theory as a framework helps us identify the root of belonging struggles faced by first-generation and minority students of color. It also points to an obvious way to disrupt the process: to have power-holding institutional agents help bridge the gap between first-generation students' cultural sensibilities and the everyday institutional demands of college life (Bastedo and Jaquette 2011; Stuber 2011; O'Keeffe 2013; Moschetti and Hudley 2015; Tinto 2017; Roksa and Kinsley 2019). I suggest concrete ways to accomplish that work in chapter 7.

Organizational Structures and Campus-Community Belonging

By "organizational structures," I am referring to the programs, policies and everyday decisions that are enacted by the administration and lived out by all members of the campus community. Schools, including universities, are organizations, and their structural features form the foundation of their organizational culture, or campus culture, as we call it. By comparing Public and Private side by side, it becomes even clearer how a campus culture is cultivated (Warikoo 2016; Reyes 2018).

First-Year Housing

At both schools, first-year students are housed on campus in dormitories. At Public, they are assigned to dorms based on their major. This way to assign housing implies an assumption that students want—*or should want*—to build relationships with people who share an academic similarity, rather than any number of other traits that might make for harmonious living arrangements. By contrast, at Private students are assigned housing based on personal interests. All first-year dorms are themed: Environmental Justice, Global Village, or Moral Universe, for example. As part and parcel of its liberal arts orientation, Private intentionally groups students in the same dorm who intend to declare a variety of different majors so that friendships can bloom across disciplinary interests. Students select into their desired themed dorm at Private, just as students select into their desired academic dorm at Public.

A key benefit of Public's major-based housing is that dorms are conveniently located near the buildings of the academic departments associated with relevant majors. The Life Sciences dorm is just steps away from the Biology building, for example. This is an effective way to create a kind of home base for first-year students by carving out a relatively small territory on Public's sprawling campus that they can think of as theirs. Each dorm has its own kind of neighborhood feel, with distinct eateries and hang-out spaces that successfully foster a sense of local community. I found the various dorm-communities all over campus to be warm and lively places, bustling with student activity in communal spaces: students were eating, studying, chatting, playing ping-pong, setting up art installations, and so on. Because they are based on majors, these dorm-communities structure campus life so that academic interests are the organizing principle for everyday social interactions—again, privileging academics over all else.

Scholars Rashawn Ray and Jason Rosow (2010, 2012) highlight the role that student housing plays in facilitating "normative institutional arrangements," which are "boundaries that shape social interactions and establish control over social environments" (2010, 525). They emphasize the way that the design and location of physical spaces (e.g., on-campus fraternity houses as opposed to fraternity members living in small clusters scattered around apartment complexes and rental homes near campus) contribute to the creation of cultural understandings among the group living there about the kinds of activities and attitudes that are possible and acceptable within the group. The administrations at both Public and Private play an important role that affects the normative institutional arrangements of dormitory life for first-year students by carefully crafting rules, policies, and programming that steer students toward particular cultural understandings about what is valued, important, and acceptable on campus.

Private's campus is much smaller than Public's, so carving out territory there is not necessary to foster community. Instead, Private's strategy is to organize events, competitions, field trips, and the like exclusively for members of the same dorm-community. These activities are often anchored in the dorm's theme, which is based on students' own interests. For example, the Environmental Justice dorm-mates may load up on buses (paid for by Private) and make the trek to the coastline for a Beach Clean Up Day, where they collect trash out of the sand for a few hours and then wrap up the day with some beach volleyball and a bonfire where they listen to professors talk about marine life and social justice while making s'mores. Such programs emphasize relationship building that is not entirely disconnected from academic learning but is focused on shared values and fun experiences. Through programs like these, Private communicates to its students that relationships are the top priority.

Dorms and Curriculum

At Public, the general education curriculum is tailored to each dorm-community. For example, students living in the Humanities dorm have different graduation requirements (more history and literature courses) than those in, say, the Life Sciences dorm (more lab sciences and advanced calculus). This makes sense, following the wisdom of the housing policy to cluster students according to similar majors. The policy reinforces the sense that academic decisions and academic identities drive college life. However, even students who come in undeclared or who change majors are obligated to fulfill the general education classes associated with their dorm-community, which can be problematic.

At Private, the academic curriculum is also tailored to first-year housing, but in a way that pays attention to relationship building alongside learning. All dorm-communities at Private have the same general education requirements, but students are automatically enrolled in one of those required classes alongside a couple dozen of their dorm-mates. The class revolves around the dorm's theme, and students from other dorms are not allowed to enroll in it. It is a mandatory graduation requirement to pass the dorm-community course, so it helps that potential study partners abound in their living spaces. This program sends an unmistakable message to students that getting to know each other is fundamental to college life at Private by ensuring that first-year students are constantly crossing paths with fellow members of their dorm-community both in their classrooms and residence halls.

Tutoring and Academic Support

Budgets are a critical way that institutions communicate their priorities. One area that stands out in communicating universities' commitments is academic support that intentionally targets students whose K–12 schooling underprepared them for college academics. Both Public and Private participate in the federal TRIO Student Support Services (SSS) program, which serves students who qualify based on a combination of statuses, including first generation, low income, and disabled. Both Public and Private have decided to generously supplement the funding for this program so they can serve a larger number of students than the federal grant funds would cover. In that way, both schools are signaling to the students enrolled that they matter, that the university values them so much that extra resources are devoted to ensuring their success. In this way, they are offering campus-community belonging directly to this population. Throughout this book I refer to both schools' expanded programs as Student Success Resources (SSR), rather than Student Support Services, as a reminder that they are wider and more accessible than the federal TRIO program. Like other universities across the United States, both Public and Private invite SSR students to campus before their first semester to participate in a Summer Bridge experience. As part of Summer Bridge, students take a special course to help them get acquainted with college academics and to get to know each other for friendship and support as they navigate the transition to college. At both universities the Summer Bridge programs are well funded and well loved by the students who attend them.

Of course, where buildings are physically located on campus is another way that institutions communicate their priorities, and in this way Public and Private send different messages to their students and contribute to the differences in campus culture at each school. At Public, the SSR Center is located in a tall impressive building in a central area of campus, just steps away from a complex of classrooms that are commonly used for intro-level classes and not far from the campus' main library. This means that first-year students likely pass by it routinely during the school week. It is where students who are enrolled in SSR come for tutoring sessions or advising appointments, or just to hang out or do homework. Public's program requires multiple hours a week of mandatory tutoring for everyone enrolled in courses that are known to be troublesome, such as Calculus I and Introduction to College Writing (Conefrey 2018), so students find themselves in the SSR Center on a regular basis. For many, it becomes a safe haven that offers social belonging. The program also pairs first-year students with peer mentors whom they meet for the first time during Summer Bridge, which at Public is four weeks long.

The prominent location of the SSR Center on campus and the intensive time commitment for Summer Bridge and mandatory tutoring both signal to students that their academic success matters at this university and that achieving it requires a serious commitment by the student. SSR resources, help, and mentorship are not available to anyone and everyone at Public but are reserved for students like themselves who need it the most. By investing in the academic well-being of SSR students, the university is offering campus-community belonging and at the same time helping cultivate the culture at Public that prioritizes academics over other pursuits.

There are similarities in the way SSR is structured at Private. The university also signals to SSR students that they are valued by investing in their academic success. Private too pairs first-year students with peer mentors in the program, providing a lifeline for support and encouragement. However, key elements communicate that Private is a place where academics are not expected to be students' only focal point in their college experience. For example, tutoring is ample and available in the SSR Center, but not mandatory as it is at Public. Summer Bridge is a successful cornerstone of the program that happens over one week, as opposed to four weeks at Public. Importantly, the SSR Center is located on the outskirts of campus in a complex of buildings that most undergraduates never have reason to enter. If students want to meet with advisors, attend tutoring sessions, or just pop by for free printing, they have to walk or take a tram to this remote corner, which separates their SSR experience from the rest of campus life. Private students experience it as somewhat isolating, even as they simultaneously experience SSR as a "lifesaver," a "family," and a "home." In terms of offering campus-community belonging, this placement of the SSR Center sends a mixed signal to students: we value you, but at the same time we hide you.

Majors and Advising

At Private, the faculty who teach the dorm-community courses are assigned as the primary academic advisors for all the students in that course until they declare a major. The assumption seems to be that this will build relationships quickly between students and their professor. The faculty member whom they see in class multiple times a week is the same person whom students should turn to for advice about which future courses to take, whether to withdraw from a class they are failing, and so on. My interview data show that this works well for some first-year students and less so for others. Sabrina, a first-generation student who identifies as "I'm Mexican," illustrates the drawbacks. She met with her faculty advisor to figure out which courses to take in planning for a neuroscience major. In particular she wanted guidance about a chemistry requirement and whether she should postpone it one semester to lighten her workload. She tells me, "I met with him to plan out a schedule and he just did not know what he was doing. I don't know if it is because of my science major and he is a literature professor, but he pretty much told me he didn't know. He didn't give me any advice. I didn't come out with a plan or anything." Sabrina says he is "a great professor" in class but does not intend to ask for advice again in the future even though he is her official academic advisor because "I don't feel like he could help."

By comparison, at Public, it is impossible to run into this kind of frustration because academic advising is done by professional staff who know the ins and outs of curriculum policies and strategies. Every student I interviewed at Public described their academic advising sessions in positive terms. They were efficient, helpful and easy to schedule. Unlike at Private where students have to stop in during their faculty advisor's limited office hours to have their advising questions answered, students at Public had access to full-time advisors who had appointments available every day of the week. The differences are sharp: Public's efficient and effective advising structure clearly communicates that academics are the top priority, and no relationship is expected to develop with an advisor. In contrast, Private's structure, in which professors serve as academic advisors for undeclared students, communicates that relationships are the top priority, even if academic oversights result.

Where academic advising was a breeze for students at Public, declaring a major was a potential landmine. Multiple majors at Public are impacted, which means there are more students who want to declare that major than there is room for. Public's admissions policy is to allow students to enter with a declared major, so some students already have a secure place in impacted majors when they arrive. However, students who do not qualify based on their GPA from high school, standardized tests scores, and the rest of their college application, are allowed to enroll at Public as undeclared and apply for the major at the end of their first or second year. Incredibly high college GPAs are needed to be successful in this venture because only a few spots are available each year. Yet several students in my sample were killing themselves in the attempt to get high enough grades to get in, like Patrick whose situation I describe in the next chapter. Most ended up facing heartbreaking defeat and gave up on their dreams in their second year. This kind of academic rejection is impossible to experience at Private where no majors are impacted nor do any majors require students to prove their worthiness before declaring.

Another landmine in declaring one's major happens when students at Public decide they want to pursue a major that is not aligned with their dorm-community. Valentina, a first-generation student who identifies as "Chicana. Yes, and Mexicana as well," is an example. She intends to be an International Relations major: "I can't remember if I chose the engineering dorm as my first choice. I'm fairly certain that I didn't because it just wouldn't make sense with my major." Valentina was failing her calculus class when we met for our first interview and was trying desperately to move out of her current dorm and into the dorm aligned with her major. If her petition to move were successful, she could drop her calculus class because it is not a graduation requirement for that dorm. After several months of appeals, her petition was denied, and Valentina then had to face multiple calculus courses standing between her and her bachelor's degree.

These kinds of experiences—Sabrina being sent off without advice from her advisor, Patrick being rejected from his intended major, and Valentina being denied a dorm change that would fit her academic talents better— are examples of the university withholding campus-community belonging from students. Sabrina, Patrick, and Valentina do not feel like their universities care about them. The message is clear: they are on their own to sink or swim, and it does not matter to the university which occurs. This echoes Violet's experience at Private in the previous chapter when she said, "It's hard to feel valued if they have the ability to do something but they don't."

Similarly, Benjamin, a continuing-generation student, laments that Public does not give enough "attention to students." He wishes the university would "cultivate a sense of 'Oh! We're proud to go here! This is where we are!' I feel students will naturally feel they start to belong. That also comes along with feeling the school wants them here." A cornerstone of belonging for Benjamin is that students feel wanted by their school. Benjamin is poised yet candid in our interviews, self-confident without a trace of arrogance. He ethnoracially identifies as "mostly I say Asian. Sometimes I say Chinese." He is an international student, a British citizen whose parents currently live in China, but he attended a private boarding school on the East Coast for high school, so he has been living in the United States for several years. His perspective reflects the characteristic focus on academic belonging that is pervasive at Public:

A lot of my friends, all I hear is about them being put on academic probation and then getting warned and not really doing anything to help them. They've been trying to switch out to different majors and they can't because the GPAs are too low. So I just feel it's definitely a very hard place to stay afloat. I think if there's one thing that I could change about Public [it would be that] the students felt the school was making a bigger effort to keep everyone afloat.

Several first-generation students echo Benjamin's sentiment. However, first-generation students are more likely to describe the institution as not caring about them personally, as opposed to Benjamin, a continuing-generation student who sees this lack of caring affecting others, rather than himself. Thus, organizational structures can offer belonging, withhold belonging, or send mixed signals to students. Organizational structures contribute directly to universities' distinct campus cultures.

Private University: Social Belonging Is Salient

Given Private's organizational structures, it is not surprising that students there commonly place social relationships front and center in their descriptions of college life. When I sat down with Dalisay at the end of her second year, she gave a typical example. Dalisay identifies as "Filipino. Asian. I also define myself as Asian American." She is a first-generation student whose energy fills up the room. In all three interviews she exuded happiness. She has a bouncing smile, a genuine laugh, and a confident voice—at times when she shared intimate details about her feelings, she used her full voice in the open courtyard where we sat together. My instinct was to feel shy on her behalf because others could easily overhear her. Dalisay was not the least bit shy, however. I found her brave and impressive. In the beginning of our third interview, before I had used the word "belonging," Dalisay makes it clear that she experiences belonging in all three realms. However, she puts social belonging first and strongest:

LN So, the first question is, How is college going for you?
DALISAY So good. It's so good. I love it here.
LN That's wonderful. On a scale from 1 to 10, how successful do you feel as a college student?
DALISAY I would say an 8.

LN Okay, tell me more.

DALISAY It's pretty high.

LN Yeah, it's very high. Why is 8 the right number?

DALISAY Socially I'm doing really well. I've made a lot of great friends. I think I found my squad here, if I could say that. Personally I think I'm doing really well too. I think I definitely learned how to time-manage really well, especially after my freshman year. And then academically it's been going pretty well too. So I think that all of those combined have really helped me like the school even more and become successful here.

Dalisay's answer to the question of whether she is a successful college student centers on social belonging: "I think I found my squad here." Academic achievement along with life balance (as indicated by her satisfaction with her improved time-management skills) are also part of her definition of success, but academics are not the first thing on her mind. When I asked directly about belonging, some students at Private did not mention academics at all, including Dalisay herself in our first interview. Instead she focused entirely on friendships.

Another typical example is James, a continuing-generation student who identifies as "As far as race goes, I mean—so, it's like—I am in the majority of being white." James has a sweet nature and is unwilling to speak unkindly in our first interview, even about people and situations that have been tough for him, such as his roommate's sleep habits. He is talkative in our interviews, and his voice has a hint of a southern accent, no doubt from living in Louisiana when he was young. He works at a nearby gym and plays intramural basketball. He told me that exercising is how he stays mentally sane. In our third interview at the end of his second year, I ask whether Private is a place where James feels like he belongs: "I mean ultimately, we're all just students looking to get a degree. But I feel that I fit in pretty well with the general demographic of Private kids and I've made a ton of great friends here. So yeah, I'd say so." He tone is casual, easy. I ask what it means to belong:

I think it's all about making relationships. For the most part, everyone at Private has been incredibly friendly. And I have made, I mean, what in high school was an unimaginable amount of connections and relationships. I'll walk across campus and I'll say hi to five people I know, which for me—I don't know, I think it's pretty cool. So I would say I do belong. I think here at

Private, really, if you're open and friendly—I think it's hard not to make a lot of friends. So belonging, just kind of—I don't know. Being happy in the community and being able to be a friendly presence and meet people. I'd say that's my thoughts on belonging.

James leaves academics out of his definition of belonging entirely: "it's all about making relationships" for him, which is fitting given Private's campus culture. For James, campus-community belonging seems to be tucked into social belonging. He has made a previously "unimaginable amount of connections and relationships," but they are not discrete individuals he has discovered in a search for people to whom he can relate. Instead, "everyone at Private has been incredibly friendly," and he suggests he is "happy in the community," which represents dynamics in the realm of campus-community belonging. Of course, continuing-generation and ethnoracial-majority students like James are the most likely to perceive it as "hard not to make a lot of friends," as I discussed in the previous chapter, but James's response also underscores the salience of relationships and friends in Private's campus culture.

That relationships are central to college life at Private does not mean that academics are altogether unimportant. Instead, relationships are seen as indispensable, even in the face of academic disaster, in much the same way that, at Public, academic success is seen as indispensable, even if one's social life is a flop. Some Private students such as Brandon describe how their friendships bolster their academics (Antonio 2004; Azmitia et al. 2018). Brandon is a first-generation student who identifies as "African-American for sure." He is energetic; his lean frame hardly stays in his chair. His whole body seems to gesture along expressively as he talks. In our first interview he speaks of his new college friends affectionately. They are "my rebound from stressful academics. They're my outlet of everything. So friendship does play a big role." Brandon has had a particularly rocky transition to college academics: "I've always been really good with my studies. So when I saw the first F or the first D or the first C, I'm like, 'Whoa something is wrong here. I'm not doing well here.' I just thought college wasn't for me." He considered giving up entirely in those early weeks of his first semester, but after leaning on his new college friends for encouragement, Brandon bounced back: "I took this weekend and got organized, and I'm actually loving the school now. I'm back up on top." Brandon offers a good example of how social belonging can engender academic belonging.

A few students at Private were frustrated by the focus on social belonging on the campus. Just as Lucia and Regina were frustrated by the academic single-mindedness they discovered at Public, Katie laments that academics are not prioritized enough at Private. We met Katie in the previous chapter. She is a continuing-generation student who identifies as "I am Vietnamese, but if I were to describe myself, I would say Asian American." In our first interview, she was feeling great about her college friendships. Recall that in chapter 1, she said, "I love hanging out with them. I feel like they want me to hang out with them. Like I'm not just there. And it just makes me happier to know that I have friends that want me there, that make me feel like I belong." However, a year and a half later, Katie felt differently. In our third interview, she says she only "sometimes" feels that she belongs:

> A lot of the people here are not people that I am similar to, especially academically. Outside of the people that I have classes with in my science courses, they're very different from me. Then the people that I was friends with, they're really different from me. They enjoy the social aspect more than the academic part. But I have goals that I want to achieve after college, so I focus more on the academic side, and a lot of people don't understand that. They write me off as just being a nerd, but—it's like they just see instant gratification—and there's delayed gratification.

Katie does not spend much time with those early friends anymore, even though she cherished them her first semester. In that first interview she unequivocally told me that she belonged at Private, and she defined belonging as "feeling happy and comfortable. So you don't walk around and feel like you want to hide." At that moment, she did not mention academics whatsoever as being part of her sense of belonging. I had to bring it up. Now, at the end of her second year, when she only "sometimes" feels like she belongs at Private, her definition of belonging includes both social belonging and campus-community belonging: "To belong, I think in the smaller aspect is to have a group of people you can be whoever you want to be around, and do whatever you want. And then belonging in the sense of on campus in general, I think just being able to walk on campus and be like 'this is where I'm meant to be.'" Just as she did in her first interview, Katie defines belonging as being able to walk around campus confidently. However, relationships come up first in her answer, and her previous comment that her former friends "write me off as just being a nerd" hangs in the air behind it.

Katie was one of three students in my random sample at Private who felt disappointed that so few of their fellow students were academically focused. Again, this is evidence that campus culture is not something that simply reflects the sensibilities that students bring with them. They learn about and discover campus culture once they are part of campus life. Katie did not register her own disappointment until she had been there for a while. Although she tells me clearly, "I am not unhappy," she agrees with me when I suggest, "But that's not quite the same thing as being happy, is it?"

Katie applied to other schools to transfer out of Private after her first year. She was accepted to two very prestigious universities and wrestled with the decision to leave. In the end she reluctantly decided to stay at Private, explaining that "the biggest factor" was that the transfer schools did not offer her academic scholarships: "I didn't want to do that to my parents." On the heels of that comment, she added, "Also, if I left, I would be starting over basically, and my GPA would just be gone, and I'd be in the worst classes, the classes that no one wants. I'd have to start over with new friends, and that's kind of, just—what made me decide not to leave in the end." Katie's situation is instructive. It helps us appreciate that campus-community belonging is not required for students to stick it out. As Javier at Public said in the previous chapter, "Just because I don't belong here doesn't mean I can't succeed here."

Campus-Community Belonging Shifts over Time

Katie is one of 12.9 percent (4 of 31) of students in my sample at Private whose campus-community belonging declined over time (see table 4). All four students are continuing-generation students, including Madison and Justine who transferred out of Private in their second year. Ideally, students' belonging would not ever decrease, and all students would experience steady belonging over time, which is the most common trajectory for campus-community belonging at Private: 58.1 percent (18 of 31) of Private students— of whom more first-generation students (61.5%) than continuing-generation students (55.6%) had this experience.

If we combine those who experience steady belonging with those whose belonging increases and the additional few who have ups and downs during their first two years at college but land with belonging at the end of that time (a total of 9.7%, or 3 of 31, have ups and downs, but one ends with no

Table 4
Campus-Community Belonging Shifts over Time

	N	Consistent Campus-Community Belonging	Improved Campus-Community Belonging	Consistent Partial Campus-Community Belonging	Declined Campus-Community Belonging	Consistent Absent Campus-Community Belonging	Up & Down Campus-Community Belonging
Public							
All students	25	12.0%	28.0%	4.0%	28.0%	12.0%	16.0%
Continuing-gen	9	22.2%	33.3%	11.1%	11.1%	11.1%	11.1%
First-gen	16	6.3%	25.0%	0%	37.5%	12.5%	18.6%
Private							
All students	31	58.1%	9.7%	0%	12.9%	9.7%	9.7%
Continuing-gen	18	55.6%	5.6%	0%	22.2%	5.6%	11.1%
First-gen	13	61.5%	15.4%	0%	0%	15.4%	7.7%

campus-community belonging), then we can see that altogether at the third interview 74.2 percent (23 of 31) of my sample at Private experience campus-community belonging (see table 5). This is a relatively strong number, and it is about the same as the 75.0 percent (27 out of 36) who experienced campus-community belonging at the first interview. Impressively, a higher percentage of first-generation students had improved campus-community belonging than did continuing-generation students.

By comparison, table 4 shows that at Public only 12.0 percent (3 of 25) experience steady campus-community belonging throughout all three points in time, the same percentage who consistently experience absent belonging. The level of others increases over time to reach belonging: 16.0 percent (4 of 25) and another 8.0 percent (2 of 25) who had ups and downs end their second year experiencing campus-community belonging. Thus, at the third interview 36.0 percent (9 of 25) of the sample experience campus-community belonging, (see table 5), which is lower than the 45.7 percent who experienced it at the first interview. We see in table 4 that equal numbers of students (28.0%) see their campus-community belonging improve over time and decline over time at Public. These shifts are more than twice as common as the steady experiences of belonging. At Public, campus-community belonging is in flux for the vast majority of students in my sample over their first two years on campus.

There are also critical differences between first-generation and continuing-generation students at Public. Table 5 gives a snapshot: first-generation

Table 5
Percentage of Students Who Experience Campus-Community Belonging

	Public		Private	
	N	Campus-Community Belonging	*N*	Campus-Community Belonging
Interview 1				
All students	31	45.7%	36	75.0%
Continuing-gen	11	45.5%	21	81.0%
First-gen	20	45.0%	15	66.7%
Interview 2				
All students	29	37.9%	34	67.6%
Continuing-gen	10	50.0%	19	68.4%
First-gen	19	31.6%	15	66.7%
Interview 3				
All students	25	36.0%	31	74.2%
Continuing-gen	9	44.4%	18	66.7%
First-gen	16	31.3%	13	84.6%

students are at near parity with continuing-generation students with 45 percent experiencing campus-community belonging in the first interview, but that figure drops to 31.6 percent by the end of the first year and hovers there at the end of the second year. In contrast, continuing-generation students experience an increase in campus-community belonging, to 50.0 percent in the second interview and then drop back to 44.4 percent in the third: this reflects some fluctuation, but continuing-generation students' percentages never drop as low as those of first-generation students.

Looking again at table 4, we see sharper differences between the belonging experiences of first- and continuing-generation students at Public: clearly, continuing-generation students fare better across the board. They have a greater claim to steady campus-community belonging, higher percentages of improved belonging, and a lower rate of decreased belonging. First-generation students at Public, in contrast, more often have campus-community belonging withheld from them. More than half of my sample experience downward shifts in their campus-community belonging or consistently live without having any belonging at all during their first two years.

I do not want to exaggerate the power of these numbers because my sample sizes are not large enough to be generalizable. However, the numbers do offer evidence that Private is cultivating a campus culture where belonging is offered to a greater share of students than at Public. This is likely due to the heavy emphasis that Private places on relationships. After all, belonging only exists in relationships with others. Private is also meeting the belonging needs of its first-generation students better at the campus-community level, both relative to Public and, by the end of their second year, relative to Private's continuing-generation students.

University Decisions and Students' Lives

To help us think about how two universities can exhibit such stark differences, it is useful to draw on inhabited institutionalism theory. Inhabited Institutionalism emphasizes the role of individuals who "inhabit" an organization such as a school; that is, the people who operate within it. It focuses on interactions among individuals and the ways that people make meaning within the organizational context (Haedicke and Hallett 2015; Leibel, Hallett, and Bechky 2018). For those of us with some college knowledge, it might feel like common wisdom that a large research institution such as Public would have a very different cultural environment than a smaller liberal arts institution such as Private and that the two would have housing policies and curriculum requirements that reflect different priorities. Importantly, policies and priorities are constructed by people, even though we often think of them as part of the faceless, institutional university landscape. Inhabited Institutionalism research shows that such policies are the result of both widely shared ideas, such as what effective university programs around the country look like, and of the particular sensibilities of the people who are in charge of making decisions (Hallett 2010; Reyes 2015, 2018). Decision makers at different organizations (in this case universities) craft policies and strategies that take into account the circumstances and tensions in their own organizational context (their campus), as well as broader wisdom on successful practices (in higher education); all of that is then filtered through the individual decision maker's own training and perceptions of what seems like the right thing to do (Binder 2007; Everitt 2012, 2017; Haedicke 2016). Thus, we should expect even similar universities—for example, three large public research universities in the same state with similar programs for first-year students—to implement the same kind of programs differently. Consequently, each campus will foster its own distinct cultural environments to which students will need to adapt.

Inhabited Institutionalism research also shows us that students' personal identities and future trajectories are influenced by the cultural ideas that exist at their school (Binder and Wood 2013; Nunn 2014; Binder, Davis, and Bloom 2016; Reyes 2018). Where you attend school shapes your ideas about success and about who you are in critically important ways. Thus, there are two important takeaways from my analysis. One is that the increased difficulty that many first-generation students and minority students of color experience around belonging is created by the university and is not an inadequacy of some kind of the students themselves (Davis 2010; Jehangir 2010; Beattie 2018). The second takeaway is that decision makers in university administrations, as well as faculty members, can make targeted changes that shift the campus culture toward greater inclusion and belonging not just for marginalized students but also for all students (Harper and Hurtado 2007; Strayhorn 2008; O'Keeffe 2013; Nunn 2019a). To do so effectively they need to understand their own campus's dynamics, specifically whether it promotes academic belonging over social belonging, or vice versa. These ideas are embedded in the suggestions I offer in chapter 7.

3

Academic Competence
and Academic Belonging

· · · · · · · · · · · · · · · · · · · ·

Academic belonging means feeling that you are an accepted member of the academic community of your campus, which is different from the wider campus community. The feeling of being accepted academically is multifaceted. First and foremost, it requires being competent in coursework. Thus, it is not surprising that many students in my study use their GPA as a belonging gauge: good grades validate their capabilities. However, there is more to it. Academic belonging includes a sense of confidence in one's own academic ability, which Mason, a first-generation student at Public, clearly lacks as he relates his worries to me: "Do I even belong in college at all? . . . Am I good enough? Am I smart enough? Just academics . . . when my grades took such a significant drop on me, despite my best efforts—it's hard to think that I belong in a university just because the fruits of my labor should have been better." Mason identifies as "Hispanic/Latino and White. . . . I don't necessarily have a set ethnic identity, because my ethnic background has never defined me, but that might just be because I look White."

His example highlights the doubts about belonging that arise for students when they face academic challenges. Brianna, at Private, a first-generation student who identifies as "I'm White," has similar doubts in her political science class: "It's all work for hours of studying and still Ds. I've never been a student who has received grades like that, so I really don't know if it's my studying methods are wrong. I don't feel like they are because I wouldn't have passed so many AP exams and standardized tests." The transition to college academics can be frustrating and confusing for students, particularly first-generation students like Brianna and Mason (Collier and Morgan 2008; Mehta, Newbold, and O'Rourke 2011; Katrevich and Aruguete 2017; Azmitia et al. 2018; Conefrey 2018).

Laura, a first-generation student at Public, also looks at class averages instead of GPA. She explains that if "everyone is struggling, you might not know them personally, but you know, 'Oh, if the average is *this*, then yeah, people are struggling with this. Wow.' So, with academics you have indicators to see if you're the only one . . . and you don't feel as alone, like, 'Oh my God, it's just me.'" Based on these measures, Laura says that she is "in the middle" when I ask her if she feels like she belongs at Public. She answers my question exclusively as it relates to academic belonging: "I think about chemistry class and how the average is something, and I don't get that [score], so I'm like, 'Oh'—I mean, I didn't get so much below the average, but it's still—I didn't meet the average." Laura identifies as "Latina. Hispanic. Because that's where my roots are from." We learn more about her in the next chapter when she talks about her favorite professor.

When students feel academically competent, they experience some academic belonging. That sense of belonging brings a certain confidence with it, a confidence that allows them to raise their hands in a lecture to ask a question or make a comment that engages the professor directly. Students feel comfortable going to office hours without feeling like their questions will only reveal their ineptitude. Such confidence also fortifies them to participate in study groups without worrying that their peers will be disappointed by how little they know, a concern that multiple students expressed. One such student is Xavier, a continuing-generation student at Private who identifies as "I use Vietnamese because looking at me you can kind of tell I'm Asian," He explains, "If I'm studying with them and I haven't really gone over the material and I'm unprepared for study session, that's going to make me more worried . . . after I've reviewed everything and now I enter the study group, it's a lot easier for me." Others like Ilana, a first-generation student at Public who identifies as "Mexican," avoid studying with others altogether: "I'm not a study group person. Why? Because—I don't want to say because I don't feel smart—but I feel like I don't have as much to offer."

Shying away from study groups is a sign that a student does not experience academic belonging. This is doubly troublesome, because engaging with peers on academic material has been shown to have a positive effect on academic performance (Espinosa 2011).

Choosing a Major Yields Academic Belonging

Another important dimension of academic belonging is connected to declaring a major, because that decision entails settling on a path that speaks to a student's personal interests and academic strengths (Chambliss and Takacs 2014). Selecting a major means that students have found their place in the academic community (Schreiner 2018). Armanda, a continuing-generation student at Public, who identifies as "Mexican from my mother's side and then German/White American from my dad," explains:

> I think that's also another big point of me not like feeling like I belong is everyone else is like, "Yeah, I know exactly what I'm doing and in what classes!" And I don't right now. . . . I don't really know any other people who are undeclared like I am. Because of that it's a little difficult for feeling like I belong. But once I know that and I make friends in the major who have similar goals to me, I think that will help in belonging.

Deciding on a major is also part of the larger project of "becoming an adult" in college, as many students describe it: doing their own laundry, managing their own finances, and getting enough sleep all while figuring out where their passion lies and what future career goals they want to pursue. For many students the road to determining a major is bumpy (Malgwi, Howe, and Burnaby 2005; Allen and Robbins 2008; Engberg and Woiniak 2013). Failing assignments in subjects they want to love, realizing that they are not cut out to be, say, elementary school teachers after observing in actual classrooms with children, or endlessly waiting for a magic moment when their true passion is revealed to them through some spark in class—these are common experiences for the students in my study.

Students believe that the spark of passion that they are looking for is striking students all around them, though that is rarer than they imagine. David is an example of a student who found his passion. He is a continuing-generation student at Private whom we met in chapter 1. David identifies as "Black and Caribbean." He fell in love with his philosophy class: "I just like the material. It's the first class I was actually really interested in, where I looked forward to doing the reading, homework, and papers and all that." Aristotle was what did it for him. "The professor broke it down—we were studying it for a good month and that's when I realized this is for me. Because this is the kind of stuff that I wanted. So that was awesome. . . . It definitely changed the way I think about things."

Tan, over at Public, switched her major early on from biology to geophysics and tells me, "I just really love it." In chapter 1, we met Tan with her dyed blue hair and foot scooter: "I just describe myself as Queer. First-generation. Vietnamese American." The joy she is finding in her new major inspired her to join a club that travels to national parks to see geological formations and to attend a month-long Earth and Energy camp during the summer after her first year. She is all in. Tan is eager for student organizations or volunteering opportunities connected to geophysics: "I'm always searching for more things to do; even though I'm already busy, I still want to do more."

A critical part of why choosing a major yields academic belonging is because students believe that finding the right major is—or should be—synonymous with discovering their passion and purpose in life (Damon 2008; Clydesdale 2015; Burnett and Evans 2016; Cairns 2017). Tomás at Private sums it up succinctly: "you should do what you love." Students are convinced that the right major would lead to the right career, which would lead to a fulfilling life. The vast majority of students in my study do not sound as sure about what they love to do as David and Tan did, however, and even students who experience that enviable spark of passion sometimes change their minds. For example, after Aristotle, David later fell in love with communications and later still, finance, officially redeclaring a new major each time. For many students, the search for the right major tends to be an anxiety-ridden journey of false starts or perpetual uncertainty.

Competitive Majors and Competitive Careers Thwart Academic Belonging

Marisol at Public is the recipient of a prestigious and competitive national scholarship that supports promising students who are underrepresented in higher education. Winning this scholarship is an indication of her intellectual talents and potential for success, yet she is struggling academically in her first year. For Marisol, the scholarship is the reason she was able to attend Public; she told me she would have chosen a much less expensive school otherwise. Marisol identifies as "I'm Mexican." Her hometown is in South Central Los Angeles; she lives in a neighborhood that I depict in the previous chapter as suffering from poverty and city neglect. She has a warmly supportive family, but they have extremely limited financial resources to draw on and no college knowledge to offer whatsoever, which is not uncommon for first-generation students (Roksa and Kinsley 2019). After Marisol struggled with classes during her first semester, she decided to abandon her life plan of becoming an engineer. I talk to her at the end of her first year, just after she had switched majors. She tells me, "I'm currently a physics major right now—so then I was thinking it would kind of be cool if I were to double major in computer science and physics, but I don't think they'll let me do that, but I'm going to talk to the department and see if they do . . . But then I don't know because it's like I'm so lost in life right now, I don't know exactly what major to choose."

As with Marisol, the most painful experiences happened to students who entered college absolutely sure of their career choice, say, engineers or physicians, only to discover that their interest flagged or their grades in their first year were not high enough to be admitted into impacted majors or into medical school down the line. These disappointments were hard to overcome, impeding such students from experiencing much academic belonging during their first year or two, because the academic community was sending them unequivocal messages that they were not cut out for the field where they hoped to build a future.

For example, Sabrina, whom we met in chapter 2, is a first-generation student at Private who identifies as "I'm Mexican"; she has a 3.1 GPA at the end of her second year. "I think it's good," she said. "But once you look into the pre-health thing, it's like, 'Oh my gosh.' It's just—it doesn't feel like it's good, you know?" She explained, "Right now I'm doing the pre-PA requirements, which is a physician's assistant, and the more we learn about it—in the club we are in—the more we have guest speakers, the harder it sounds to get into a program. . . . They are just super high. They are 3.4 and above for everything." Sabrina has not given up but is worried as she looks toward her junior and senior years: "I know the classes are just getting harder." The goal of being admitted to a graduate school in health and medicine is a common one for students in my study at both schools. Like Sabrina, many were discouraged by the daunting statistics for admission.

A problem specific to Public is the difficulty of being accepted into impacted majors: many students in my study worked tirelessly their first year to earn a GPA high enough to be accepted into those majors, as I briefly discussed in the previous chapter. When I ask Patrick at the end of his first year whether he has settled on a major, he responds that it is a "touchy" subject for him. We met Patrick in chapter 1 where he shared his disappointments as a "shutout" in the social realm of his dorm. He is a first-generation student who identifies as "I'm an Asian American. I still hold close ties to my Asian culture because that's what I grew up with, but I've deviated from it. That's why I feel like I'm an Asian American." Patrick explains why choosing a major is "touchy" for him: "I talked to the advisor and I got some statistics on acceptance rates. . . . They were extremely deflating. . . . They only accept people once a year, which is already bad news. This academic year they have only taken in 10 people. It's based off of GPA and it's 10 people . . . for the entire body trying to apply into it."

Based on these numbers, Patrick tells me that his GPA would need to be in the top 2–3 percent of applicants next year to follow his dreams. "My grades aren't all that great," he admits. Then, with a heavy voice he tells me that he does not want to talk about it anymore. "I want to finish up on the topic," he says and then moves our conversation along with this comment: "I'll still try, but I'm pretty much tossing it out of the window for now and switching over to psychology with a minor in business . . . my college advisor recommended it." Patrick had yet to take a single psychology course.

Patrick's experience shows us how defeating it feels to be denied academic belonging in this way. Recall from chapter 1 that at this same time—the end of his first year—Patrick was also feeling socially ostracized. Yet when I ask Patrick whether Public is a place where he feels like he belongs, he answers, "Yeah. I still say I belong here. What path I'm going to be walking on has changed a bit." He clarifies that he is talking about both his change in major and changes in "my social half." Patrick experiences neither social belonging nor academic belonging at this moment, but with resilience that is characteristic of first-generation students, he refuses to give up (Stuber 2010; Azmitia et al. 2018; Covarrubias et al. 2019). He claims campus-community belonging.

A year later in our third interview, Patrick again claims that Public is a place where he belongs: "Yeah, sure. I would say it would be. I don't think I can imagine myself going anywhere else at this point." At the same time he still does not experience social belonging nor does he experience academic belonging. Yet that does not erase his sense of having at least some campus-community belonging.

That's not to say that nothing has improved for Patrick. He is happier because switching majors freed up a lot of time for him and also allowed him to improve his GPA. However, he feels like he is spinning his wheels taking prerequisites for the psychology major, which he still does not know if he will enjoy. His low GPA at the end of his first year continues to haunt his sense of accomplishment. "It was a 2.014," he admits softly to me, adding on the extra digits no doubt to emphasize that it was higher than 2.0. Importantly, in this third interview when I ask Patrick what it means to belong, he answers, "Quite simply, I'm just here. That's all I can think of really, that I'm just here. That's how things are." His definition sets a rather low bar for belonging, much lower than set by other students in my study. I see it as a sign of his determination to stick things out. Although it might be tempting for us—looking in from the outside—to think that this does not actually count as belonging at all, I am committed to allowing students to define belonging for themselves in this study. At this moment in Patrick's life, "I'm just here" is enough for him to feel some campus-community belonging, that he is a part of Public University, minimal as his part might be. Thus, I coded his third interview as having partial campus-community belonging (see "Methodological Appendix" for more details on coding).

Whereas Patrick demonstrates that academic belonging is not required for persistence, Marisol instead shows how valuable it is. For Marisol, the situation with her major was not as clear-cut as Patrick's. When I asked her why she decided against engineering, she replied,

> I kind of think it's the lack of confidence now, honestly. Because I feel like I can still go for engineering, I feel like inside I still think that that's what I should do, but, I don't feel confident enough to pursue it anymore. Everyone that's pursuing that major now, their parents are engineers or they're prepared, they know what they're doing. I'm just—I don't know what I'm doing. This is a trial-and-error process. . . . I knew we were coming from different backgrounds, but it's crazy because they are so much more prepared. And I feel like I have to do a lot more to get—to be on par with them. You know? And sometimes it's frustrating, and you're just like why do I have to do all of this? When they just got it like nothing because they were already taught this before.

Marisol does not experience academic belonging, even though she has mentors—professional engineers—who partner with her program and routinely give her advice and guidance. "I am so grateful for that," she says. Nonetheless she feels disheartened. She sits across an outdoor picnic table from me on a cloudy afternoon, her shoulders slumped over in an air of defeat, so droopy in fact that I could not read the bright logo of her prestigious scholarship on her sweatshirt until we both stood up to leave at the end of the interview. "I just don't feel supported, and I think that's the worst part." She adds,

> Because there are so many incoming students and we're all at different levels. Even though we have our highlights in different areas and we're good at different things, we come from different backgrounds and I feel like sometimes Public doesn't acknowledge that—that there are incoming students from poverty-stricken communities, or from various communities who didn't have all the resources and they weren't privileged. Students like myself. I feel like I'm at a disadvantage. I do have to put a lot more work in to try to be on par with my other peers.

Marisol points to the role that the university can take to foster academic belonging in students. As I explained in the previous chapter, Public and Private both offer campus-community belonging to students like Marisol by generously funding Student Support Resources (SSR) programs. Indeed, Marisol is an active member of SSR. Thus, she is a bit unfair in her characterization of Public as not "acknowledging" the backgrounds and differences that put students like her "at a disadvantage" academically. Regardless, Marisol feels frustrated by the extra burden of having to scramble to catch up.

Marisol's answer to my question about whether Public is a place where she belongs centers immediately on her feeling ethnoracially isolated: "Not really. I don't feel like I belong, at least not yet. I haven't found that home away from home. And aside from that, looking at the demographics, it's only a few Latinas here. It's hard to find people like myself, and it does make a difference. When you see other people like yourself, you're just like, 'I'm not alone in this.' You know?"

That is what belonging does for us: it makes us feel that we are not alone. I discuss ethnoracial dynamics in greater detail in chapters 5 and 6, because they are central to many students' belonging experiences. What I want to highlight here is that, despite taking advantage of campus programs like Student Success Resources, a professional mentoring program, and generous scholarship funding, Marisol feels unsupported: her academic belonging needs are not being met. In addition to wishing there were more Latinas around, she aptly zeroes in on one of the main challenges that first-generation students in my study face: their high schools did not prepare them for college academics the same way their continuing-generation classmates' high schools did (Martinez et al. 2009; Davis 2010; Fletcher and Tienda 2010; Jehangir 2010; Ward, Siegel, and Davenport 2012; Katrevich and Aruguete 2017).

The Effects of K–12 Preparation on Academic Belonging

First-generation students are likely to come from low-income backgrounds. That is because adults who have a college degree generally earn more money than those without one. Therefore, if neither of one's parents has a college degree, one is more likely to grow up in a low-income household. That means that first-generation students are also more likely to have attended modest or poor-performing K–12 schools (Bui 2002; Duncan and Murnane 2014; Redford and Hoyer 2017), which has an effect on college enrollment (Bastedo and Jaquette 2011; Roderick, Coca, and Nagaoka 2011; Radford 2013; Holland 2018). It also means that they are less familiar with the pace and rigor of college academics. What it does *not* mean is that they are less intellectually capable of doing the work, of course; it simply means that they have not been coached in critical thinking, critical analysis, writing, and other skills as much as a typical student has who attended high-performing schools that are often located in more affluent neighborhoods (DeRosa and Dolby 2014; Flores 2014; Clark 2017; Beattie 2018; Covarrubias, Gallimore, and Okagaki 2018). In the United States, the overall pattern is that the more affluent the neighborhood, the higher the quality of the public schools that serve the neighborhood (Kozol 2005; Lareau and Goyette 2014)—not to mention that affluent families frequently do not even rely on their local public schools but instead send their children to exclusive, college-preparatory private schools.

At both Public and Private, most first-year students I talked to struggle to "figure out how to study" in college. They often learn the hard way when they fail an assignment, a midterm, or an entire course that their high school study methods are inadequate. Easton, a continuing-generation student at Public, had such an experience in his first term: "I failed the class I put all my time into, and I could have saved the entire thing. I think 10 days of all-nighters . . . studying nonstop. I redid the entire course . . . [I had] no discipline at the beginning, but the final was weighted high enough that I could actually pull off an A. . . . It's a very dangerous gamble and it paid off terribly. But back in high school it worked out, better than it probably should have." During our final interview more than a year and a half later, Easton was still lamenting "that awful, awful class" from which his GPA had not yet recovered.

Although failure can be emotionally demoralizing for anyone—and it happens to continuing-generation students like Easton too—first-generation students are more likely to face failure in their first year because of their inadequate high school preparation, rather than a lack of self-discipline, which was Easton's problem. Marisol is not mistaken when she says that many of her classmates "were already taught this before." Amy, a continuing-generation classmate of Marisol's at Public, describes what it feels like on the other side of the experience in her introductory physics class:

> The material is not too difficult, and it's something we kind of covered in high school. But it's funny because the professor—he understands the material, it's just he'll present it up front in a very confusing manner. I think he just doesn't know how to walk students through things very well. He'll just say, "This is what it is," in a very complicated way, and then he'll be like, "Don't worry. You'll understand it by the end." It's like, okay, you've lost the students already. . . . Then he goes rather quickly, too, because he's like, "All right, now I've covered that. I can move to the next thing." I think some of the people beside me are like, "What's going on? I don't know anything!" . . . I'm really fortunate to have gotten the material beforehand and to have gone through it once . . . It's not too stressful. But I was a little deer-in-the-headlights when he went over certain concepts that I was shaky on in high school—so I was like, "Oh, he went so quickly! I might need a—I'm not sure."

Students at both schools told me story after story of professors who "move too fast" through material, "go off on tangents," "don't explain clearly," and have test questions on concepts or operations that "weren't anywhere" in the lectures or books. Although both continuing-generation and first-generation students alike experience these same problems because they are enrolled in the same introductory courses their first year, continuing-generation students, as Amy shows, are more likely to be able to jump these academic hurdles easily because they are already familiar with the course content (Mehta, Newbold, and O'Rourke 2011; Katrevich and Aruguete 2017). For others, such classroom experiences leave students feeling confused and dismayed. It undermines their sense of academic competence, which constrains their academic belonging.

Amy identifies as "I'm three quarters Japanese and one quarter Chinese. Yeah, so I'm Asian American." She experiences social belonging and campus-community belonging at this first interview and throughout her first two years at college. Although Amy experiences only partial academic belonging after her first term, it improves over time to a resoundingly strong level—so much so that in hindsight she describes her transition to college as "struggle free," both socially and academically.

At the end of her second year she does not seem to remember how challenging it was in the beginning for her to be diligent in her schoolwork. In her first semester she told me, "When it's a bigger lecture hall I find myself falling asleep even if the content was kind of interesting. Why am I falling asleep?" She also told me, "I think I learned in high school how to fudge it—smudge it, not fudge it—I mean you learn how to try and get by, just be able to sort of pull it off without really carefully doing the homework." She had to push herself to develop new habits of prioritizing academics, to get out of "my senior in high school mentality." Yet her high school years overall served her well: "I think that I was very well prepared by my teachers. My parents helped prepare us too." As evidence of that preparation, Amy's academic belonging was not threatened by the content of the physics class in her first semester. She found it "not too difficult" and "not too stressful," because she was "really fortunate to have gotten the material beforehand and to have gone through it once." Amy has an enviable 3.7 GPA at the end of her second year. She says casually, "It's pretty high. I feel like it could be higher."

First-generation students are likely to be on the opposite end of the spectrum: their high school teachers and parents laid less college-level academic groundwork for them (Engle and Tinto 2008; Conefrey 2018). Sometimes it is the fast pace of the class that is challenging for first-generation students, and other times it is the professor's poor teaching methods. Many students related to me examples of faculty failing to deliver material with pedagogical competence. Some instructors seem to simply not be good at teaching, and others seem, quite frankly, not to care about student learning. Serena, a first-generation student at Private, offers a typical story. She described her history professor who "didn't seem to care" about the course she was teaching, even to the point of telling the students, "'At the end of the semester when you have to rate me I don't care what you rate me because I'm retiring anyway.'" Serena thought it was a funny comment at first, but soon came to realize that the professor was genuinely not invested in the students' learning. Serena identifies as "African American. Also my grandpa was Chinese, and my grandmother was Native American and Black."

Like Marisol, Serena also won an enviable, prestigious national scholarship. She chose Private over her other top two schools, even though they were more selective and had "better" reputations, because "I just felt like before I even came here, I had people that were calling me just to check on me and stuff. I think that kind of made all the difference, just kind of having the support that worked before I got here, as opposed to the other schools." Each of her top three schools "have the really small class sizes, and that was something I definitely wanted." After arriving on campus, Serena feels a bit let down by Private, because she was expecting that same level of support in her classroom experiences that she got before enrolling. Yet her history professor

> just kind of goes off on tangents, so we get behind, and then there's a lot of work—I have to do twice the amount of work I'd have to do outside of class because she'll go on tangents. She's older, she's retiring, and . . . it's kind of related but not like what we cover in the book or the actual material. One time at the end of class there were like two minutes left and she literally went through twenty slides within the two minutes and she was like, "I can't really go through these" and was just kind of clicking through them and saying, "Okay so these are going to be on the test."

For Serena this was frustrating, not the least because she had never taken a European history class before, so she did not have prior knowledge to draw on to master the course content. Because AP European History is offered very commonly by well-funded high schools around the country, it is likely that some of Serena's classmates needed less from the professor than Serena did to do well in the class.

First-Generation Students Are Impressively Self-Reliant

Serena was determined not to let her nearly retired and checked-out professor get in the way of her learning history. She tells me it is her favorite course that semester: "I'm not a fan personally of the teacher, I don't like the way it's taught, but I like reading about it. I'm really interested in the subject material." She explained that to keep up she spends a lot of energy reviewing the lecture slides, which her professor posts online. "But the thing is, she changes them a little bit every year, so they're not the exact same all the time . . . she'll have old ones [posted online]. Once I email her, she'll update them, but they aren't automatically updated." In addition to essentially teaching herself material that is not covered well during lecture, Serena has to spend her time most weeks chasing down her professor for the right slides.

Serena is a great example of two key traits that first-generation students often have. First-generation students are highly motivated to succeed and are also incredibly self-reliant (Davis 2010; Jehangir 2010; Calarco 2018; Covarrubias et al. 2019; Marine Nin and Gutierrez Keeton 2019). Serena is less typical of first-generation students because she was not intimidated by her professor and emailed her time and time again to request updated slides. However, the fact that Serena took it on herself to figure out how to succeed in the class—even though it meant doing "twice the amount of work" outside of class because the professor's lectures routinely strayed away from explaining the material—is very typical of first-generation students.

Marisol over at Public offers another example of self-reliance. Recall that Marisol felt "unsupported" and "lost" despite the institutional resources she routinely accesses. When she found herself struggling in chemistry class, she figured out a way to solve it on her own. "Okay, so in high school—I came in honestly with no science background. I didn't know a thing about science. I was like, literally, what is science? I didn't know but it intrigued me because it just explains everything and I love it. Now that I've learned by reading the textbook it's awesome . . . what I ended up doing was I got a high school version of the chemistry textbook." She is proud of herself for thinking up this solution, and it seems to have worked: "The high school textbook, it explains it. It applies things . . . With the college version, it's just theories, theories, theories, and they're just like, 'Okay, how do you apply this?' That's what was hard for me in chemistry class because I didn't know how to apply things."

Marisol's ingenuity is not only an example of self-reliance but it is also clear evidence that students who arrive at college academically underprepared are not intellectually incapable of the work: they simply have not had enough practice at "applying things," as Marisol phrases it, or enough exposure to concepts that college introductory courses assume have already been learned. With the right support and some time, students like Marisol can catch up to be "on par with my other peers," as she phrased it. It requires enormous effort, but that is one of first-generation students' strengths: the willingness to do "whatever it takes" to succeed. The trouble is, that first-generation students do not always intuitively know what to change or how to strategize effectively in a way that enables enormous efforts to pay off (Collier and Morgan 2008; Kim and Sax 2009; Moschetti and Hudley 2015).

One example of not strategizing effectively for success is the reluctance of first-generation students to reach out to faculty for help (A. Yee 2016). Remember that Serena is atypical in repeatedly emailing her history professor for the lecture slides. Part of this reluctance stems from the fact that, in addition to figuring things out on their own, first-generation students' self-reliance includes taking responsibility for their mistakes and missteps. Taking responsibility for one's actions is unquestionably a strength, but counterintuitive as may seem, it can also be an obstacle to success. Ilana, whom we met earlier—a first-generation student at Public who identifies as "Mexican"—gives a typical example:

> One time I was doing my chem homework and it was due at 11:00 P.M. on the laptop. I was doing it and I was in the last question and it was 10:55. So I was like, "I got this!" And then it shuts me off. . . . It shut me off and said "your professor has canceled the session" or something . . . in the syllabus it says that you need to complete all of it or either you get no credit . . . And I haven't gone to the professor . . . because I was going to look like I was probably lying. She's going to be like, "Girl, you are lying."

Because Ilana did not have any "proof" to show the professor that the system shut down five minutes early, she was convinced that there was no recourse, given that the syllabus was so clear about the rules for submission. She told herself, "I was like, you know what? It's your fault for obviously not time managing well. I know that there is a higher risk if I work on my homework late at night." Then she admits sheepishly that it happened twice. That second time made her even more certain that she had to take ownership of the experience as her own mistake: "Yeah, I was like, 'Girl, no! You need to stop crying because it was your fault.' It wasn't the teacher's fault anymore. She could shut it down at 10:30 if she wants. 'You should have known already that it's not enough time from when you start doing your homework.'"

If Ilana had "college knowledge" about online course platforms, she might have realized that her professor can look up whether she was logged onto the system at 10:55, how long she had been logged on, and exactly which pages or portals she worked on. "Proof" existed, but Ilana did not know that. From her perspective, the professor had no reason to believe her and no reason to make an exception to her clear homework policy. Ilana did not view such policies as negotiable. A great deal of sociological scholarship on education shows that middle-class and (would-be) continuing-generation students are much more comfortable asking teachers and professors for special requests when something goes wrong for them, compared to lower-class and (would-be) first-generation students (Lareau 2003). This pattern also has a racial component: Whites and Asian Americans secure advantages that African American and Latinx students do not, both through their own requests and through teachers' implicit biases and assumptions. These dynamics are evident in elementary school (Calarco 2018), as well as in high school (Ochoa 2013; Castagno 2014; Lewis-McCoy 2014; Lewis and Diamond 2015) and college (Collier and Morgan 2008; Stuber 2011; Smith 2013; Thiele 2015; A. Yee 2016; E. Yee 2016; Hamilton, Roksa, and Nielsen 2018).

Much of this research points to cultural capital as the explanation. Middle- and upper-class White and Asian American continuing-generation students learn from their parents and families how to negotiate with authority figures and to expect accommodations that meet their individual needs. Meanwhile, lower-income and first-generation students learn from their parents and families that "bothering" the teacher is disrespectful and asking for special favors when you make a mistake is not admirable. Indeed it is a kind of moral failing, whereas doing your work on your own shows high moral character. Students in Anthony Jack's (2019) study of an elite college saw it as "kissing ass" to talk to professors and avoided it even when they saw their peers benefiting from their relationships with faculty (108). Importantly, Jack demonstrates that cultural capital can be gained from sources other than your family. The "privileged poor" students in his study who attended elite high schools on scholarships were just as comfortable interacting with faculty and asking for help and favors as their affluent classmates, and they explained that they had developed those habits in high school. Poor students who had not attended elite schools, however, experienced interactions with faculty as "tense, off-putting, and anxiety inducing" (92). Jack calls this group the "doubly disadvantaged" and argues that elite colleges are failing to adequately support them. Like the first-generation students in my study, the doubly disadvantaged found dignity in being self-reliant.

It is evident that the trait of self-reliance can bolster first-generation students' experiences of academic belonging when it helps them overcome challenges in courses, as Serena and Marisol show us. Academic belonging involves being interested in and connected to the material, and it yields the confidence and inspiration that come from understanding exciting new subjects. However, self-reliance can also work to constrain students' sense of academic belonging when it serves to stop them from talking to professors about their struggles and perhaps even lodging legitimate complaints that might yield results, such as having homework points count, as in Ilana's case. Not only did Ilana's grade suffer from the missed points but also her confidence in her academic competence was shaken: "I've cried more times these eight weeks than my whole entire life. I swear . . . I don't feel like I can't do this because I'm dumb. I just feel like I can't do this because I'm not prepared. Where I come from—my high school—you are not prepared." Thus, the extra obstacle to academic belonging that comes from being underprepared for college is not always overcome through self-reliance. In some circumstances, ironically, self-reliance adds to it.

What It Means to Be First-Generation

Although it is true that first-generation college students are more likely to have attended low performing K–12 schools, that is not all that comes along with that status. It also means that neither parent has completed the four-year college experience. Therefore, parents might not know anything about how to navigate the system themselves, which makes it impossible for them to pass on "college knowledge" as useful advice, such as pushing their daughter to tell her professor that the online system closed five minutes early and to show the professor her completed homework.

In my interviews, I asked students whom they turned to for college advice. Some continuing-generation students, such as Emily at Public and Julianne at Private, unhesitatingly responded "my mom" and "my parents," respectively, however, not surprisingly first-generation students almost never answered that way.

Marisol gives a very typical, self-reliant answer to that question among first-generation students: "I don't talk to anyone, honestly." She explains,

> Well my parents didn't go to college. They didn't—I think they just had like a third-grade education. So they—through that side they can't really help me, because they weren't prepared you know. They didn't go through the entire process. So they understand that for me it's very challenging. Sometimes they're just asking me, "So how are you doing? Have you fully adapted yet?" And I'm like, "I'm still trying." They're used to me just acing my classes and doing so well, so . . . sometimes I feel bad telling them. [pause] I don't, honestly. I just stopped telling them about how I feel emotionally because I know my mom gets worried. I don't want her to be worried. So I don't even tell her anymore. I'm just like, "Oh yeah, I'm fine."

Marisol is not the only first-generation student to say that sharing the emotional ups and downs of college is too difficult to do with parents. Violet is another typical example. We met Violet in chapter 1 as she was realizing she might not return to Private for her second year because her financial aid package was reduced. She told me then that she was putting on a brave face for her mom: "I don't think she knows the extent of my disappointment because I feel like if she knew how much I was bummed about it then she'd feel more upset."

Violet wants to protect her parents both emotionally and financially: "If I can't afford this school, I don't want to stay here another year and put that burden on my family. . . . It's very stressful but I'll figure it out." She ethnoracially identifies as "I'm Indian." Her dad grew up in India before emigrating to the United States. Violet relied on her SSR advisor for help with "my financial situation," just as she relied on that same advisor for help choosing her international relations and French double major and registering for classes. Violet says that she does not talk to her parents about those things: "I don't think they really understand the stress of college and things of that nature. . . . I'd say I rely on my friends more so for emotional and life advice. Because my parents grew up in a different world. They can't relate . . . Since they've never been to a four-year university, there's like a gap."

Violet's comment—"It's very stressful but I'll figure it out"—is yet another example of the ubiquitous trait of self-reliance among first-generation students. I found that many students described that sensibility as connected to their family upbringing. Brandon at Private, whom we met in chapter 1 and who identifies as "African American for sure," tells me in our first interview,

> I don't like to ask for help. I'm just very independent. All throughout high school and everything—since my mom didn't finish high school and I lived with my mom, everything was on me. And I figured high school out. I knew how to get the good grades and the extracurricular activities and the letters of recommendation. I figured it out. So I don't like to ask for help. And if I do, it's like, "Oh my goodness, this is serious." Because I don't like it at all.

Similarly, Patrick at Public shares, "I was brought up with the idea, mostly from my parents, that you try to figure everything out on your own first before asking others for help. Because a lot—in the real world—you are expected to know what you're doing and work on your own. So, I try to do that first."

For both Marisol and Violet, hiding their feelings from their families takes an emotional toll. They are distancing themselves from people who love and support them, which puts them in a lonely and isolating place. This dynamic is not completely independent from the characteristic of self-reliance. Like other first-generation students, including Brandon and Patrick, they seem to believe that it is their own responsibility to handle their college experience and not burden their parents with worry when it is not going well. Importantly, they are not only saving their parents from concern but they are also saving themselves from the additional task of managing their parents' feelings. Handling that task can add stress, as Brandon implies when he tells me he does not share "anything" with his family: "I would rather not, because then it would get her to worry, my mom to worry, or my family to worry. And I'm not in the mood for that."

Despite these complicated dynamics, many first-generation students describe their parents as incredibly supportive and a strong source of motivation for them, because they want to make their parents proud (Dennis, Phinney, and Chuateco 2005; Gofen 2009; Azmitia et al. 2018; Roksa and Kinsley 2019). Marisol tells me that she calls her mom every day and talks to her dad regularly too. "They don't really offer much advice," she says. However, "what they do—what my mom tries to do though, is motivate me. She always—oh my gosh, she's so cute!—sometimes she texts me little motivation quotes. I'm just like, 'Aw, she's so cute.'" Brandon also communicates with his mom every week. He smiles sweetly as he describes it: "Oh, she loves FaceTiming. Loves it." He affectionately exaggerates his mom's voice: "She's like: 'Oh, I get to see your face! You are alive!' and she asks, 'How is everything???'"

Not all first-generation students can rely on their parents for that kind of support, however (McCarron and Inkelas 2006). Laura Hamilton (2016) found that some parents of first-generation students are absent in terms of support or even sabotage their children's college success. Although none of the students in my study described being sabotaged by their families, some had to contend with serious and destabilizing family circumstances. One student's parents were losing their house. Two had parents who were in the process of being deported from the United States. Another student's legal guardian was her sister, who had to drop out of college to take care of younger siblings when their mother disappeared from their lives unpredictably. Yet another had recently been informally adopted by a friend's family when her mother was institutionalized in a mental health facility. One's father could not pay the tuition bill on time, so the student had to sit a semester out. Two others had parents who lost their jobs and worried constantly whether they too would have to stop out of college. Although these circumstances certainly could also befall continuing-generation students' families, in my sample these kinds of disruptions of family support networks occurred only in first-generation students' lives.

By definition, parents of first-generation students cannot pass on their own college wisdom, but many did provide emotional encouragement, as complicated as it might be. Other first-generation students were cut off from their parents by forces they could not control. Ilana's mother was one of those being deported, and she told me that her family was reluctant to keep her updated on the details: "I feel left out because they don't tell me as much. As parents you don't want to worry your child. She's in college, you don't want to distract her. That's another thing. I didn't tell my parents I was struggling because I didn't want to worry them also."

Self-reliance involves independence, resilience, and also a sense of pride around what it means to conquer challenges on one's own. Thus it is a positive trait even though it sometimes has unhelpful effects. Ilana brings it up again when she explains why she does not go see professors during their office hours, even for math and chemistry, which she is failing at the time of our interview. Recall Ilana's rough experience with the online portal shutting down on her chemistry homework. She says, "I'm going to tutoring at SSR, and I'm going to discussions and everything. I don't go to office hours though. I'm not going to lie. And that is because I feel—how to say it, not scared—I want to say scared." I suggest "intimidated?" and she responds, "Yeah, intimidated. That's the word . . . the feeling of—I guess because they are a professor. They are really good professors . . . I feel like if I were to talk to them—I guess it would be easier for—the thing is—I feel like for some reason—if I go to them I'll feel like they will think, 'Oh she wants me to have pity for her," or something. And I don't want that. Because I am used to doing stuff for myself." The way Ilana struggles to find the words to admit why office hours are intimidating to her is indicative of how uncomfortable she feels, which is also a sign of a lack of academic belonging. Like other first-generation students, Ilana does not want special favors based on the professor feeling sorry for her. Instead she wants to be successful the "respectable" way, by accomplishing things with her own skills and merit.

Continuing-Generation Students' Greater Academic Belonging

Continuing-generation students are not immune to roadblocks to academic belonging, as Easton and Amy showed us earlier. However, they often were able to navigate them fairly easily by simply by changing their study habits and becoming more self-disciplined. As table 6 shows, striking differences exist between Public and Private around academic belonging. Public's campus culture is heavily focused on academics, and students experience it as fiercely competitive (see chapter 2). Accordingly, it seems that academic belonging is rather hard to come by, especially at the start of the first year. Students at Public experience it at much lower rates at the time of their first interview than do students at Private: 29.0 percent (9 of 31) compared to 61.1 percent (22 of 36), respectively. This leaves the overwhelming majority of Public's students with partial (38.7%) and no academic belonging (32.3%), compared to Private where only 25.0 percent have partial and 13.9 percent have no academic belonging (not shown in table 6). Although both continuing-generation and first-generation students at Public see improved

Table 6
Percentage of Students Who Experience Academic Belonging

	Public		Private	
	N	Academic Belonging	N	Academic Belonging
Interview 1				
All students	31	29.0%	36	61.1%
Continuing-gen	11	18.2%	21	66.6%
First-gen	20	35.0%	15	53.3%
Interview 2				
All students	29	37.9%	34	58.8%
Continuing-gen	10	50.0%	19	73.7%
First-gen	19	31.6%	15	40.0%
Interview 3				
All students	25	52.0%	31	61.35%
Continuing-gen	9	77.8%	18	66.7%
First-gen	16	37.5%	13	53.8%

academic belonging over their first two years, continuing-generation students have stronger gains. They start very low at 18.2 percent at the first interview but jump to 50.0 percent by the end of the first year and increase again to 77.8 percent at the end of their second year. The change in first-generation students' belonging is more modest: from 35.0 percent to 37.5 percent over the two years, with a drop down to 31.6 percent at the second interview. At Private, academic belonging moves up and down among continuing-generation students, but they consistently have higher percentages than do first-generation students.

What It Means to Be Continuing-Generation

Just as first-generation students have typical traits, experiences, and forms of family support, so do continuing-generation students. The previous chapter discusses the cultural alignment that many middle-class and affluent continuing-generation students experience between the lives they grew up in and campus culture. This chapter has shown that continuing-generation students' educational histories also often set them up for success in college academics. Recall Amy's advantage in her introductory physics course at Public: "I think some of the people beside me are like, "What's going on?

I don't know anything!" . . . I'm really fortunate to have gotten the material beforehand and to have gone through it once." Amy's experience is common for students who had access to high schools with strong AP curricula. As discussed earlier, Amy went to a good high school largely because her family—and families like hers—was able to afford to live in a neighborhood that is served by a well-resourced and high-performing public school district (Owens 2017). College-educated Americans earn higher salaries than those without a college degree, so it is not surprising that continuing-generation students come from financially advantaged backgrounds.

In addition to having access to strong K–12 schools, having a family with greater financial resources also typically leads to a host of other advantages in college and afterward (McCabe and Jackson 2016; Rauscher 2016; Roksa and Kinsley 2019). Taking advantage of private tutoring and other test preparation such as for the SAT makes a student's college application more competitive (Buchmann, Condron, and Roscigno 2010). Research also shows that students with lower levels of college debt are more likely to complete their degrees (Dwyer, McCloud, and Hodson 2012), so having a family that can shoulder some or all of the costs of college is an important advantage for persisting to graduation. Natasha Quadlin (2017) shows that it also allows students to have greater freedom in choosing what to study. She found that students who have substantial student loans are more likely to major in applied non-STEM fields such as business, communications, nursing, and health, and they are less likely to be undeclared during the first term. These fields have "financial appeal with few barriers to entry" (99), which makes them strategic choices for students saddled with college debt. Quadlin argues, "Because students know they will be responsible for payments after leaving college, they may gravitate toward majors they perceived as practical because they facilitate the transition to full-time employment. Students may also choose these fields because they have few major requirements, which can shorten their time-to-degree and, in turn, their college costs" (113). Meanwhile students with low levels of debt or no debt at all are more likely to enter college undeclared and to major in a much wider set of fields. They are freer to explore their interests and choose a major accordingly, without taking future financial constraints into account.

Although this greater freedom is certainly a boon, it also has downsides. Studies of college life show that academics are often not students' main priority (Nathan 2005; Grigsby 2009). Many students "spend far more time socializing than studying" (Arum and Roksa 2011, 120), which is especially true for students from more affluent families (Armstrong and Hamilton 2013). Laura Hamilton (2013) shows that greater financial aid from parents can actually decrease the college GPA, because some students strategize to "perform well enough to stay in school, but dial down their academic efforts" to focus their time and energy on social endeavors (70). Similarly, Quadlin and Rudel (2015) find that many more debt-free students focus on extracurricular pursuits in a "socially engaged" lifestyle, which entails spending more time on partying, athletics, and student group activities compared to their peers who have college debt. Additionally, Hamilton (2016) found that some students strategically neglect to complete all the required credits for their major in four years to "get an additional, purely social, semester of college" on their parent's dime (128). It is clear that being financially supported by one's parents, as many continuing-generation students are, directly contributes to social relationships in college (McClure and Ryder 2018), which students experience as positive even though we might rightly be concerned about it, because too much socializing can detract from their academic performance.

In the last decade or so, some parents of continuing-generation students have been criticized for being "helicopter parents" who intensely monitor their children's success and swoop in to solve problems for them (Hunt 2008; Odenweller, Booth-Butterfield, and Weber 2014; Reed et al. 2016). Some are even considered "snowplow parents" who take helicoptering a step further and attempt to keep their children's paths to success free of obstacles (Miller and Bromwich 2019). Often called "overparenting," these high levels of intervening in students' college lives can have serious negative consequences, such as a lack of resiliency, increased anxiety and stress, and "higher levels of narcissism and more ineffective coping skills" (Segrin et al. 2013, 569; see also LeyMoyne and Buchanan, 2011). Yet, overparenting can also yield tangible payoffs (Lipka 2007). Hamilton, Roksa, and Nielsen (2018) find that affluent parents serve as a "college concierge," using resources of both money and knowledge about how college works "to provide youth with academic, social, and career support and to gain access to desirable infrastructure that maximizes their investments" (125). This includes strategizing how to get into competitive majors that offer career placement opportunities, securing private tutoring, arranging internship opportunities on their behalf, and paying for them to relocate geographically to relevant job markets after graduation. We also know that continuing-generation students are more involved on campus (Lundberg et al. 2007) and that students from higher socioeconomic backgrounds report stronger sense of belonging (Ostrove and Long 2007; Soria and Stebleton 2013; Jury et al. 2019). Therefore, it is not surprising that continuing-generation students in my study follow the same pattern.

Even after graduation, continuing-generation students experience greater benefits from their parents. Silver and Roksa (2017) find that parents play "an important role in providing resources to help students manage uncertainty. Continuing-generation students typically expected a significant amount of financial support from their parents and the added security of being able to acquire employment or developmental opportunities via their parents' social connections and the information they could provide about postgraduate options" (255). By contrast, first-generation students "valued the support their parents provided, but most were aware their parents would not be able to facilitate their senior-year transition with information or finances, which added to the uncertainty many first-generation students faced" (256).

The heart of what it means to be a continuing-generation student is that one has at least one parent who has successfully completed a bachelor's degree. That means one has a parent who can give tips, advice, and strategies for how to succeed in college (Schwartz et al. 2018). Continuing-generation students in my study routinely turned to their parents for academic advice—everything from what major to choose, to reading over essays before submitting them, to guidance on how to talk to professors one on one. For example, Hazel at Private, who identifies as "Well, I know I'm White," tells me in her first interview, "I think academics are the hardest part right now." I ask her, "So when a class is hard, what do you do?" and she responds: "I'll talk to my mom and ask her for advice." Emily at Public, who identifies as "I'm White," has a similar response: "I talk to my mom first. I am like, 'Mom, I'm struggling' . . . definitely if the class gets hard, I'm going to first complain about it to my mom. Of course, ask her for help."

Several continuing-generation students describe how they followed their parents' lead. For example, in his first semester at Private, Zach tells me, "I'm thinking about majoring in something similar to economics or finance. I'm obviously interested in that kind of stuff because it's what my dad majored in . . . and that's what he thinks I should do." Zach identifies as "I would say I'm pretty much just White. My mom is 50% Hispanic but I don't personally identify like that, even though it is in my background a little bit.

I personally just identify as White just because people see me and that's probably the first thing they're thinking." A year and a half later, at the end of his second year, Zach had just declared his finance major, smiling as he announced, "I am happy with it. That's what my dad did."

Other continuing-generation students in my study describe a balancing act where they not only rely on their parents' college knowledge but also try to feel independent from them. Kenadee at Private, who identifies as "I'm technically African American because that's how people label it, but I'm actually Caribbean," for example, acknowledges that she appreciates her mom's wisdom: "I definitely go to her for advice. Like when I was thinking about switching from an English major, I had to talk to her for a while about it." Kenadee's mom "worked at different colleges for 16 years so, she knows everything." But sometimes Kenadee would push back: "I'm like, 'Listen, I get it, but I'm trying to do my own thing.' She is like, 'Listen you should take my advice.' I'm like, 'I am taking your advice but with a grain of salt because I have to make my own decisions.'"

Tyler at Public, who identifies as "White," has a similar dynamic, though he sees his parents as less intrusive than Kenadee sees her mom. He says, "They're not here to tell me, 'Here's what you should be doing in college.' But if I have a question, they'll definitely offer me some type of advice. They don't necessarily expect me to have to follow it, especially now that they know, 'Yes, you're your own person.' But I really respect them because I know that they're very intelligent people. I hold them in very high regard. I will go to them." Tyler relies extensively on his parents for his schoolwork: "When it comes to, say, college advice and stuff like that, I definitely use them, especially my mom, because she likes hearing all these cool ideas and stuff for my essays. She loves hearing about what I like to write about for essays, so I like to go to her, especially if I'm stuck on something. It's like, here's my idea, and let me tell it to you." Tyler seems to genuinely enjoy his parents' input, and both of them have PhDs so they are very familiar with the kinds of critical thinking and writing that higher education demands. He tells me. "I love discussing things with my parents in deep intellectual conversations. In that sense, they're great as whiteboards for that kind of thing. It's a lot of fun."

Not all continuing-generation students have parents with PhDs like Tyler or whose careers revolve around college campuses like Kenadee, of course. Yet, they all know how the system works. At the end of her first year, in our second interview, Hazel shares with me she now avoids reaching out to her parents for academic help: "With grades I am just so worried about disappointing them that I don't want to be like, 'Okay, I'm struggling in this class. I don't know what to do.' Because then they would be like, 'Oh, but you haven't gone to office hours' and then they guilt trip me." Clearly Hazel's parents are well versed in what it takes to do well in college courses, so much so that Hazel can anticipate their scolding her if she has not sought out available resources such as office hours.

Katie Lowe and Aryn Dotterer (2018) suggest that "parental involvement" in college should be defined in a multifaceted way to capture the range of benefits it can confer on students. They highlight three categories: parental support giving, parental–student contact, and parental academic engagement. Thus, although both first-generation and continuing-generation students may receive emotional encouragement from their parents, continuing-generation students also have access to much greater financial and cultural resources and, perhaps most importantly, educational wisdom.

Academic Belonging Shifts over Time

Like social belonging and campus-community belonging, academic belonging also shifts as individual students' situations change. As table 7 shows, the most common pattern at Private is for students to experience consistent academic belonging across all three interviews (48.4%, or 15 of 31), whereas the most common pattern at Public is for academic belonging to increase over their first two years (52.0%, or 13 of 25), though 12.0 percent (3 of 25) only improve to partial belonging (not shown in table 7). However, it is clear that continuing-generation students fare better. At Private, nearly half the students in my sample had steady academic belonging, but that half is comprised of 55.6 percent (10 of 18) of continuing-generation students and only 38.5 percent (5 of 13) of first-generation students. Similarly, at Public just over half the sample increased academic belonging over time, and that half is comprised of 88.9 percent (8 of 9) of continuing-generation students and only 33.3 percent (5 of 16) of first-generation students.

At Public, the academic belonging of the first-generation students in my sample changes in a variety of ways, whereas only one continuing-generation student, Easton, saw his academic belonging move up and down over the first two years. All the other continuing-generation students experience improvement. At Private, academic belonging numbers overall are stronger

Table 7
Academic Belonging over Time

	N	Consistent Academic Belonging	Improved Academic Belonging	Consistent Partial Academic Belonging	Declined Academic Belonging	Consistent Absent Academic Belonging	Up & Down Academic Belonging
Public							
All students	25	12.0%	52.0%	4.0%	16.0%	12.0%	4.0%
Continuing-gen	9	0.0%	88.9%	0.0%	0.0%	0.0%	11.1%
First-gen	16	18.8%	33.3%	6.3%	25.0%	18.8%	0.0%
Private							
All students	31	48.4%	12.9%	6.5%	19.4%	3.2%	9.7%
Continuing-gen	18	55.6%	16.7%	5.6%	16.7%	0.0%	5.6%
First-gen	13	38.5%	7.7%	7.7%	23.1%	7.7%	15.4%

than at Public, but the road is also rockier for first-generation students: they experience less stable academic belonging, less improvement, more ups and downs, and more decline than their continuing-generation classmates.

Neither school—not the one that emphasizes the importance of academics nor the one that emphasizes social relationships instead—is doing right by its first-generation students in terms of academic belonging. Better understanding of the common experiences and traits that first-generation students bring with them, such as determination and self-reliance, will allow universities to better strategize to meet their belonging needs. I take up this discussion in the next chapter.

4

The Academic Community
and Academic Belonging

• •

Like the other forms of belonging, academic belonging is something that is extended from the community to an individual member, so it makes sense that grades and other indicators of academic competence are interpreted as signals of acceptance and belonging because these signals come from faculty and classmates. However, members of the campus community can also offer academic belonging. Emily at Public, whom we met in earlier chapters, offers an example. She is a continuing-generation student who identifies as "I'm White." When I ask in our first interview whether she feels like she belongs, she tells me about a key interaction she had before applying to Public, when she was being recruited by her athletic coach. She expressed to him her doubts about being capable of handling the academics at such a selective school. "My coach is like, 'No. I wouldn't recommend you coming if your grades were too low.' So I was okay. That comforted me." Emily needed an official member of the Public community to reassure her that she would academically belong there.

She follows that story with more details that speak to the way her team's collective academic experiences also help her figure out whether she academically belongs at Public. "Whenever I hear my teammates say, 'Oh, I had to retake this class,' it gives me comfort because we are all human. Everyone will goof up sometimes. It's fine. Everyone is there for you, and not everyone will be a perfect, straight-A student. No one is going to be a straight-A student here. It kind of proves to myself that I think I do belong here." Just as students in the previous chapter used GPA or average scores on class assignments as signals from the academic community about whether they belong, Emily relies on comparisons within her trusted community of teammates as signals of academically belonging.

Emily, however, is the exception in looking to her coach for reassurance of academic belonging. Most students interpret signals from their professors instead because they are prominent authority figures in the academic community of any campus. An important element of students' descriptions of academic belonging is feeling comfortable in class or confident enough to talk to a professor one on one—whether during office hours, by raising their hand in class, or approaching the professor before or after a lecture. As discussed in the previous chapter, this comfort tends to come along with feeling academically competent. We also saw how, for first-generation students, self-reliance can either contribute to a sense of competence by fostering learning and good grades or undercut it by discouraging habits of reaching for help, especially directly from professors.

Remember that belonging comes from the community and is not willfully acquired by individual students, which might seem counterintuitive. Students are working hard to perform well in their classes and strong performance is part of academic belonging, so it might seem as if students were indeed able to acquire academic belonging of their own volition. However, grades are not synonymous with academic belonging. Belonging is more comprehensive and more holistic than mere performance. In fact, it is often in moments of failure when academic belonging is generously extended to students, as Tomás shows us in the next section.

Professors' Contributions to Academic Belonging

Students at both Public and Private discussed at length with me the interactions they have with their instructors and how it makes them feel. Having a professor who shows interest contributes to belonging (Maestas, Vaquera, and Zehr 2007; O'Keeffe 2013; Hurtado, Alvarado, and Guillermo-Wann 2015). Students feel encouraged by professors who make them feel seen and who acknowledge their efforts; they take this as a sign of their academic worth, regardless of the outcome. Tomás, a first-generation student at Private, who ethnoracially identifies as "I am really proud to be Colombian. I love everything about our culture," recounted the "biggest disappointment" of his first year to me: he had to withdraw from a math class he was failing, leaving a W on his transcript. He smiled and told me and how much better he felt when his professor, who is also his academic advisor, shared that he too had failed a class his first semester in college. It was a relief for Tomás because he takes his education seriously: "This is a dream that came from a generation before me . . . my parents are immigrants and it's a dream carried on from them. They're like, 'I want to send my son to college.' That's why they came over and they wanted to make their family take a different path." Tomás's parents earn a comfortable middle-class income working in blue-collar industries, even though he says, "Obviously they don't like what they do, but they sacrifice and do it for me. . . . They are still supporting me, especially by paying for me."

Tomás is thriving at Private, and he is aglow with happiness in all three of our interviews. He speaks warmly and positively about every aspect of college, except for the fact that he is the only one among his roommates who cleans the bathroom. "I think the first thing is just being happy. It's really hard to do things in life if you can't smile," he tells me. He has a close relationship with his parents: "I actually keep in touch with my parents a lot. I'm an only child so they feel like they have an empty nest." He adds sweetly, "When I got accepted to college, God, it was a celebration for my family. It was a really happy moment."

As his parents did not attend college, he cannot rely on them for college advice and support: "unfortunately they can't help me out too much in that area. . . . I guess it's mostly like an emotional thing." Thus, when his faculty advisor made him feel "comfortable" about withdrawing from his math course that he was failing, assuring him that he would be able to make up the units, it encouraged Tomás. He felt cared about. His faculty advisor was offering academic belonging to him, signaling that he is accepted as he is, stumbles and fumbles and all.

Serena at Private, who in the previous chapter described the history professor who was openly disinvested in teaching, also had a physics professor that same semester whom she adored. He was one of the people who convinced her that attending office hours was worthwhile: "He's really funny, you can tell he just really cares, and he's passionate about the material. And he understands that it's hard. So even with his tests, even though they're difficult, I feel like he just prepares us really well for them, especially if you make the effort to go into office hours and get the extra help." Several students at both Public and Private echo Serena's comment that they like it when professors "understand that it's hard." It makes them feel less "alone" and less "lost" when faculty express in a straightforward way that they do not expect students to already know the material or to find the material easy. Hearing this validates students' experiences, particularly first-generation students who are less likely to be familiar with the content of introductory courses. It contributes directly to their sense of academic belonging.

Abundant scholarship demonstrates that positive student–faculty interactions yield many benefits for students, including better grades and increased self-confidence, motivation, and well-being (Halawah 2006; Kuh et al. 2010; Brint 2011; Kim and Sax 2017; Schreiner 2018). These positive interactions can be especially beneficial for students from marginalized backgrounds (Strayhorn 2008; Anaya and Cole 2001; Morales 2014; Thiele 2015; Vetter, Schreiner, and Jaworski 2019). Micari and Pazos (2012) show that, the more students admire a professor and feel that the professor respects the students in return, the stronger those students perform in the course. This is particularly true for those courses in which many students struggle, such as organic chemistry. Dachner and Saxton (2015) find that professors who highly rated their own commitment to teaching were perceived positively by students and that these positive perceptions pay off: "Students who believed that their instructor cared about their well-being and valued their contributions were more satisfied with their course and had higher commitment to the course" (560). The reverse is also true. Hawk and Lyons (2008) demonstrate that, when students feel that their professors have given up on them, they become less engaged, experience lower self-esteem, and are less likely to complete the course. Disinvested or dismissive faculty make students feel small and full of self-doubt. Despite overwhelming evidence of the benefits of positive student–faculty interactions, unfortunately many faculty members are unmotivated to engage in interpersonal relationships with students (Einarson and Clarkberg 2004; Hoffman 2014). Although there is rightly some debate over where the boundaries should be drawn for relationships fostered outside the classroom (Chory and Offstein 2017), even when interactions are limited to class time and office hours, some faculty are unwilling to devote their energy toward making students feel cared about and valued.

In my study, students' experiences seem to match these same dynamics. They deeply appreciate professors who are invested in them. Those faculty inspire students. As I show throughout this chapter, students experience professors' and TAs' behavior and demeanor toward them as unmistakable signals of whether they are wanted and valued by the academic community on their campus, of whether they belong.

Consider how Laura at Public describes her favorite math professor: "He's really, really good, oh my God. Yeah, I go to his office hours all the time and we developed a close relationship, so it makes me—seeing how passionate he is, and how much I love math, it just makes the class even—it makes it so good to be in there. It's at 8:00 A.M. and I don't even mind waking up at 8:00 A.M. for it." This professor offers academic belonging not only through his "passion" and his approachability but also through his willingness to go slowly and carefully through the material. Laura is a first-generation student who identifies as "Latina. Hispanic. Because that's where my roots are from." She has bright brown eyes. and when she talks about math, her whole face lights up. She continues to tell me about her professor: "He's always really well prepared. He comes in before class starts, and he already has notes on the board for us to copy down. He always does a lot of examples, which I like to see, because then if I see step-by-step methods, if I see a problem similar to it, then I know, 'Oh, it's something like this I saw before.' And then I can apply that to this."

Laura receives the gift of academic belonging from this professor. He shows how much student learning matters to him, and by extension, Laura feels that she matters. She is touched by his willingness to devote extra time and energy to help ensure his students' success: "He personally holds—before each midterm and final—five-hour review sessions. Yeah, like Friday and Saturday. Personally. It's not even the TA. So, he goes out of his way, and sometimes he—not all the time—but he prints out handouts for us to follow along with him during the review sessions, and I'm just like, 'Wow.' That takes a lot of dedication and passion to do that. To take time out of your day to do that."

On the flip side, Kevin, a first-generation student at Private who identifies as "I am Vietnamese," explains what it feels like when a professor does not offer belonging by validating students who struggle with the material or who are seeing it for the first time:

I had a professor who last semester who was just—he is a genius, he is definitely a genius like there's no question about it, he is a genius, he's smart but he teaches students as if we are geniuses or that we understand the material already. I mean yes, there was reading and yes, we read it, but it doesn't necessarily mean that we are able to absorb everything and understand it fully. And so when he explains it to us it's as if he's talking gibberish because we don't understand what the heck he's talking about. He definitely is a genius but like I said, he teaches us as if we're all geniuses as well. And I am not going to lie. I am nowhere near genius. So, when you try to teach me in that manner you can't expect me to understand you right away.

Kevin, like many others, says he feels "lost" in such a class and frustrated by the assumption that all the students in the class are "geniuses." How can one possibly feel like they belong if they are neophytes among geniuses? Or, as Kevin aptly notes, when the professor assumes "that we understand the material already," as some of his continuing-generation classmates likely do from their excellent high school training. Kevin struggled on multiple fronts in his first year in college. His financial aid package was pulled out from under him just after the school year began, and he has had serious concerns over money ever since. He has had to pick up extra work, which undercut his ability to focus on schoolwork and attend his classes.

Kevin was in his second year when he took this class from the gibberish-talking "genius" professor. He had just come off academic probation and was still working multiple jobs because he had not been chosen to be an RA in the dorms (which would have gone a long way toward solving his financial problems). To make matters worse, Kevin was lonely. Between financial stress and school stress, Kevin could not find time to build friendships, though he did join a local church: "Besides being at work and church during the weekend, I don't hang out with anybody. I don't necessarily feel like I am belonging, but I am not necessarily feeling I am shunned. I am just someone." He elaborates what it means to be "just someone": "I don't know, it's just I feel like I just walk past people all the time, and I never get a chance to get to know them." For students like Kevin, being denied academic belonging by his "genius" professor makes the classroom yet another place on campus where he feels lonely and lost.

Just as students often use the word "comfortable" to define belonging in general, when they talk about professors who "care" about their students and "care" about the material, they are describing interactions through which they receive the gift of academic belonging (Noddings 1984; Valenzuela 1999; Schreiner and Tobolowsky 2018). Valentina, a first-generation student at Public who identifies as "Chicana. Yes, and Mexicana as well" and whom we met in chapter 2, illustrates this in a typical way: "Just caring for students, genuinely caring for students, for me is really important to have from my professors. I know they are busy and stuff too, but there's small ways to show up." Valentina's voice suddenly gets hard: "like not talking down to students when they ask questions." Several students such as Serena and Laura also use the word "passionate" to characterize professors who offer academic belonging. They feel included and validated by faculty whose excitement for the material extends to a desire for students to get excited about it too, regardless of whether they are particularly good at it. Valentina highlights this in her disdain for professors who make students feel small for asking questions by "talking down" to them.

In addition to faculty who do not care or who expect students to already know the material, students also tell me about faculty and TAs who directly discourage students by pointing out their incompetence, rather than encouraging them to try to improve. Unfortunately, existing scholarship indicates this type of interaction occurs often (Hawk and Lyons 2008; Dachner and Saxton 2015). Carlos, a first-generation student at Public who identifies as "Hispanic and my father is Persian, so I am kind of a combination of both," shares a striking story: "I had a TA who made me feel like I was really dumb. I told him I'm a math major. . . . I went to him to pick up my final exam. I didn't do as well as I thought I did, and I wanted to see my mistakes. So, as I get it, we're looking it over and he's like, 'If you're struggling at *this* then you are not going to—you're going to have trouble.'" It was easy to hear the hurt in Carlos's voice.

Carlos was a commuter student during his first year. His family had only one car, so his dad would generously drive him to campus and wait for his classes to finish and drive him home. As a result, Carlos had few opportunities to get involved in campus life at Public. Happily, "my dream came true," and he was selected to be an RA his second year, allowing him to live on campus without paying out of pocket for room and board. However, during that first year, classes were Carlos's main arena for connection and belonging, which made his TA's comments all the more biting. In addition to already feeling disappointed by his grade on the final exam, the TA made

Carlos feel that he was entirely inadequate for the major. Instead of offering academic belonging, he extended to Carlos a definitive sense of rejection from the academic community of the math department.

These discouraging experiences with instructors who withhold academic belonging sometimes happen to continuing-generation students too, though less often in my data. Hazel at Private, who identifies as "Well, I know I'm White," tells me the following story from her first semester: "I went to office hours one day, this was a horrible day . . . I had no idea, no idea what was going on in the class. And I got myself to go to office hours. So proud of myself. I peeped my head in, and said, 'Hi, Professor, could you help me with this question? I don't really understand.' He was like, 'There's someone outside around the corner working on the same problem, you can go ask them.'" Here Hazel pauses dramatically to emphasize her surprise in the moment: "I was like, 'What?!' And then he munches on his trail mix and turns away. I was like, 'Oh my gosh!' So I didn't go ask them, because the other students in that class were kind of that same way. . . . They weren't going to help."

Hazel's, Carlos's, and other students' experiences are a good reminder of just how impactful small interactions between faculty and students can be. As authority figures in the academic community on a campus, instructors, including TAs, play an important role in extending academic belonging to students or actively denying it to them. Negative interactions can be confusing and sometimes painful experiences.

Some good news here is that students often have at least one professor or TA who does offer belonging. Hazel also told me about her favorite philosophy professor, whom she describes as habitually validating students in class: "Sometimes she would say like, 'Oh, that's not exactly what I'm trying to get at,' but you still felt important all the time. She was just very understanding and helpful for everything I would ask her about or comment on." When instructors make students feel "important all the time," as Hazel describes it, students feel valued. They feel seen. Karla, a first-generation student at Private who identifies as "I'm Puerto Rican, African American and Nicaraguan. I'm very proud of all of those," similarly explains what makes her best professors great: "just constantly telling your students that you're available for office hours and you want them to succeed really helps. Even if they don't go to office hours, I feel like just knowing that they're there to just work with you is always so great" That is what belonging feels like. That other people are there for us. That they want us to succeed. That we matter.

Organizational Structures Affect Academic Belonging

When I designed this study I expected to find that interactions and relationships between faculty and students would differ between a big school
like Public, where faculty are hired, promoted, and rewarded for research
rather than teaching (Einarson and Clarkberg 2004; Hoffman 2014; Chory
and Offstein 2017), and a smaller liberal arts school like Private where faculty are hired with the expectation that they will prioritize teaching and
student mentoring alongside research. To my surprise, students at both
schools seemed to have strikingly similar experiences: they each seemed to
have a few professors who cared and others who did not. As we saw in the
previous chapter, students at Private experience academic belonging at
higher rates than do students at Public, thus perhaps more faculty at Private are extending belonging than students described in their interviews
with me. I explicitly asked them to talk about both their favorite and least
favorite professors, so it is possible that they shared examples of each without mentioning whether, overall, they had more favorites than least favorites. Yet I maintain that the clearest explanation for the higher rates of
academic belonging at Private lies in the differences in organizational structural and campus cultures at the two schools, some of which directly promote or discourage interactions between faculty and students.

Private is much smaller than Public. It advertises small class sizes, which
are known to promote more student–faculty interaction for first-generation
students (Beattie and Thiele 2016). Serena in the previous chapter, along
with several others, mention small classes when they answer my question
in the first interview about why they chose Private. Thus, students expect
faculty to be accessible and perhaps even get to know them a bit, or at least
students expect not to feel completely anonymous. I thought more students
would sound like Jeff—a first-generation student who identifies as "I just
say White, but I'm also an eighth Lebanese. I try to include that"—who told
me, "I like class sizes a lot. I like how all my professors know me by name.
If they see me on the street, they'll say hi to me. I like that." Instead, evidence that students expect professors to know who they are often came in
the form of complaints at Private. Sabrina, a first-generation student who
identifies as "I'm Mexican," lamented to me in her first semester that her
dorm-community course professor (who is also the assigned academic advisor for every student in the class) is the only professor who asked students to
introduce themselves: "The other three classes we didn't introduce ourselves.

I thought that was really strange because we are in a small class and you didn't even bother to do that."

James, a continuing-generation student, expected not only to be invited to introduce himself but also that his professors would learn and remember his name. In our third interview, he shares this experience: "I have had a professor tell me straight up in the beginning of semester that they weren't going to remember my name. The excuse was that they weren't good at matching faces and names." James identifies "as far as race goes, I mean—so, its' like—I am in the majority of being White." We met him in chapter 2 when he told me that belonging "is all about making relationships." The sense of community he found at Private is important to him, and he found it quite easily. Recall his earlier comment: "Here at Private, really, if you're open and friendly—I think it's hard not to make a lot of friends." Now, at the end of his second year, James shares with me his reaction to this particular professor who declared that he would not remember students' names. He admits, "It's not huge," but it bothers him. "At the same time I kind of thought, you're sort of paid to teach me, and, I mean it's helpful if you remember my name so that if I have my hand raised in class you can know what to call me, not just, 'Okay, *you* talk.' I don't know. Just kind of helpful. I don't mean to sound spoiled or stuck up." James laughs self-consciously as he says this. His peppering of "sort of," "kind of," and "I don't want to sound spoiled" indicate that he was aware that it might not be appropriate to feel entitled to having every professor know his name. Yet he does feel entitled to it.

As Private's campus culture prioritizes relationships, it is fitting that students who came in expecting their professors to get to know them a bit continue to expect it and feel slighted when those expectations are not met. The fact that James feels it warrants complaining when those expectations are not met indicates that most of the time his professors do learn his name. I take this as evidence that Private's small classes do seem to foster academic belonging, which helps explain its higher rates compared to Public.

By contrast, Public is a much larger school with large classes. Students do not expect faculty to learn their names or anything else about them. As Ling, a first-generation student who identifies as "I'm an Asian, I mean it's not like I need to hide myself, like 'Oh, I'm so ashamed to be Asian.' I'm me and I'm just Asian" tells me in his first semester. "It's really hard to get professors to notice you." Nevertheless, several students at Public do feel noticed by their professors. For example Joaquin, a first-generation student who identifies as "personally, I just use Hispanic," already felt like he was building relationships in his first semester: "I've gotten to know some of my professors—two of my professors—on more than just, you know, attending class basis." Also recall Laura the first-generation student who adores her math professor: "I go to his office hours all the time and we developed a close relationship."

The key difference here is that students at Public clearly seem to feel that they are responsible for initiating an interaction if they want a professor to know who they are. This is fitting given not only the academically competitive campus culture at Public but also the organizational structure of large lecture halls that do not easily facilitate interpersonal discussions. Thus, there are fewer opportunities for professors to offer academic belonging directly and personally to an individual student. Yet when that does happen, students relish it, as Marisol did in her Spanish class: "That's why it was my favorite class of all, because in the other classes you just feel like a number, and then in that class you felt like you actually belonged and you actually—like your voice mattered." Meanwhile at Private, students expect professors not only to know them but also to *want to* know them as a routine part of teaching and learning in the classroom. As faculty are a key source of academic belonging for students, these differences in campus culture influence the academic belonging rates at the two schools.

Student Support Resources Offer Academic Belonging

Class size and campus culture are two important organizational structures that affect academic belonging. Another is the Student Success Resources (SSR) program. In chapter 2 I discussed how funding SSR is a way that Public and Private offer campus-community belonging to students. Naturally, because it provides academic support, SSR directly contributes to academic belonging as well. Students on both campuses express gratitude for SSR resources. For example, Laura describes herself as "blessed enough to get accepted. I know they can't accept every single person." She bubbles with enthusiasm as she explains, "They offered me so much. I can get a writing tutor, a chemistry tutor, a math tutor, basically anything you need they're there. To me that's amazing. . . . That's why I am also like, 'Oh my God, this is so great!' Because I have—basically if I need something, I will have it within reach."

On the day of our first interview, Laura had just met with her writing tutor for the first time and was already working with a math tutor and chemistry tutor. "My math tutor was very helpful, he helped me study for my midterm and I did well on it. So, I was like, 'Wow.' Again, I really love math, so even better." Her chemistry midterm, in contrast, did not go so well. "Honestly, I—well, yeah—I failed my chemistry midterm." Just two days before our interview, Laura went over her disastrous midterm with her SSR chemistry tutor and was planning to get even more help. "I seriously never want to feel like that on a test again. I don't think I've ever felt that lost within a test." Recall in chapter 3 when Laura answered my question about belonging, she said that she was thinking about the fact that her chemistry score was below the class average. She did not feel that she could claim strong academic belonging with such a score and instead said that her belonging at Public was "in the middle."

It requires trial and error to figure out the demands of college academics if those demands have not already been modeled by one's high school. Public's SSR Center is aware of this and so intervenes with mandatory tutoring. However, even that is unable to prevent every episode of failure and the negative emotions that go along with it. Thus, Laura's academic belonging is threatened by her chemistry exam, but it is skyrocketed by her math exam. All the while the tutors and mentors at SSR work to scaffold Laura's success, and by doing so, they nurture her academic belonging. Many months later, in our second interview at the end of her first year, Laura tells me, "Since I got the opportunity to be in SSR, I think I'm very, very lucky. Because they give me so much support . . . that's been a big part for me that's really helped me this year. But if I didn't have that, I think"—here Laura pauses for a long moment—"I don't know." She cannot find the words to imagine what her college life would be like without it.

Other students I talked to at Public express similar gratitude for the academic help and the sense of community offered by the SSR Center, describing it as a place where they feel at "home" and "where my friends are." Alma, a first-generation student who identifies as "Chicana and Latina. Chicana because I was born here, but my family comes from Mexico, but I'm also from here, so it's the best of both worlds. And Latina too because I am from a Latin American country in the sense of my family and my ancestors, I'm proud to say" demonstrates that the staff at SSR extend academic belonging to her in the same way that faculty can: "I feel like they do really care about their students a lot. . . . I'm very close to one of the directors. I've asked him for help a few times and he's never been shutting me down. He's always there to help, like 'Yeah, so I can help you with this,' and 'Whatever I can.' So that is very nice as well." Alma feels important to this director at SSR.

Although at both schools the budgets for SSR have been generously expanded, those funds still do not enable every student who could benefit from these resources to enroll in their programs. Joaquin is such an example. He is a first-generation student who identifies as "personally, I just use Hispanic." We met him earlier in the chapter; he is the student who had already started making relationships with two professors in his first semester. I was surprised to learn, when I interviewed Joaquin at the end of his second year, that he failed the same math class three times. "Math isn't particularly my strong suit," he admits. Technically, he dropped the class twice as soon as it was clear he would fail, and then he failed on the third go-around. He took Ws (withdrawals) on his transcript both times he dropped the course. He confesses, "I didn't really tell anyone that I was doing pretty badly. I didn't really go to anyone for help until pretty late into the semesters. . . . At first when I started to slip up, I was like 'No, no, this is fine. I don't need help.' It's just maybe I just have to stay up another night, and then I'll get it done and I'll catch up with this and it won't be a problem."

Joaquin eventually turned for help to his older roommates, people he sees as "very on top of their academics," but each time it was too late. "I felt really embarrassed because I was like, 'Man!' Because it's not even a particularly difficult math class. It's Pre-Calculus." Mandatory tutoring might have spared Joaquin this humiliating journey if he had been enrolled in SSR. It might also have spared him the stressful semester he spent on academic probation. His experience highlights the critical role that SSR plays in offering academic belonging both by developing students' skills and by signaling to them that they are valued members of the academic community at Public—so valuable that SSR refuses to let them slip through the cracks. First-generation students like Laura find SSR "helpful," and Joaquin illustrates that such help is in fact imperative for academic survival (Mehta, Newbold, and O'Rourke 2011; A. Yee 2016; Schwartz et al. 2018).

I focus here on Public students' experiences with SSR offering academic belonging because Public is the more academically intense campus and overall students similarly describe the SSR support they receive at both schools. Indeed, students at Private rely heavily on SSR as well. For example, when I ask Brandon whom he turns to when a class is hard, he is quick to respond, "Student Support Resources, for sure. Go to them first." Brandon identifies as "African American for sure" and is a first-generation student. We met Brandon in the previous chapter as he described how self-reliant he is. Recall his comment, "I don't like to ask for help. I'm just very independent." Yet Brandon's answer to my question emphasizes how comfortable he feels at SSR. He says he can just show up in the office and "vent" with confidence that the staff will "lead me" to the right person, right resource, or right advice to resolve his problems. "I'll be like, 'I'm kind of struggling with this,' and they'll help me out." Brandon is just one example. Students who are enrolled with SSR at Private find the program invaluable academically and emotionally because SSR offers academic belonging at every turn. It even fosters social belonging, as Karla at Private illustrates. She said that people always ask her, "'How do you know so many people?' I'm like, 'SSR.' They are like, 'What is that?' I'm like, 'You have to be a part of it to understand.'" She raises her eyebrows and flashes me a knowing smile.

First-Generation Success Stories

My depiction of first-generation students' experiences would be incomplete if I did not also share the examples of students who navigated academics easily and seamlessly in their first two years. Certainly, most first-generation students encountered the kinds of obstacles that I have been describing, but not all did: 18.8 percent of first-generation students in my sample at Public have strong, steady academic belonging at all three interview points, as do 38.5 percent of first-generation students in my sample at Private. Here I highlight one student from each school, Ramon and Isabella, each of whom has not only strong academic belonging but also soaring academic performance to boot.

Ramon at Private identifies as agender and uses the pronouns they, them, and theirs. They go by Ramon, their birth name, and ethnoracially identify as "Latinx." At the end of Ramon's second year the only class they describe "struggling with" in their engineering major was one where they had earned a B+. Ramon explains that this class was not much of a struggle: "It was really not that stressful. The material wasn't really that hard. I knew what I was doing, but the test came, and I just didn't have enough time to do all of them." I ask if they had ever gone to tutoring or office hours or SSR, and they responds, "Not really, no ... Maybe only once and that was the first semester for chemistry for one problem." Ramon works as a math tutor on campus and seems to enjoy that job: "A lot how I learned math was helping other people try to understand it and that's been working for me." Their first-semester GPA got them into the honors program. Ramon did not share their exact GPA with me but acknowledged that it had to be above 3.65 to qualify for honors.

In our first interview, Ramon is equally nonchalant about how easily academic success came for them. They tell me they like to study with friends sometimes, even though they most often study on their own: "I like to help them out sometimes because I feel bad for breaking curves." Ramon laughs good-naturedly here. "In math class, I saw a lot of people get 12 out of 30 on the calculus test. And then I got a 31 out of 30 and I felt really bad." They laugh again, betraying a sense of shy pride but without a trace of haughtiness. "I try to help them out usually—or sometimes they help me out with chem."

During that first interview they tell me that college academics are "not too different" from high school "because I went to a pretty rigorous high school. I did the IB [International Baccalaureate] diploma." Thus, Ramon felt prepared for their college courses and indeed is successful in them. Even in chemistry, the one class they went to office hours for and asked friends for help in, Ramon scored above their classmates. They describe a recent homework assignment: "I only got a 97 or something percent. I felt like I missed a couple of answers. And I see others got a 75 or something like that. I'm like, 'Oh, okay.'" Ramon is not boastful: they are simply excelling without enormous effort or stress.

Isabella at Public is another great example. She identifies as "Mexican or Latina" in our first interview, but in her third, she says, "I identify as Chicana 100 percent of the way. Because I am American." It is not uncommon for students to go through a process of self-discovery about themselves and their heritage in college, leading to changes in the ethnoracial identities they hold and how they describe themselves (Harper 2014; Johnston et al. 2014; Johnston-Guerrero and Renn 2016). This seems to have been true for Isabella. By the end of her second year, she is debating whether to add a second major in political science or to graduate a year early.

Like other first-generation students at Public whom I highlighted in the previous chapter, she originally came to college with an impacted major in mind but changed course in her first year. "It didn't work out for me," she tells me. What is less common about Isabella's situation is that she did not struggle in her classes for that impacted major; instead she found them uninspiring: "It was easy. But I was like, 'I don't feel I'm going to be happy doing this forever' . . . it was too dry . . . I could do the math. I could do the calculations." She shrugged her shoulders with disinterest.

Isabella discovered the field of urban planning and was drawn toward that major instead. "Urban planning is more like my passion. It's more of a, 'I care about my community. I'm going to fight for my people' type of thing. . . . Will it be functional for the people that are going to use it? . . . Will it suit the people? Do the people want it in the first place?" Isabella sees a future in urban planning as a vehicle for social justice, an opportunity to improve communities like the one she comes from. She recounts an episode from a recent class discussion:

> We were talking about ghettos. We were talking about Jewish ghettos and that's the beginning of ghettos and then some kid was like, "Oh, well I've never been to a ghetto, so I don't know what it's like." And I was laughing, I was laughing . . . my TA already knows me from being with me for two semesters, and he's like "Oh Isabella, how do you feel?" I was like, "Well, I live in the ghetto and I know what it's like and I know what these people are suffering because I've seen it happening." And it's like, who are you taking out into the world that don't know what other people need? They are going to be building things that don't need to be built. It's just frustrating . . . there are specific things that a community needs that *you* will always be ignorant to because *you* don't know about it or never learned about it.

Isabella has found a major that is meaningful to her. She sees it as "work for a purpose." Most other students in my study would be envious to hear what Isabella is telling me because they themselves long to discover their passion, purpose, and calling and to identify the major that will unlock it for them.

Isabella's grades are very strong and have been rising every semester. She proudly shares her GPA with me down to the thousandth place: 3.456. She is considering applying to the honors program. As we know, success in terms of GPA promotes a sense of academic belonging for students. Isabella also feels very competent in her coursework. She tells me that tutoring resources "don't really make sense for me . . . I don't really need it." When I ask Isabella how successful she feels as a college student on a scale from 1–10, she answers with a buoyant smile, "Nine and a half."

Her confidence and strong sense of academic belonging are also evident in her descriptions of interactions with faculty. I ask her whom she turns to when she has academic challenges, and she responds, "I don't really struggle with content, it's more like when I have questions, like 'But what if *this*?' or, you know, 'But this doesn't make sense.' [or] 'This angers me.' I go directly to the professor." Isabella feels comfortable approaching her professors in person: "If I can't go to office hours then I'll email them. But if I have time for office hours, then I'll go." She told me about "a really long email" she sent to her professor about an injustice that was presented in the course material: "This doesn't make sense. This isn't right" was the tone of the email. "And she used my email as an example in her next lecture." Isabella is beaming as she tells me. "And I was laughing . . . I found that positive because she discussed it. She was like, 'This is a real question.'" Exchanges such as these with professors and TAs give Isabella the gift of academic belonging, which is reinforced by her easy grasp of course material in classes both inside and outside her major.

Academic Belonging Does Not Equate to Campus-Community Belonging

Interestingly, neither Ramon nor Isabella claims that they belong when I ask them directly about it. Although they both demonstrate unfettered academic belonging and seem content with their academic success, they also affirm unequivocally they do not experience campus-community belonging. Ramon is consistent throughout each of the three interviews, saying, "I don't belong anywhere."

In our third interview, Ramon explains, "I don't really feel like I could say this is my home. Feel like anyplace really. And after 18 years or 19 years, I've been doing fine without it, I think. It would probably be nice to say this is a place I think is home, but I'm not there and I don't need it." Ramon is sitting comfortably across from me in a gray hoodie. They seem at peace with this, casually discussing not belonging anywhere as a fact of life. I follow up and Ramon elaborates, "Private is familiar now, but it still doesn't feel like a home. Because, I think that home—I think people associate—kind of like a retreat, I guess. And then, my house was never really that. School wasn't that all the time. . . . There wasn't a place where I really felt safe." Ramon's answer reminds us how complex students' lives are and how multidimensional belonging is. No matter how much academic belonging Ramon experiences, it is not a bridge to a wider feeling of being accepted, valued, and wanted for who they are at Private as a whole.

Isabella, in contrast, points directly to the campus culture and the university itself to explain why she feels the way she does. At the end of her second year, she answers my question, "Is this school a place where you feel like you belong?" this way: "I don't know. It's weird . . . Because I feel like Public is very—and learning about it too—it's like they don't care about majors like mine. They really don't care. They are built on a pride of elitism. It's still there. They don't care about the humanities and stuff. It's pretty evident." As Isabella continues on about things she has learned about the history of Public in her urban courses and about social injustice more broadly in her Chicana Literature class, which is her favorite. I ask her again, "So back to this question of belonging. Do you feel like you belong here?" In response, she tells me the following story about a conference she attended:

> Over winter break I presented on clubs and branding for your own club for Latino organizations. I used to be a part of it in high school. . . . I was talking with one of the [presenters]. He came to Public, but he dropped. He said, "No. I'm not going here anymore." And I was like, 'Why didn't you stay?' because he was a STEM major and was doing good. He was like, "I just felt like I didn't belong." I was like, 'Why?' He [said], "I don't know. I didn't see any brown kids so that was really hard." And I was like, 'Oh.'

Isabella said that she immediately understood what he was talking about. Yet, she adds,

> My experience is so different because as soon as I came here, I found where all the brown kids were and I followed them. I stayed there and I'm still there, all my friends are brown. All that parties I go to, all you see is brown kids everywhere. So I'm always in that environment, but then I understand because you have to look for it and a lot of people don't find it . . . You have to work for it. It's not just going to happen for you on this campus . . . and it's pretty obvious that this campus doesn't care about the brown kids, seeing the percentages that are there and everything.

Isabella quickly found a social scene that suits suited her, which gave her a steady sense of social belonging at all three interview points during her first two years. And we already know how strong her academic belonging has been. Yet, the wider campus culture that she perceives as not valuing "brown kids" like herself or majors like her own thwarts campus-community belonging for Isabella. Being part of the Latinx student community has made it "bearable" to be at Public, but she does not describe her experience there as comfortable or satisfying. Isabella's example highlights the important role that ethnoracial dynamics play in campus-community belonging, which is the topic of the next two chapters.

For college students, the experience of belonging not only happens in three distinct realms but also is multifaceted within each realm. Part of what sparks passion for Isabella in her major is that she brings her personal history to the table as a "Chicana 100 percent of the way" woman from a low-income neighborhood, a place she refers to as "the ghetto." Her insights into urban planning and the validation she receives from professors and TAs come directly out of her ethnoracial identity and lived experiences. Yet, that identity is one that her university and campus culture "don't care about." Precisely what makes her feel valued in her academic community and social community is what makes her feel not valued by the campus community. She does not plan to leave but she resents Public for it.

5

Ethnoracial Diversity
and Belonging

● ● ● ● ● ● ● ● ● ● ● ● ● ● ● ● ● ● ● ●

Neither Public nor Private have student bodies that are as ethnoracially diverse as the U.S. or California population. Low and lopsided representation on campus affect students' access to belonging, as do campus tensions and national political tensions around race. Students' experiences according to my sample are largely similar at Public and Private, so throughout this chapter I draw on data from both schools to demonstrate the dynamics I found, rather than contrasting them. The similarities speak to the wider, enduring ethnoracial issues that exist in the United States today; even though Public and Private have markedly different campus cultures, they seem to overwhelmingly share similar ethnoracial dilemmas.

Friendly and Not-So-Friendly Perceptions of Campus

Members of the ethnoracial majority perceive both campuses as warm and welcoming, which signals to them that they belong in the campus community. Emily identifies as "I'm White." She is the continuing-generation student whose athletic coach extended academic belonging to her in chapter 4.

She tells me that the best thing about Public is that "there are a lot of nice people here. They have been so sweet, so kind to me. The people hold doors for you and it's the little things. 'Wow. You guys are so nice!'" Emily smiles broadly, yet shyly, as she talks about her new campus home: "This is a wonderful social atmosphere. I love this place. Everyone is so kind. Everyone gets to know each other." Emily's impression largely holds for both those first- and continuing-generation students who are in the ethnoracial majority on their campus. Ethan, a first-generation student at Private who identifies as "Caucasian," tells me that he feels like he belongs at Private because "the people are really similar to me." I ask him, "In what way?" and Ethan answers, "I don't know. They are all nice. Most people that I've met are really welcoming. And they are open to everyone." This is how ethnoracial-majority students describe campus-community belonging, and at both Public and Private, they perceive the welcoming feeling to be universal. They imagine that everyone else on campus feels it too.

However, they are wrong. We know that students of color generally do not perceive their campuses that same way (Harper and Hurtado 2007; McCabe 2009; Yosso et al. 2009; Gusa 2010). There are many studies analyzing these dynamics. Shaun Harper (2013) observed that Black students at predominately White institutions often experience their campus climates as "toxic" and exclusionary (188). Daisy Reyes (2018) found that Latinx students at the small, predominately White university in California she studied were the targets of overt racist accusations, as well as more subtle microaggressions and tokenization, making the environment "at times hostile" both on campus and off (90). Lerma, Hamilton, and Nielsen (2019) found that Black and Latinx students at the large, Western, public, majority-minority university they studied experienced their campus as "unsafe" due to racial discrimination, anti-immigrant sentiments, online attacks, and no accountability when campus police shot and killed a student of color who was armed with a knife (6). These issues are widespread nationwide, so it is not surprising that they hold true at Public and Private as well.

Teagan, a continuing-generation student at Private who identifies as "I'm Black and Mexican," struggled at the start of her first year. She perceived people whom she met around Private as being disinterested in her or standoff-ish. "You can tell—for instance where I didn't feel like I fit—is when you have a conversation with somebody while you're getting to know them or meeting them," she said. She then voiced both parts of a conversation, where she mimicked herself asking questions in a friendly, inviting tone and then answering them in a clipped, monotone voice: "Oh, do you have any siblings?"—*Yeah*. "Brother, sister?"—*One brother, one sister*. "How many classes do you have?"—*Five*." Teagan sighs, "You can tell when it's like, 'yeah, good-bye. Why are you talking to me?'"

Teagan was acutely aware that she did not blend in (Horvat and Antonio 1999; Ispa-Landa and Conwell 2015). She tells me, "I didn't feel like I belonged here because number one, I don't look like everybody else." When she first arrived, she straightened her hair, but then decided not to do that again because she was disappointed in herself for trying so hard. "I thought, 'No.' I'm Black and Mexican. I'm not about to make myself imitate even more. I have a different skin tone. I act different. I'm not going to add another factor to being different." It was not just her hair; Teagan also worried that she needed "nice shoes and nice clothes and all this stuff" to "fit in" at Private. "I really cared at first. I was like, 'Wow, people aren't going to like me . . . this is not where I fit.'"

Eventually she sat herself down and decided not to care anymore. "You kind of have to make it where you fit. I'm going to go here for probably the next four years. You're going to go here. This isn't high school. Who cares if people like you. Who cares if you fit in. Who cares if you're a different skin tone. We're all still the same." Here Teagan takes a long pause and then says definitively, "It's where I belong." She exhibits the same determination we saw in David at Private who "tricked himself" into belonging and in Alma at Public who said, "I had to make myself belong here," in chapter 1. Teagan did not experience her campus as a friendly and welcoming place the way ethnoracial-majority students commonly do. She was offered neither social belonging nor campus-community belonging as abundantly as she had hoped in her initial weeks and months as a new college student. Like others in her shoes, she had to decide what do to about it.

Small Numbers: Is the University to Blame?

Some majority students recognize that it must be hard for underrepresented students. Brianna at Private who identifies as "I'm White" tells me, "I would hate being Black here. Everyone's White." Both Public and Private have robust numbers of White students. Both campuses have Latinx populations that are roughly proportionally close to the national level of 18 percent, but neither is anywhere near the proportion of Latinx population of 39 percent in California, where Latinx have outnumbered Whites since 2014 (Panzar 2015). Both campuses have about 4 percent African American students, compared to more than 13 percent in the nation and 6.5 percent in California. The biggest demographic difference between the two campuses is that Asian students make up more than 30 percent of the student body at Public, not including international students—a strong overrepresentation given that Asian Americans comprise less than 6 percent of the U.S. population (which is approximately the percentage of Asian Americans at Private) and just over 15 percent of California's population. This is why they are perceived as an ethnoracial majority at Public alongside Whites (Park 2013; Reyes 2018).

Ethnoracial-majority students in my study are largely unaffected by their school's diversity numbers, and many even seem to be willfully unaware of the demographics. Shaun Harper (2013) reminds us that this lack of awareness is not uncommon for White students at predominately White institutions (PWIs): "Extreme underrepresentation is usually accompanied by a set of experiences that undermine espoused institutional commitments to fostering inclusive campus climates; these are challenges from which White students at PWIs are almost always exempt" (189). For example, Zach, a continuing-generation student at Private, says, "I feel like the campus is pretty diverse. I mean I don't really notice, I don't go out of my way to like notice, or like obviously I'm not counting or anything. I mean, I just kind of assumed that it's balanced and it's how it should be." Zach identifies as "I would say I'm pretty much just White. My mom is 50 percent Hispanic but I don't personally identify like that, even though it is in my background a little bit. I personally just identify as White just because people see me and that's probably the first thing they're thinking." We met Zach in chapter 3 as he followed in his dad's footsteps by majoring in finance.

In contrast to White students, those who identify as members of minority groups tend to be painfully aware of the small numbers. They also tend to blame the university for their underrepresentation. Dannisha—"I identify as African-American because both my parents are immigrants from Africa but I grew up here"—who is a continuing-generation student at Public, says, "For me, I've always grown up where I've seen faces like mine going to class. But coming here, that's a little bit of a shock to not see that at all. And I feel like they have the diversity, inclusion and equity clause that they just input. But I thought they were making an effort to fully do their jobs. Which is if you want to create a more diverse campus you have to bring in different people. I don't feel like they are trying to do that."

Sara Ahmed's (2012) work helps us understand Dannisha's frustration with the administration "not fully doing their job" but instead "just input[ting]" a claim to diversity, inclusion, and equity. Ahmed argues that the "lip service model of diversity" (58) is not uncommon in higher education, and the people hired to do diversity work at universities often find themselves "banging their head against a brick wall" (26) to accomplish structural changes that would bring not just diversity but also equity to their campuses. Ahmed asserts that "having an institutional aim to make diversity a goal can even be a sign that diversity is *not* an institutional goal" (23) and, that in some cases, "diversity is incorporated as an official term insofar as it is made consistent with the organization's goals" (57), thereby undermining or removing the power of diversity work to confront and change inequities on campus. Of course, equity involves a great deal more than having enrollment numbers that adequately represent the nation's ethnoracial demographics. Yet, neither Public nor Private have accomplished it, and many students like Dannisha point to the need to "bring in different people" as a critical step.

In contrast ethnoracial-majority students do not think that the lack of diversity is the university's fault. They seem unable or unwilling to recognize that the university leadership has the power to effect changes in the enrollment of the student body. Spencer, a continuing-generation student at Private who identifies as "I can't really identify as anything other than White," says, "I think that the university is doing everything it can to make this a place that would be as welcoming as possible to diversity but, I think as it stands, it's not all that diverse. But I don't think that could be attributed to a failure on the part of the university. I think it's just a socioeconomic fact about life. I don't like it when people say that the university isn't doing enough."

Eric, a first-generation student at Public, who identifies as "I'm Chinese. Asian. Cantonese specifically," sees things similarly to Spencer: "I guess the political answer would be that of course we need diversity in colleges, but part of me also says if you're intelligent enough to come to Public then you belong here. And I guess you could say it just so happens to be that this many people of this race got in." Like Spencer, Eric also makes it clear that he is aware that additional explanations complicate the matter: "But then there is also the argument that people of color are known to have . . . more obstacles that they have to overcome to get to college. So of course we should be providing programs to help these people of color improve and better themselves. So, I don't know. I don't know where I stand on that idea."

This tension around who deserves to be admitted to college is a long-standing issue in the United States. It is part of what Natasha Warikoo (2016) calls "the diversity bargain" among students at elite colleges. She finds that "White students support affirmative action insofar as it benefits themselves" (75); thus, tensions remain around merit, race, and college admissions at both of the universities in her study, as well as most others around the nation. I discuss Warikoo's insights into "the diversity bargain" further in the next chapter, but here I emphasize students' ideas about merit and deservingness as being part of the cultural landscape of higher education; as such, they form these ideas partly by what they absorb from their college's campus culture (Feagin, Vera, and Imani 1996; Reyes 2018). As W. Carson Byrd (2017) argues, the experiences and perspectives that students gain on "highly selective college campuses downplay students' consideration of social structures perpetuating racial inequality in their social world as well as in broader society" (2). He argues that elite college environments teach students to develop a sense of "ease" with which they "can rationalize race and inequality in their social world to mean meritocracy and individuality" (4), rather than due to social forces beyond individuals' control. Byrd says this is partly because students are able to identify themselves as "the best and the brightest," as Eric suggests when he says, "If you're intelligent enough to come to Public then you belong here." Importantly, Byrd emphasizes that at the same time that highly selective colleges are making visible diversity efforts, they simultaneously reinforce racial ideologies as campuses that "were specifically created for and continue to be dominated by Whites" (4).

Navigating Campus in the Minority

Although Latinx students at both campuses are not dramatically underrepresented in comparison to the national proportion, many Latinx students come from California, often from communities that are predominately Latinx, and it is a big adjustment for them. Daisy Reyes (2018) heard similar experiences of "alienation and culture shock" (87) from Latinx students at both the small liberal arts college as well as the large public research university in her study. She describes Latinx students feeling "disoriented in the new racial landscape . . . where Latinos and blacks are in the minority" (94–95). Valentina at Public, who identifies as "Chicana. Yes, and Mexicana as well," says, "I came from a high school where it was mostly Filipinos,

Latinos and African American students. That representation is not equal at all here. So that was just very wow! I'm not hitting on other cultures. . . . It was just a really huge change in so little time. That really did hit me and was a struggle during my first year. I felt the lack of support from the university too."

As Valentina hints here, Latinx students experience a general sensibility that they are not valued by their school. This sentiment surfaces more often at Public than Private. Recall Isabella who said straightforwardly in the previous chapter, "It's pretty obvious that this campus doesn't care about the brown kids." Isabella points to her group's low representation among the student body as evidence that the university "doesn't care about" them. "It's hard to find a brown person," she says. Sometimes Isabella and a friend joke together when they spot a fellow Latinx student on campus: "We'll both tell everyone, 'Oh my God, there's another Mexican kid or Latino kid. Like oh my God!'"

Small numbers can make students feel invisible in some ways and conspicuously visible in others (Feagin et al. 1996; Moore 2008; Ray and Rosow 2012; Givens 2015; Means and Pyne 2017). Kenadee at Private, a continuing-generation student who identifies as "I'm technically African American because that's how people label it, but I'm actually Caribbean," insightfully says, "It would be nicer if there were more people who were similar to you around, because it feels—when there's so many of the people who aren't like you, it gets to be this Us–Them vibe."

Javier describes another aspect of Public that makes him feel unimportant. He is a first-generation student, who identifies as "Latino—well, I'm American like everybody else here. But both my parents are from El Salvador. And keep in mind that Latino is very different from Chicano, because Latino is Latin America, anything in Central America. And Mexico is part of North America, a lot of people get that mixed up." Javier shows how Latinx students are rendered less visible at Public, even though their numbers are not all that low. He says that, when he looks around, he sees "mostly White and Asian students. . . . I feel like a lot of things are catered to them mostly. Even in the markets and stuff, almost every market on campus it's always stuff that they would get in an Asian market. You wouldn't see a Latino [market], or let's say an inner-city place where Latinos and African Americans are from."

When Javier tells me this, I know exactly what he is talking about. Public is a large campus, and it often takes fifteen minutes or longer to walk from wherever you are to the next place you need to be, whether a classroom, the library, a dorm, or a professor's office. I routinely stop into the small markets around campus for a drink or snack as I walk, and I have often happily noticed selections of Asian foods available. I saw it as a sign that Public cared about the tastes and habits of its students, and it struck me as something to be proud of.

I felt a pang of embarrassment when Javier made that comment, because I had never noticed the absence of Latinx food items. In the neighborhood where I live, I am a regular customer at our corner carnecería, a Mexican grocery and butcher shop. I am familiar with the aisle dedicated entirely to Mexican candies, the vast selection of tortilla options, and the containers of fresh guacamole sitting in an ice bucket near the cash register, being sold almost as fast as the staff can make it in the back of the store. I recognize that these are items I do not see in grocery stores that predominately serve Whites. Yet, it had not occurred to me to expect campus stores to offer them.

As a White person, it is part of my racial privilege to move through the world unaware of the many instances where my race's tastes, preferences, and cultural sensibilities are "catered to," as Javier puts it. For many Whites like me, those instances feel invisible, natural, and normal, because cultural Whiteness is reflected, expected, and validated almost everywhere I go (Feagin 2013; Johnson 2017; Wise 2011). As a sociologist who cares deeply about racial injustice, I make efforts to be aware of my White privilege so that I can do my best to disrupt its dynamics. Javier helped me see that I had failed in this instance, even though I should have been aware enough to notice because I had spent time in my neighborhood carnecería. To that point, Javier also mentions the absence of items from "an inner-city place where Latinos and African Americans are from." To be perfectly honest, I do not know what items he might be referring to. I have precious little experience shopping in inner-city stores. I mainly know what I have read about them in sociology books or seen in movies.

Like me, university administrators may or may not have repertoires of personal experience that allow them to easily see the many ways that routine aspects of campus life reinforce Whiteness, thereby creating what scholars such as Wendy Moore (2008) call "white institutional spaces." These include, but are not limited to, institutions of higher education such as the two law schools where Moore conducted her research. She argues that in White institutional spaces, White students automatically feel they belong, whereas non-White students are routinely identified as bringing "diversity" to the school, which affirms over and over again in everyday thinking that they are not the students for whom the schools were intended: they are the "other." Moore further points out that it is not just everyday norms and discourse that make many schools and universities White spaces; it is also their physical space. She describes how elite law schools like those in her study have "portraits of important legal actors lining the halls and classrooms . . . and nearly all of these are portraits of white men" (28). As students navigate their campus, they are surrounded by the message that it is White people who are admired for their valuable contributions to knowledge and history. Moore asserts, "As institutional spaces descended from explicitly racist institutions, they retain the remnants of the historical legacy of racial exclusion. The physical structures of the buildings that make up these schools reveal the connections between elitism and whiteness, and they present a selective memory in which the racism that defined their histories gets minimized or ignored" (60). Similarly, James Thomas (2018) describes the university he studied as a place "where the legacies of Jim Crow remain inscribed in its traditions and iconography" (144; see also Harper 2013; Meyerhoff 2019; Ray 2019). Of course, many schools that were built in states outside the Jim Crow South also bear histories and markers of racial exclusion.

White spaces exist all over community life, not just on university campuses. These spaces include neighborhoods, workplaces, restaurants, parks, and even grocery stores. Elijah Anderson reminds us, "White people typically avoid black space, but black people are required to navigate the white space as a condition of their existence" (2015, 10). On campuses like Public and Private, this seems to hold true for all ethnoracial minorities.

Conversely, spaces can also validate the presence of ethnoracial minorities. Returning to Javier's complaint about Public, the staff who are hired to manage and stock campus markets and eateries might not have personal experiences that make it easy for them to recognize these dynamics, so university administrations could create policies or other initiatives that require training or direct implementation of practices that students such as Javier would find welcoming. This idea is included in my list of suggestions in the final chapter.

Lucia at Public presents another campus dynamic that goes beyond the small numbers of minorities: "It goes beyond just students; it goes to faculty and who's working, and it breaks my heart to see the custodial services on campus. They're all Latino folks. What's making so many Latino folks be custodial services? Clearly there's Latino folks here, but why aren't they coming to school here? And is it students don't want to come here? Or the school doesn't want us to come here?" Lucia is a first-generation student whom we have met before. She identifies as "I have African ancestors, I have Spanish ancestors, and indigenous Native American ancestors. So it's not as easy to just say, 'Oh I'm just this.' I'm all three. I'm both. I'm a Black Cuban, I'm an Afro-Latina." Her observations of the staff are accurate. At both Public and Private many of the Latinx people whom I routinely see around campus are not students but service workers, such as custodial staff, cafeteria workers, and groundskeepers.

Lucia ties this underrepresentation of Latinx students directly to her sense of belonging: "Talking about racial diversities, it's not, in my opinion, where it needs to be. And if it were, it'd be more comforting for me. I'd feel more accepted. I'd feel like I did belong. I'd say, 'Okay, I do belong here. They have more students like me that they want here.'" Students who are members of ethnoracial minorities, such as Lucia, Javier, and Dannisha, unmistakably see the university as withholding campus-community belonging from them. It happens partly by not "catering to" them with foods and items that feel familiar to them and by hiring abundantly from their group for manual and service labor while not admitting greater numbers into the student body. It makes them feel unimportant to the institution. And feeling important matters for anyone's sense of campus-community belonging.

Indeed, campus-community belonging is markedly lower among students who identify as ethnoracial minorities at Public, as table 8 illustrates (see chapter 6 for the more complicated discussion of demographics at Private). It starts out at a mere 28.6 percent in the first interview and drops steadily to 20.0 percent in the third. Notably, both minority and majority students decrease in campus-community belonging over time at Public, but majority students are consistently at approximately double the rate of minority students. Despite the many structural obstacles, some ethnoracial-minority students blame themselves, not the university, for their personal lack of campus-community belonging. Marisol, a first-generation student who identifies as "I'm Mexican," whom we have met several times in previous chapters, tells me, "I honestly—I don't feel at home. I haven't felt at home with it. Sometimes I think about it, and I get so sad because I'm like, 'I wanted to come here! What's wrong with me?'"

Table 8
Percentages of Students Who Experience Campus-Community Belonging at Public

	Public University	
	N	Campus-Community Belonging
Interview 1		
All students	31	45.7%
White & Asian	17	58.8%
Ethnoracial minority	14	28.6%
Interview 2		
All students	29	37.9%
White & Asian	16	50.0%
Ethnoracial minority	13	23.1%
Interview 3		
All students	25	36.0%
White & Asian	15	46.7%
Ethnoracial minority	10	20.0%

Small Numbers: "I'm Used to It"

In the literature, many underrepresented students of color profess that the "lack of diversity" is tolerable because they are "used to it" from having attended predominately White high schools (Ispa-Landa and Conwell 2015; Jack 2019). David is a good example from my study: "I hear a lot of my Black friends saying that there's not a lot of Black people here, and I agree there's not a lot of Black people here. It's not something that bothers me though just because I went to boarding school." David is a continuing-generation student who identifies as "Black and Caribbean" whom we met in previous chapters. Tomás, a first-generation student who also went to private school, echoes David's sentiments: "I don't really pay too much attention to it. My high school growing up, my elementary school, middle school, it was really similar to the way it is now. . . . It doesn't feel any different. I don't feel like an outcast"—although he admits, "I don't feel like there's an overwhelming amount of Hispanics." Tomás identifies as "I am really proud to be Colombian. I love everything about our culture."

Emily, the continuing-generation student who identifies as "I'm White" and who experiences "a lot of nice people" at Public who "have been so sweet, so kind to me," gives the majority perspective. She had the same experience of attending predominately White suburban public schools growing up: "I think it's just kind of, whatever. I've never really paid too much attention. I feel like we have a pretty decent diversity—which I like. . . . It actually reminds me of my high school." She adds, "I guess it was just a sweeter transition from high school to college because I'm already used to this."

In contrast, Nicole shows us why the transition to college is so much harder for minority students of color, even those who are "used to" being a minority. In her first semester at Private she shares, "I guess it's different because I came from a private school. Most of my friends are White back home. I'm half-White, half-Black but I live with my mom, who is Black. It hasn't been a problem or anything." However, by the end of her second year, Nicole sees it as somewhat of a problem: "I'm used to it. I have a better experience than other people, but I'm very sympathetic. . . . If I looked different than I do, I would feel very uncomfortable, you know?" I follow up because I am not sure that I know what she means, though in my mind I am guessing that she is referring to skin tone and the racial dynamics of colorism. I ask her, "Different how?" She explains, "If I was darker . . . I'm lighter skin than a lot of other half-Black, half-White girls and it's definitely different. I know that I have a different experience, and I'm very aware of that. My friends are always like, 'No, you look exotic. You look White but exotic.' It's this whole thing." Her voice suddenly becomes tired: "I'm like, 'Okay, good. That's great. But what if I didn't?'"

It seems that for Nicole, colorism is indeed tied up with her experiences at college. Colorism is "skin color stratification . . . that privileges light-skinned people of color over dark" (Hunter 2007, 237); it is not only manifested in U.S. culture but also happens across the globe (Glenn 2008; Dixon and Telles 2017). In the U.S. context, colorism is part of the racial dynamics that allows some light-skinned African Americans and light-skinned Latinos to benefit from White privilege and be treated as Whites, according to Eduardo Bonilla-Silva's (2002) theory of contemporary race relations. Skin tone has a host of effects among people of color in the United States (Hunter 2005). Research shows that African American high school students with lighter skin have lower rates of being suspended compared to darker-skinned African American students (Hannon, DeFina, and Bruch 2013); Latinos with lighter skin have better health outcomes (Garcia et al. 2015; Cuevas, Dawson, and Williams 2016), as do lighter-skinned African Americans

(Monk 2015). African American women with lighter skin are more likely to find marriage partners (Hamilton, Goldsmith, and Darity 2009). Lighter skin tone boosts African Americans' "educational attainment, household income, occupational status and even the skin tone and educational attainment of their spouses" (Monk 2014, 1313). Colorism shapes a range of Latinx and African American students' experiences in school and college (Hunter 2016; Monroe 2017). Thus, Nicole is not wrong to imagine that "if I looked different than I do, I would feel very uncomfortable, you know?" Social belonging from friendships with White students and campus-community belonging at Private would likely pose different challenges for her if she were not perceived as "White but exotic."

These dynamics are embedded in Nicole's experiences, reminding us that coming from a demographically similar high school might make a student "used to it," but it does not mean that the problems that come with being Black or Latinx on campus are eliminated. The problems are still there; they are simply are not new to the student. At the same time, ethnoracial-majority students who come from largely White high schools have a "sweeter transition," as Emily describes it, in which they can continue to "not pay too much attention" to the lack of diversity.

Small Numbers: Sticking out "like a Sore Thumb"

Many students of color also feel conspicuous, which is perhaps part of what Nicole meant when she said she would "feel very uncomfortable" if her skin were darker. Serena is a first-generation student who identifies as "African American. Also my grandpa was Chinese and my grandmother was Native American and Black." Soon after she joined Greek life, she tells me, "I stick out like a sore thumb" in photographs alongside her overwhelmingly White sorority sisters. "Going through rush, that was really intimidating for me because I was like, 'Well I kind of like the group of girls but maybe they won't like me because all of them are blonde hair, blue eyed.'" At our third interview, I ask how it feels for her now that she has been a member for more than a year. She replies, "I don't really feel a difference. No one really treats me differently or anything, which is nice. And I was really worried about that. But I still just notice it from time to time." Although Serena sounds relieved that "no one really treats me differently," it is something that she is on the lookout for and is "worried about," which means that she cannot experience social belonging in the way that many students define it: as letting one's guard down or, in Haley's words, "feeling comfortable. Feeling like you can truly be yourself. You don't have to put on any sort of façade or mask. Yeah, and just being able to express yourself how you want." This level of comfort and acceptance does not seem to be available to students like Serena who "worry" and "notice" whether they are treated "differently," even within the smaller communities they join. Janice McCabe (2016) found similar dynamics at the large Midwestern research university she studied. She described students experiencing "race-based marginality," even those who were involved on campus and were members of multiple student organizations; some still felt that they "did not quite belong anywhere" (118–120).

Joining Identity-Based Student Organizations and Resource Centers

Marginalized students often find social belonging and the freedom to let their guard down when they are around fellow members of the same group who share their identity (Tatum 1997; Ozaki and Johnston 2008; Park 2013). Dannisha at Public articulates why this dynamic works: "We look the same, you understand my struggles, how I'm perceived in the world. You understand everything about me. We can make a connection here." Teagan at Private agrees: "All the Black people, they hang out together. It's fun because I can relate to them and stuff." Even students like Nicole at Private, who easily develops friendships across racial lines, agrees: "Obviously I do feel like a minority. . . . Even talking to my friends—even my best friend [who is White] isn't going to understand what I'm saying from my perspective."

Universities today often provide student organizations, resource centers, and other spaces for members of marginalized groups, though they are not easily won on all campuses (Lipson 2007; Ahmed 2012; Berrey 2015; Warikoo 2016; Reyes 2018). At the large public research university in Lerma, Hamilton and Nielsen's (2019) study, the Multicultural Center was entirely student-led and student-run: "Many different groups of students have spent years fighting for safe spaces to learn and celebrate their cultural histories, engage in intersecting identities, recognize and confront inequities in university policies and infrastructure and receive culturally informed support services" (2019, 7). Once established, these become spaces where students can build relationships with people they can "relate to," as Teagan phrases it.

And these centers often live up to the task (Museus 2008; Cerezo and Chang 2013), as Daisy Reyes explains, "The underrepresentation of Latinos gave my respondents a feeling of not belonging. Externally ascribed as 'other' on campus, they found refuge in Latino organizations. Joining a Latino student organization helped ameliorate the feeling of being out of place" (2018, 95). Similarly, as we learned in chapter 2, Dannisha relied on the Black & African American Student Resource Center, known by students as "BAfA" as she made the transition to college in her first year: "That's a family I have now." Such centers, as well as less formal circles of friends who share a common identity, are critical sources of social belonging for students.

Yet, such centers and student organizations can also be points of conflict (Moore 2008; Warikoo 2016; Reyes 2018), even as they are part of wider efforts to "institutionalize diversity" on university campuses (Ahmed, 2012, 22). As Sara Ahmed points out, administrations often undermine and coopt efforts of their own diversity workers: "Diversity might be promoted because it allows the university to promote itself, creating a surface or illusion of happiness. . . . Diversity provides a positive, shiny image of the organization that allows inequalities to be concealed and thus reproduced" (72).

What does this mean for belonging? Students at Public and Private demonstrate that these centers and organizations are crucial sources of social belonging; yet the social belonging that they are offered there does not lead to a wider sense of campus-community belonging. In fact, participation in culturally specific organizations can highlight campus hostilities, which are experiences that withhold campus-community belonging from marginalized students. Valentina, at Public, tells me at the end of her second year that she is exhausted by the racial tensions on campus. "There's days that are so intense," she begins. Valentina works at the Latino-Chicano Resource Center, which Public students affectionately call "Lati-Chi." She loves the space and the community she has found there: they provide her safe haven. But, as Valentina describes some of the "intense" days from the past year or so, it becomes clear that her safe haven is not always all that safe. She told me about students "storming in" to Lati-Chi, "asking why there isn't a White resource center." Valentina's voice gets tight as she talks about it: "It's really frustrating. And it's also really scary, to be honest—for students. Students were in there studying."

"I think it's interesting," Valentina continues, "because really? You want to come to the only space within an institution that was never built—or made—for having women, women of color, first-generation students, and claim this? When this entire [campus] space is you!" She pulls on her long braid and laughs lightly as she tells me about other times when unfriendly White students entered Lati-Chi: "They come in there to instigate, but they're so nervous." She chuckles and then becomes serious, saying, "They're still asking and prodding those questions. Most of it was during the elections, pre and post, but it still happens."

Ethnoracial Tensions on Campus and in the National Political Arena

My fieldwork was conducted during both the 2016 rise of the controversial Black Lives Matter movement and the contentious presidential campaign and election of Donald Trump. As was happening at colleges all over the country at this time, graffiti started popping up on both campuses carrying anti-immigrant and pro-White sentiments, including swastikas, hate speech, and references to Trump's promises for a "Muslim ban" and a border wall. Simultaneously, racist episodes circulated rampantly on anonymous social media platforms. On both campuses, student groups organized protests, sit-ins, and other public demonstrations to express their discontent. They also expected the administrations to step in but were disappointed by the official response.

Both the Public and Private administrations issued statements via email after each racial incident, but they were little more than boilerplate responses reiterating "Our Community Values." Students complained that they came several days too late and that they affirmed the value of free speech, rather than denouncing acts that targeted fellow campus members. Wendy Moore reminds us that U.S. laws such as the constitutional right to free speech are not simply racially neutral expressions of our national ideology. Laws also carry "the force of the state to shape racial structure" by, for example, "legally protecting the right of white people to publicly express racial hostility" (2008, 16). We are not free from the ongoing legacy of our national origins. Historically, constitutional law explicitly protected White elites' ability to exploit both "human beings and land, while simultaneously asserting the rhetorical principles of freedom, democracy and equality under the law" (14). In more recent rulings on First Amendment cases, the Supreme Court has affirmed racist speech as protected free speech on college campuses, as Moore and Bell (2017, 114) discuss,

The practical result is a post–civil rights constitutional right to be racist in colleges and universities that administrators may not restrict in any meaningful way. The legal result is that whites can invoke state-centered protection for their racist speech and expression on college and university campuses, whereas students of color have no right to attain higher education free from dehumanizing, oppressive, and tacitly threatening communications. The broader outcome is that U.S. courts have created an interinstitutional symbiosis that reifies color-blind racism and white institutional space. In creating a state protection for explicit racist expression on college and university campuses, the courts protect a powerful mechanism of white institutional space, ensuring that administrative discourse rebuking such racist activities never goes beyond rhetoric.

Not surprisingly, many students at both Public and Private feel that their administrations are not concerned enough about racial aggressions and are not taking seriously how hostile the campus climate has become. Students of all ethnoracial identities whom I interviewed describe the email statements as "pointless," "weak," and "a joke." Alma's comment is typical among ethnoracial minorities: "It just makes me so sad to see not only students think this way, but our own administration thinks this way, too. Or they claim they don't think this way, but they kind of do. . . . They said, 'Oh you know, the Constitution, freedom of speech.' But I just personally feel like that doesn't give you the right to bully someone else." Alma, a first-generation student, identifies as "Chicana and Latina. Chicana because I was born here, but my family comes from Mexico, but I'm also from here, so it's the best of both worlds. And Latina too because I am from a Latin American country in the sense of my family and my ancestors, I'm proud to say."

The campus administrations at the two law schools in Moore's (2008) study also dismissed and diminished racial aggressions when students of color raised complaints and concerns, asserting that it "would not be fair to *other students*" if consideration or reparations were afforded to the injured party (136; emphasis in original). Moore also conducted her research during a racially contentious political moment, when landmark affirmative action cases were before the Supreme Court in the early 2000s. Similar to Private and Public's administrative responses, one dean in Moore's study sent out a vague email about some "unfortunate incidents" and reminded the student body that "the law school was committed to diversity and that he wanted the students and faculty to work to create a friendly and cooperative law school community" (136). Nearly two decades later, many universities, particularly predominately White institutions, have administrative "bias response teams," and yet they still struggle with "balancing free speech and diversity" (Miller et al. 2018, 29). At Public and Private, these efforts fell short of what students of color expected from their administrations, which was, to use Moore and Bell's words, to assert and protect their "right to attain higher education free from dehumanizing, oppressive, and tacitly threatening communications" (2017, 114).

As mentioned, the years of my study were a time of elevated ethnoracial tensions. The number of White supremacist displays on college campuses nationwide doubled from 2016 to 2017 (Smith 2017). Yet, we should not be tempted to think that Valentina, Alma, and others in my study simply had the bad luck to arrive at college during such a racially fraught moment in U.S. history, just as the students in Wendy Moore's study had the misfortune to be at law school during the contentious debates on affirmative action. Although we might hope that college life for Latinx and other minority students of color during less politically divisive times is tension-free at universities like Public and Private, that is simply not true. Scholarship on the years before my study show that similar dynamics were commonplace (McCabe 2009; Park 2013; Franklin Jeremy, Smith, and Hung 2014; Gin, et al. 2017).

Ethnoracial Tensions: "Huddling off" Together

Valentina's experiences show that Latinx students' campus-community belonging is vulnerable to direct attack, even in the very space designated to support them: the Lati-Chi center. Paradoxically, their vulnerability is heightened by their support space. Students at both Public and Private see their campus as a place where different racial groups segregate themselves (Tatum 1997; Villalpando 2003; Carter 2012), something that White students have a long history of "attacking" students of color for doing (Feagin et al. 1996, 71). Patrick, a first-generation student whom we met in previous chapters, explains, "A lot of these minorities, ethnic minorities on campus, they tend to huddle off with themselves, because they share the same culture and that's how it is. And it's very hard to get them to open up to others . . . It's just each culture has their own little corner on the campus." Patrick identifies as "I'm an Asian American. I still hold close ties to my Asian culture because that's what I grew up with, but I've deviated from it. That's why I feel like I'm an Asian American," which puts him in the ethnoracial majority at Public.

Lily, a "White" continuing-generation student at Private says, "I feel like here you see a lot of the different nationalities hanging out together, or you have the different resources you can go to if you were that nationality. I'm sure that they do that so that you can feel comfortable in the space if you're a certain nationality. But I just feel like it's just very segregated." To be clear, Lily is not talking about international students. Instead she seems to be conflating ethnoracial heritage with nationality, perhaps somewhat intentionally, because many White students perceive that it is not "nice" to directly bring up race, as I discuss in the next chapter.

Julianne at Private describes the situation similarly. She is a continuing-generation student who identifies as "I would definitely say White. I am half-Mexican. My mom is Mexican and my dad is White, but I'm very White. I was definitely raised very, just—I don't know—White." Julianne says, "I mean even if you just go to the dining hall, you'll just see all the kids kind of grouped together. . . . People make jokes about how, you know, everyone on the campus that's not White, you can count them and blah, blah, blah. I think Private wants to be diverse, and I think they are trying to . . . but it's still such a small population."

Julianne continues but struggles to articulate her thoughts: "I can't put this into words. I think that it is signaling them out as not being diverse. I don't know how to explain it. I feel like they are kind of grouped together instead of being able to immerse with everyone else." Among many others, Ryan, a continuing-generation Public student who identifies as "White," echoes the same frustration and also implicates the university: "By trying to promote diversity and inclusion they are actually promoting separate groups. There is rarely interaction between different groups."

One noticeable dynamic that none of the students in my study mention is that clusters of exclusively White students can commonly be seen around both campuses walking in groups, sitting together in eateries, studying together in libraries, and so on. Yet somehow, they are not perceived as self-segregating when they do so. It likely has something to do with ethnoracial-majority students' sensibility that it is the task of minority students to integrate themselves into the flow of campus life, as I discuss in the next chapter. However, that does not explain why ethnoracial-minority students do not recognize Whites' behavior as "huddling off" when they see all-White or nearly all-White circles of friends or student clubs.

When ethnoracial-minority students bring up dynamics of segregation in interviews, they also acknowledge that there are particular locations on campus where they can find fellow Latinx or African Americans. For example, Laura, a first-generation student, asserts, "I'm Mexican and the only Mexicans I've met are people in SSR." However, when Laura says this she is expressing frustration at how few fellow Mexicans exist on her campus, which is different from Julianne, Patrick, Ryan and others above who are frustrated that their school "promotes separate groups" when it promotes diversity. Here Laura is echoing Marisol's comment in chapter 3: "Looking at the demographics, it's only a few Latinas here. It's hard to find people like myself, and it does make a difference. When you see other people like yourself, you're just like, 'I'm not alone in this.' You know?"

At the same time, students like Teagan at Private feel conflicted about their own participation in the segregating dynamics: "I look around and like there's so many groups and cliques, but that's basically me doing the same thing." Teagan's experience is a telling example because she finds herself "huddling off," as Patrick at Public describes it, with other African Americans because they are people she can "relate to." Yet she also desires a wider set of friendships, but she was not made to feel wanted when she made efforts to acquire them, as we learned earlier. Social belonging was not offered to her in those circles.

Violet is the first-generation student at Private who identifies as "I'm Indian" whom we met in chapter 1, who ultimately left Private when her financial aid package was reduced. She acknowledges her own participation in self-segregating dynamics. Violet is a member of three ethnoracial student organizations, none of which target her own identity:

> I feel like a lot of the minorities kind of stick together. I don't know how much we actually mix in the school, I'm not sure. I know I'm part of Associated Black Students, even though I'm not Black. And then there's a Native American—it's an indigenous organization. And I'm part of that too, even though I'm not Native American. So, I don't know, just, when I look around campus, I mostly see minorities with minorities."

In her sweet, sincere manner, Violet explains further,

> For me, personally, a lot of times I feel more comfortable with minorities because a lot of times we come from the same socio-economic background. But at the same time, sometimes it doesn't feel very inclusive. I don't know if people have, just stereotypes—ideas based off of looking at people who are minorities? I'm not sure. But I know a lot of people were worried about joining sororities and things like that because they didn't know how inclusive it would be.

The perspectives of students like Teagan and Violet help us understand that there are multiple dynamics that lead students to "huddle off." They do so not only to spend time with those who share common ground but also to avoid experiences of rejection in the wider campus community (Moore 2008; Museus 2008; Ozaki and Johnston 2008; Reyes 2018).

Nonetheless, the overarching sensibility is that ethnoracial groups are purposefully detaching themselves from the rest of the student body when they self-segregate. That rubs majority students the wrong way. Of course, many marginalized students badly need these friendly spaces where they feel at home on campus, where they are offered abundant social belonging. Yet in heated times when they are accused of "huddling off" together, marginalized groups can feel not just unwanted by the larger campus community but also as physically unsafe, as Valentina relayed when she described White students "storming in" to Lati-Chi.

Tensions: Secondhand Stories

Another factor that posed an obstacle to belonging for several students of color I talked to was hearing secondhand stories of racism. Students' direct experiences may sometimes be confusing or vaguely racialized, leaving them uncertain whether particular interactions are related to their ethnoracial identity. However, multiple students recounted stories they had heard from friends that were unambiguously racist.

Nicole gives an example: "I heard last year there was a whole problem with a certain frat—that isn't even on campus anymore—not letting Black people into their parties. Not letting some athletes in. There was this whole fight between them. The school didn't even know about this. . . . The whole student body knew." Karla, a first-generation student at Private, who identifies as "I'm Puerto Rican, African American and Nicaraguan. I'm very proud of all of those," tells me a story she heard while hanging out at the Associated Black Student Center: "This girl was saying she was walking down the street—or down the path and someone came up to her and said, 'Do you know your dad?' Because she's Black and people say crazy stuff like that. I was like, 'What?!' That is so wrong."

Javier at Public tells me about his friend: "He said that he'll go play basketball with a Black Lives Matter shirt. And then, every—like 95% of the Asian students that get mad at him during basketball will be like, 'Hey, all lives matter!' And they'll say things like that. They don't understand . . . people shouldn't do that. You should be more aware."

Xavier, a continuing-generation student who identifies as "Vietnamese American," which puts him in the ethnoracial minority at Private, has heard similar stories: "I was talking to one of my friends and she's African American, and one day she just recounted something. She was talking with someone and then the person said, 'Oh, you speak rather articulately for a Black woman.' And that shocked me." Importantly, Xavier admits that it affected him too. "Having that in the back of my mind [pause] that kind of makes me a bit more skeptical around people now. Because honestly I don't know who's good or bad. What are they saying behind my back?" These secondhand stories become part of the campus culture for minority students of color. Like Xavier, they know that such comments and attitudes exist all around them, even though they do not necessarily experience them in blatant words or behaviors every day. Such stories make minority students of color feel at best uncertain and at worst unwelcome and unvalued, even if these kinds of incidents never happen to them directly (Moore 2008).

Lucia at Public shares with me a story that is very different from Xavier's but that had a similarly profound and negative impact on her:

> I was talking to so someone, and someone said that they went to a meeting with [the university president] and they asked, "Why are my people so underrepresented on campus? What is the problem? Why is there nothing being implemented to help these people?" And [the president] said, "Well, this school isn't for everybody." . . . When I found out I was very offended. Okay, so there's a reason why people like me aren't here and it's not because they can't be here. It's because other people don't believe they should be: "The school is not for everyone." Which I found very upsetting.

She goes on to say: "I'm dealing with it . . . but I feel like the campus climate that's here, not a lot of people would be able to survive it. It can be extreme. And it can be very easy to feel alone or like someone doesn't belong." Although she asserts that she personally has the fortitude to "survive it," her description of Public's culture reminds us again that first-generation students often struggle to "make themselves belong" to the campus-community. Lucia says, "I feel like I can handle it, but I don't necessarily feel like I belong perfectly. But I'm the type of person who even if I don't belong I am going to make it work and I am going to work hard and get where I need to get." His comments echo those of Javier in chapter 2: "Just because I don't belong here doesn't mean I can't succeed here."

The research shows us that sense of belonging is positively associated with persistence to the second year and graduation (Freeman, Anderman, and Jensen 2007; Hausmann, Schofield, and Woods 2007; Martinez et al. 2009; Morrow and Ackermann 2012). That does not mean, however, that when students from minority groups persist that we can assume that universities have effectively met their belonging needs. Many are simply determined to graduate, no matter the emotional toll (McCabe 2016; Jack 2019). Universities can and should feel obligated to foster those students' sense of belonging in all three realms, at least as effectively as they already meet the belonging needs of racial majority and continuing-generation students.

Tensions: Cross-Ethnoracial Roommates

Not only do ethnoracial tensions exist out in the campus community but they also exist in students' private living spaces (Harwood et al. 2012; Haynes 2019). Dannisha describes her two assigned roommates in her first year: "One of them is okay and the other is just rude." She explains, "When you see someone you say hi, or you say good morning or you acknowledge their presence and she just doesn't do that." Her roommate's behavior goes beyond being "awkward," Dannisha says she can sense her "side-eyeing me sometimes, I see her from my peripheral vision staring at me." It is not only uncomfortable for her, but also "confusing."

Dannisha then recounts multiple instances when her two roommates have minimized the territory that she should occupy in their shared dorm room. For example, one day, "I came home to find all of my stuff moved. They rearranged all my things and they were like, 'Oh yay! Now we have space!' And it was like, mmmm—It wasn't your space to make." Dannisha is unwilling to directly address her roommates or bring in an RA to help resolve things. She explains, "I am not good at confrontation. . . . If we start this, I will start yelling at her and I don't want any of that." Instead, Dannisha is simply waiting for the school year to be over so she can move in with new roommates in the fall.

It is easy to see how unwanted she feels in her dorm home: "I almost moved out so many times." In the beginning of the year, "I avoided going home a lot. . . . I would get anxiety getting into my room, like 'Oh fuck, is she going to be there?'" Dannisha does not bring up racial dynamics as she talks about her roommate conflicts; however, being a member of such a small racial group on campus, it seems unlikely that her roommates were fellow African Americans.

In my data it was much more common for minority students of color to have roommates who made them feel unwanted. Not all ethnoracial-majority students got along well with their assigned roommates, of course, but it was more typical for them to say that they did not like their roommate, rather than that they were disappointed or confused that their roommate did not like them. Also, they rarely mentioned race directly in stories about roommates. Sabrina was an exception, explicitly naming her roommate's Whiteness: "I have two roommates; one of them came here with people from high school and she's just been with them. She hasn't even tried to get to know me. She's just sticking with the people she came with and I feel like there's a lot of people like that." Sabrina is a first-generation student at Private who identifies as "I'm Mexican." She connects her roommate's disinterest in her directly to racial dynamics: "Well her, she's White and I know she went to a private high school. I don't think she's racist, but I don't think she'd try to get to know someone besides her group, and all of her group is a lot like her. I feel like there's a lot of people like that." What is frustrating for Sabrina is that, like Teagan, she desires a wide range of friendships but they just do not seem available to her:

I'm really open to getting to know a lot of people from different backgrounds and in SSR through Summer Bridge everybody was like that. And when everybody else comes here and they say, "I already have my friends so I'm good," yeah that was disappointing. It bothers me a little. I have my roommate; we don't really talk at all. I didn't know her major until last week, and that was just because I asked. I live with her and she's not interested in getting to know me. My other one I talk to a little more but we're still not friends. . . . That makes it really awkward when we're in the room because we don't talk. I get along with them. I've seen other people having problems with their roommates. I don't have any problem. We just don't talk.

We saw in chapter 2 how Patrick was denied social belonging by his floor-mates, but in my sample it was more common for minority students of color to have social belonging withheld from them in their living spaces. Like Dannisha, Sabrina does not feel welcomed and wanted in her dorm home. It is not a space where she experiences social belonging. Importantly, however, Sabrina does not see it as a "problem" akin to the kinds of room-mate strife that might require RA intervention: she views it instead as a dis-appointment that she simply must endure. This means that it will likely never register on the administration's radar at Private. From the universi-ty's perspective, if there are no formal complaints or RA reports of conflict, it might appear as though cross-ethnoracial roommate matching was suc-cessful in Sabrina's case (Shook and Fazio 2008).

Tensions and Belonging

The ubiquitous ethnoracial tensions that students experience in their cam-pus lives can take a heavy toll on minority students. These dynamics cut across first-generation and continuing-generation students alike in my data. Minority students of color encounter obstacles to social and campus-community belonging at both Public and Private. Some of these obstacles are due to organizational structural features such as the foods that are stocked in campus shops, as Javier mentioned. Other obstacles are embed-ded in the interpersonal interactions between majority and minority stu-dents such as Sabrina's disinterested roommate and Valentina's retelling of White students "storming in" to Lati-Chi. Both of these experiences are examples of social belonging being denied to minority students of color by their peers; both also simultaneously contribute to a campus culture that withholds campus-community belonging from minority students as well. It is no wonder that Lucia describes it this way: "I feel like the campus cli-mate that's here, not a lot of people would be able to survive it. It can be extreme." Franklin, Smith, and Hung (2014) describe this feeling as "racial battle fatigue." Their research demonstrates that "racial microaggressions impact the psychological, physiological and behavioral stress responses" of college students of color (304). Racial battle fatigue is something that White students do not experience. Quite the opposite: Joe Feagin argues that "at the level of everyday interaction with black Americans and other Americans of color, most whites can create racial tensions and barriers even without conscious awareness that they are doing so" (2014, 146).

We know that the tensions that minority students of color experience are often not systematically addressed by the diversity efforts of university administrations. Despite visibly and repeatedly espousing diversity goals and initiatives, many universities fail to make changes that would result in structural equity and meaningful gains for inclusion (Ahmed 2012; Berrey 2015; Byrd 2017). Thomas calls this a "diversity regime" that "consists of set of meanings and practices that works to institutionalize a benign commitment to diversity, and in doing so obscures, entrenches, and even intensifies existing racial inequality by failing to make fundamental changes in how power, resources, and opportunities are distributed" (2018, 145). Students at both Public and Private have described for us what it feels like to navigate schools with diversity regimes. They show us how it damages their ability to access social belonging and campus-community belonging.

6

"Nice" Diversity

● ●

Although small numbers and the contentious national political climate that I discussed in the previous chapter lead to tensions on campus, another layer of tension is connected to ethnoracial-majority students' discomfort or unwillingness to acknowledge that small numbers matter. In interviews I ask students, "What do you think about the racial diversity on campus?" Perhaps not surprisingly, students who identify in the ethnoracial majority generally express a sense of contentment with the level of diversity they perceive, as Zach at Private did in chapter 5: "I feel like the campus is pretty diverse. I mean I don't really notice. . . . I just kind of assumed that it's balanced. and it's how it should be." This holds true whether they are continuing-generation students like Zach or first-generation students like Patrick at Public who says, "It's pretty even, I guess. There's a lot of people of Asian ethnicity and I'm one. So, I would know." Patrick acknowledges the large numbers of Asians like himself, but at the same time he indicates that the distribution feels reasonable to him, even balanced, by calling the racial representation "pretty even."

A few majority students acknowledge that representation is not "balanced" or "pretty even," yet they assert that it is not an issue of concern. For example, James is a continuing-generation student who identifies as "As far as race goes, I mean—so, it's like—I am in the majority of being White."

When I ask what he thinks of the racial diversity at Private, he states unequivocally, "We don't have any." Then, with dramatic effect, he takes a long, slow drink from his smoothie bottle, as though to let his statement hang in the air. When I ask, "How do you feel about that?" he responds, "I don't care, personally. . . . I mean—I don't know. It's whatever to me." He shrugs his shoulders and then elaborates, "Back home four out of five of my closest friends are ethnic. Here my friends are White. . . . It would be cool if we had a student body more representative of the—I don't know, the national population. . . . Ultimately, though, my roommates are White, my friends are White. They are great people though. So, I could care less at the end of the day."

Ling sounds similar to James. He is a first-generation student at Public who identifies as "I'm an Asian, I mean it's not like I need to hide myself, like 'Oh, I'm so ashamed to be Asian.' I'm me and I'm just Asian." He responds this way to my question about diversity: "I'm indifferent about it. I mean people—it doesn't matter where they come from really. To me they're all people. So, it doesn't matter to me."

Students such as Haley take it a step further. Haley is a continuing-generation student at Private who identifies as "Caucasian or White." Whereas Ling, James, and others say that the lack of diversity does not bother them, Haley, and others like her, says it does not even cross her mind: "I think it's good. I don't—I don't really think about different races. I mean, I just have my friends. I don't even consider what race they are." I argue that this kind of denial of the importance of race is understood by Whites as taking the moral high ground. They believe that race *should not* be important and, if everyone would just stop focusing on it, we could move beyond racism. As Eduardo Bonilla-Silva (2018) argues, this is a form of racism because the reality is that denying that race matters inadvertently produces a racist outcome. It allows the racial status quo to remain unchallenged, which preserves existing racial inequities as they stand. Nonetheless, many White Americans are convinced that forgetting about race is the obvious and only way out of the problems created by our White supremacist history (Johnson 2017; Feagin 2013). Natasha Warikoo (2016) calls this a "color-blindness frame" for understanding diversity: it embodies the idea that race "does not and should not play a role in society" (46). As in my data, Warikoo also finds this to be a common perspective among the White and Asian American college students she studied at Harvard and Brown.

Eric, a first-generation student at Public who identifies as "I'm Chinese. Asian. Cantonese specifically," also claims it has never crossed his mind: "You know honestly that is not something I've really thought about. . . . Now that you've mentioned it, I don't know. I really don't have an opinion on that." To be fair, several Latinx students I interviewed gave me similar responses. For example, Joaquín, the first-generation student at Public whom we met in chapter 4 and who identifies as "Personally, I just use Hispanic," answers, "I see all kinds of folk. What should I say? I've never thought of it as being a problem." However, this kind of response is more common among students in the ethnoracial majority or among students who are "used to it" from attending a predominately White high school, as discussed in chapter 5.

Discomfort Naming Whiteness

Ethnoracial-majority students whom I interviewed, particularly Whites, often displayed uncertainty and uneasiness talking about race (Sue 2015; Pollock 2004; DiAngelo 2018; Ochoa 2013). As for their own identities, several White students exhibited deep discomfort naming themselves out loud as White in interviews with me. I asked everyone the same question: "How do you personally identify in terms of race?" Some White students froze in place, unsure how to respond. Haley lightly rubbed the skin on her arm as she tentatively asked, "You mean like—," unable to say anything but hinting that she meant skin color. Shane said, "Ummm—." Pause. Then he answered, in a questioning tone, "Conservative male?" which of course is not a racial identity at all.

When I encountered such responses I did my best to put students at ease by saying, "For example, when you fill out those forms, what box do you check?" and then I would share my own experience: "I always check Caucasian, but that word isn't really a word I use to describe myself. I use the word 'White.'" In these moments it helped me as an interviewer to have racial affinity with White students. I could successfully reassure them that it was okay to name their Whiteness. Sometimes all it took was a supportive smile while nodding my head as they awkwardly answered with phrases such as "I'm your typical, I don't know—White guy. Your everyday guy." Or "I'm just White. Nothing unique about me." Ryan, a continuing-generation student at Public, sighed, "White isn't a comfortable box to check." Similarly, Hudson, a continuing-generation student at Private acknowledged the same sensibility, even as he personally defied it: "I'm not ashamed to check

White." Some dove into a list of the European countries that make up their heritage without ever saying the word "White" at all.

As we see later, this prevalent sense of discomfort and uncertainty over race, in particular over Whiteness, is compatible with a desire for campus diversity to play out in nonconfrontational ways; that is, a diversity that does not name Whiteness as a factor. Students who hold a color-blindness frame want a form of ethnoracial diversity that does not name any race at all as a factor—which is rather difficult to do. They want diversity to simply exist without needing to be named or recognized. Accordingly, this avoidance leads to withholding campus-community belonging from students of color, especially when they join student organizations that name their race. Ethnoracial-majority students tend to see it as divisive any time that race is acknowledged as a relevant factor in social life. It makes them uncomfortable. Warikoo argues that youth in the United States learn this sensibility well before arriving at college. K–12 history lessons have imparted the notion that "naming race was itself racist—that calling attention to someone's race was behaving in a racist way, because after all it was differentiating people by race that led to the heinous system of racial injustice they learned about in school" (2016, 113). She asserts, "Given the history of slavery and racial segregation in the United States, a shared understanding that 'racism is immoral' develops at a young age" (114) and one readily available and appealing way that Whites attempt to disavow racism is by professing color-blindness; that is, that they do not see race, because race does not matter for how they treat others.

Further, Feagin, Vera, and Batur (2001) assert that "relatively few whites think reflectively about their whiteness except when it is forced on them by encounters or challenges" (191). They explain that this allows "sincere fictions of the white self" to exist in Whites' self-perceptions: "white individuals usually see themselves as 'not racist,' as 'good people,' even while they think and act in antiblack ways" (187). Thus, color-blindness has an additional dimension of appeal, because it justifies not giving thought to anyone's race, including one's own.

Multiracial Heritage and White Identities

Not all students who identify as White are uncomfortable naming their Whiteness, and White identities are not monolithic (McDermott and

Samson 2005). Several students in my study identify themselves as multiracial, including partly White. Some, like Nicole, are fluent in discussions of racial dynamics and racial identities in interviews. We met Nicole in the previous chapter: "I'm half-White, half-Black but I live with my mom, who is Black." Recall that Nicole said, "I would feel uncomfortable" at Private "if I was darker." She freely shared her conflicted feelings over the fact that her friends at Private tell her, "You look White but exotic." Yet Nicole unhesitatingly includes Whiteness as part of her description of herself and her lived experiences.

However, not every multiracial student is like Nicole. Several acknowledge their multiracial heritage while at the same time claiming an entirely White identity. We saw examples of this previously with Zach and Julianne. I quickly began to realize that these students are a category of their own. Recall Julianne's explanation of her identity: "I would definitely say White. I am half-Mexican. My mom is Mexican and my dad is White, but I'm very White. I was definitely raised very, just—I don't know—White." Another example is Gavin: "I would say White. Sometimes I throw in Hispanic. I think I'm like a quarter Hispanic or something, but I don't really culturally or racially identify as Hispanic." He adds, "So, you can use that on scholarships and stuff like that. But, if someone were to ask me my race I would say White. I don't really consider myself Hispanic." These students are also a bit more comfortable discussing Whiteness than Haley and James, who answer my racial identity question with a hand gesture and a political-gender description, respectively. However, it is clear from their interviews that students like Zach, Julianne and Gavin had belonging experiences and perspectives on racial dynamics that were largely indistinguishable from their classmates who identify monoracially as White.[1]

One notable difference between Public and Private in terms of ethnoracial dynamics is the number of multiracial students who identify as White. Although only one student at Public held such an identity (3.2%), eight students at Private did, comprising 22.2 percent of my original sample at that school. To be clear, I am not counting students like Charlotte from chapter 2 who identifies as "half-Japanese, half-Caucasian" because at Public, those are both majority identities. Nor am I counting students like Nicole, who claims White heritage alongside Black heritage but does not assert a White identity.

The one I am including at Public is Mason. Early in our interview he describes himself as "Hispanic/Latino and White . . . I don't necessarily have a set ethnic identity, because my ethnic background has never defined me, but that might just be because I look White." Here he disavows that his Latinx side defines him, but he also recognizes having a "mixed ethnic background." Later in the interview he gives a clearer sense of his self-perception when talking about his discomfort in one of his classes when they were "talking about institutional racism and discrimination." He tells me,

> I don't feel comfortable discussing anything about race. Simply because my heritage—coming from Latin America, my heritage traces back to the original Whites—Whites from the South, and conquistadors. So, no matter where I turn, I am oppressor . . . It's difficult to have a discussion about race without wanting to be apologetic. And being a White apologetic is not necessarily healthy to the discussion about race. . . . I'm not against having the discussions, but I certainly get concerned that I have the face of the enemy.

Mason's claim that his Latin American heritage is a White heritage confirmed for me that he fits in the category with Zach, Julianne, Gavin and others. He also characteristically expressed discomfort "discussing anything about race," which is common among majority students, because he sees himself as "a White apologetic" in such discussions.

As Marc Johnston-Guerrero and colleagues argue in their study of college students, it is critically important to "represent individuals in ways that align with their underlying meanings of race" rather than take at face value the boxes they check on forms, otherwise it could "potentially negate the usefulness of collecting racial data in the first place (Johnston et al. 2014, 66). This is particularly important for universities when "designing practices to meet the needs of multiracial students" (Johnston-Guerrero and Renn 2016, 143).[2] From here forward, I refer to this as a White* identity, allowing the asterisk to signal, as a kind of shorthand, that it is a more complicated racial identity than monoracial Whiteness.

The eight White* students at Private include six who acknowledge Latinx heritage (ranging from one-quarter to 100 percent), one who acknowledges Black heritage (half) and one who acknowledges Middle Eastern heritage (one-quarter). All but one could easily be visually perceived as White, and most openly commented on the fact (Vargas 2015). The one remaining is Cristian whose skin is darker than other White* students and who shares matter-of-factly that all four of his grandparents were born in Mexico, but he also unambiguously asserts, "I'm a Mexican kid but culturally I don't

Table 9
Percentage of Students Who Experience Belonging in Each Realm at Private

	N	Private University Campus-Community Belonging	Social Belonging	Academic Belonging
Interview 1				
All students	36	75.0%	58.3%	61.1%
White identity	11	90.1%	72.3%	63.3%
White* dentity	8	87.5%	87.5%	100%
Minority identity	17	64.7%	47.1%	41.2%
Interview 2				
All students	34	67.6%	58.8%	58.8%
White identity	11	63.6%	63.6%	63.6%
White* identity	7	85.7%	85.7%	85.7%
Minority identity	16	62.5%	43.8%	43.8%
Interview 3				
All students	31	74.2%	61.3%	61.3%
White identity	11	72.7%	63.6%	63.6%
White* identity	6	100%	100%	100%
Minority identity	14	64.3%	42.8%	42.8%

identify with that at all. I'm pretty culturally White. So that's where I'm at. I'm not like, 'Oh,' you know, 'I'm going to go out to my cousin's quinceañera' or whatever. I'm here. I was never really raised like that. I'm just culturally White." In addition to his claim to a "culturally White" identity, Cristian's attitudes and experiences align with the White majority at Private; thus, I count him in the White* category. Additionally, three of the eight White* students at Private are first generation, as is Mason, the only White* student at Public. I mention this to underscore again that the ethnoracial dynamics of belonging exist alongside and in addition to the dynamics of generation status. They do not seem to systematically overlap.

As table 9 shows, White and White* students at Private experience belonging at higher rates than ethnoracial-minority students do in all three realms of belonging and at all points in time. The proportions of students who hold minority identities hover in the low 60s for campus community belonging and in the 40s for both social and academic belonging, approximately twenty to thirty percentage points below White and White* students in nearly every instance. These are differences worth paying attention to.

Table 10
Misleading Percentage of Students Who Experience Belonging in Each Realm at Private

		Private University		
	N	Campus-Community Belonging	Social Belonging	Academic Belonging
Interview 1				
All students	36	75.0%	58.3%	61.1%
White	11	90.1%	72.3%	63.3%
Ethnoracial minority (including White*)	25	72.0%	60.0%	60.0%
Interview 2				
All students	34	67.6%	58.8%	58.8%
White	11	63.6%	63.6%	63.6%
Ethnoracial minority (including White*)	23	69.6%	56.5%	56.5%
Interview 3				
All students	31	74.2%	61.3%	61.3%
White	11	72.7%	63.6%	63.6%
Ethnoracial minority (including White*)	20	75.0%	60.0%	60.0%

For comparison, in table 10, I show what the data would look like if White* students were categorized in my analysis as ethnoracial-minority students due to the fact that their multiracial heritage includes a non-White category. I include this for two reasons. First, because it mirrors a common shorthand measure of diversity in schools, including colleges: Whites-compared-to-everyone-else. Second, because I had access to (limited) admissions data on the students in my samples at both Public and Private, I discovered that these nine students are counted at both universities as minorities. The results in table 10 are nothing short of misleading. Although White students' rates of belonging are still higher in most instances than those of ethnoracial-minority students, the differences become relatively small, particularly in interview 3; in some places minority students appear to experience campus-community belonging at higher rates than Whites. Classifying White* individuals as members of a minority does not accurately reflect the belonging experiences that students described to me at length in their interviews. These numbers are deceptively positive.

It is evident that we need to pay attention to this difference between White* identified students and ethnoracial-minority identified students. Otherwise, a school like Private might easily misunderstand the reality of belonging among its minority students. The data, as it is presented in table 10, might convince Private that minority students' belonging needs are being met on par with majority students' needs by the end of their second year. What the previous chapter and the rest of this chapter demonstrate is that how students are perceived and treated in the campus-community is more important for belonging than a strict accounting of their heritage in ethnoracial categories.

It is valuable to understand that White* students are on our campuses and that they navigate campus life differently than do other multiracial students, regardless of the boxes they check on their admissions forms. We also know that multiracial students' identities can change during their college years as they learn more about themselves and the world around them (Harper 2014). Paying more attention to White* students in future research might very well reveal that they are not always as similar to monoracial White students as they are in my belonging data at Public and Private. In addition, perceptions of them by others might be more complicated than we imagine. For example, in Warikoo's study, two White Harvard students complained in interviews that they knew people "who are, like, a quarter Mexican, who got the Latino Scholarship award, but their entire experience has been a white experience" or someone who "even though he was black . . . he was the whitest kid people knew" (2016, 106–107). Warikoo found these descriptions to be accusations that such students did not deserve to be afforded extra considerations in Harvard's affirmative action policies; that they were cheating in "the diversity bargain" because they did not bring rich cultural differences to the campus community. Importantly, Warikoo only documented the negative perception of what I am calling the White* identities of others; she did not present interviews with students who claimed it as their own identity. Clearly, White* Americans deserve to be recognized so we can better understand their experiences (Johnston-Guerrero 2017). In my study, distinguishing them from others helps us more clearly recognize that students whose lives are anchored in their identities as ethnoracial minorities face stumbling blocks in all three realms of college belonging. Those stumbling blocks are less present for students in the ethnoracial majority, including Whites.*

Table 11
Public Student's Belonging by Ethnoracial Identity

		Public University		
	N	Campus-Community Belonging	Social Belonging	Academic Belonging
Interview 1				
All students	31	45.7%	41.9%	29.0%
White & Asian	17	58.8%	41.2%	29.4%[a] (25.0%)
Ethnoracial minority	14	28.6%	42.9%	28.6%
Interview 2				
All students	29	37.9%	48.3%	37.9%
White & Asian	16	50.0%	62.5%	37.5%
Ethnoracial minority	13	23.1%	30.8%	38.5%
Interview 3				
All students	25	36.0%	63.0%	52.0%
White & Asian	15	46.7%	73.3%	46.7%
Ethnoracial minority	10	20.0%	50.0%	60.0%

[a]If the one White* student is counted separately, this number would become 25.0%. No other numbers in the table would change.

Even though my data only shows one White* student at Public, that university still needs to pay attention to the belonging experiences of its ethnoracial-minority students compared to majority students. As table 11 shows, there are stark differences between the two groups in social belonging and campus-community belonging. (We saw the campus-community data in chapter 5 in table 8, but I am including it here again alongside social and academic belonging for handy comparisons.) Although students at both Public and Private describe the ethnoracial tensions and obstacles to belonging similarly, the data in tables 9 and 11 illustrate that minority students have lower belonging outcomes at the two universities.

The Desire for "Nice" Diversity

When I asked students what is gained by having a diverse student body, ethnoracial majority students reveal that they desire "nice" diversity on their campuses (Castango 2014). By "nice" I mean that they want diversity that is not divisive or disruptive. They agree that diversity is important because students can learn new things from each other, but they assert that the differences between people should never cause conflict or make anyone feel uncomfortable. Ethnoracial majority students' responses illustrate why they are bothered by minority students' self-segregation into ethnoracial clubs, groups and centers. They see the proper outcome of the process of sharing ideas and perspectives is that it leads to acculturation to a majority campus culture not a perpetuation of distinct clusters of students. Patrick at Public uses the phrase, a "blending of cultures" to describe the desired outcome. It is "like a merging of culture kind of thing, which is what the end goal is when we come to having an ideal diversity." We know Patrick from previous chapters. He is a first-generation student who identifies as "I'm an Asian American. I still hold close ties to my Asian culture because that's what I grew up with, but I've deviated from it. That's why I feel like I'm an Asian American." His and others' viewpoint assumes that racial differences should just work themselves out, because as people get to know one another they will harmoniously find common ground. Inherently, this attitude supports the White dominant cultural status quo because differences are confined to interactions that do not disrupt existing inequities (Hill 2008; Collins 2009; Feagin 2013; Bonilla-Silva 2018).

Lily, a continuing-generation student who identifies as "White," tries to articulate how Private falls short of her vision of ideal diversity: "I feel like it's all very separated and I'm not sure how I feel about that because I feel like diversity is supposed to be something that you don't even really notice. It [should be] very integrated . . . I know that there's racial diversity on campus, but I don't even really feel it because everything's just so not integrated. It's not a mix."

Lily is not alone in her desire to have diversity be both present and invisible, "something you don't even really notice." Similarly, Noah, a continuing-generation student at Public who tells me, "I identify as Korean-American," explains what would be gained with a more diverse student body: "I don't want to say it's assimilation, but rather bringing together a coalition of people. Because the Black—specifically the African American, the Latino and Mexican American communities are so small, they have their own created groups . . . Because Asians and Whites dominate most of the area, we have select groups already. And I think it's easy for the Asians and the Whites to permeate within those groups, but not the other way around."

Hudson at Private, phrases it slightly differently: "I don't think that [race] should be ignored, I think that it should be embraced. I don't know. I do think that there are differences between people. It's just that that should not be a bad thing. It should be a constructive learning or like fusion experience where people of different types and backgrounds can coexist peacefully." Hudson is a continuing-generation student who identifies as "I'm German, Swedish, English and Dutch. That's about as White as it gets, with some Irish and Scottish somewhere in there."

Noah wishes that student groups were "coalitions" that included members of multiple races, echoing the idea of "integration" that Lily desires and the "fusion" and peaceful coexisting that Hudson can imagine. Ethnoracially specific organizations and centers strike majority students as moving in the opposite direction from ideal diversity: intentionally not integrating with others. Many have grown up in a world where they rarely—if ever— felt excluded or penalized for their racial identities. Thus, a club or a resource center that is not meant for them seems, well, impolite, even abrasive.

The overwhelming response to my question, "What do we gain from having a diverse student body—or what are we missing out on now because we don't have one?" is thus an optimistic description of interacting with others from different backgrounds and learning from those differences. They see such interaction as having the potential to expand horizons and dismantle stereotypes. As Kenadee says, more diversity would bring "different perspectives in classrooms. Stuff that would be interesting to hear." Kenadee is a continuing-generation student at Private: "I'm technically African American because that's how people label it, but I'm actually Caribbean."

I heard similar ideas across the board from members of all ethnoracial groups at both universities, just as Natasha Warikoo (2016) found in her study. She calls this the "diversity frame," which is held by those who believe that there is value to diversity. This frame "views race as a cultural identity that shapes individuals and world views in positive ways" (50). She found that more than 90 percent of the U.S. students in her study hold this frame. They desire to learn from members of other groups because it benefits their own personal growth and their development as "cultural omnivores," as befitting the identities of elites (61). The diversity frame is part of "the diversity bargain": White students are willing to accept affirmative action efforts to bring more ethnoracial minorities into the student body in exchange for being able to benefit from the knowledge and expanded perspectives that diversity will bring to their own lives.

Warikoo aptly demonstrates that one person can hold multiple frames simultaneously, and it was not uncommon for White students to hold both the "color-blindness frame" and the "diversity frame" in interviews with her, drawing on each frame separately at various moments. In my interviews I noticed an additional dynamic. When White, White*, and majority Asian students at Public and Private use the diversity frame, their descriptions often carry the sensibility that diverse perspectives are welcome and wonderful only if they do not cause conflict; that is, if they are "nice." In her book, *Educated in Whiteness: Good Intentions and Diversity in Schools*, Angelina Castagno (2014) writes about the concept of "niceness" that is a cornerstone of Whiteness in the United States:

> To be nice is to be pleasing and agreeable, pleasant and kind. . . . A nice person is not someone who creates a lot of disturbance, conflict, controversy or discomfort. Nice people avoid potentially uncomfortable or upsetting experiences, knowledge, and interactions. We do no point out failures or shortcomings in others but rather emphasize the good, the promise, and the improvement we see. Niceness compels us to reframe potentially disruptive or uncomfortable things in ways that are more soothing, pleasant and comfortable (9).

Castagno argues that "being nice is intimately tied to engaging whiteness and whiteness itself is aligned with niceness" (8). This helps us understand why it makes intuitive sense to White and White* students that conflict and friction are antithetical to the goals of diversity: causing discomfort runs counter to their fundamental cultural sensibilities about how to behave in the world. It helps us understand why they are offended by all the "huddling off" in organizations and centers: they do not feel invited and it is not "nice" to exclude anyone. By contrast, Warikoo found that many White students at Harvard and Brown are frustrated by student organizations where students of color congregate because "interactions with peers of color is a *resource* some white students feel entitled to—or sometimes wrongly deprived of" (104; emphasis original). I did not hear that particular sense of entitlement from the students at Public and Private. However, in my data, majority Asian students hold the same view as their White classmates that it is not "nice" to make people feel excluded from an organization, because it serves a specific race. The solution is for African

Americans and Latinx students to embrace niceness like everyone else and stop making others feel uncomfortable.

The difficulty is that ethnoracial diversity is not always "nice." Nor should it be. White, White*, and Asian-majority students in my study want others to blend in. Words such as "integrated," "merge," "fusion," "mix," and "coexist peacefully" make sense to them, because those ideas are aligned with the White cultural value of niceness. Yet for many, "nice" diversity is impossible in a cultural context such as the United States where historical and present racial injustices and racial inequities shape all of our lived experiences, some for the better and others for the worse. Many members of marginalized and disenfranchised ethnoracial groups are unwilling to simply ignore their racial reality just so that they can be "nice" and not challenge contemporary White America's view of itself as not responsible for racial disparities.

Warikoo calls this "the power analysis frame," which is a "view of race as inherently based in group struggles for power" and rooted in efforts toward social justice outcomes (2016, 54). She found it to be fairly common among Black and Latinx college students in her study and rare among Whites and Asian Americans. My data show the same pattern. Warkioo does not analyze dynamics of belonging, but her work helps us understand why some Black and Latinx students do not experience campus-community belonging, regardless of whether they experience social or academic belonging. It is clear to them that, to be accepted by the campus-community, they are required to "merge" themselves into mainstream campus life and not make people uncomfortable by talking about racial injustice or even just by naming race out loud.

Ethnoracial-majority students articulate how distasteful they find behaviors that raise discomfort over ethnoracial injustice. Shane, a continuing-generation student at Private who identifies as "just White," has an annoyed tone in his voice when he mentions the list of grievances that Associated Black Students (ABS) presented to the administration in a recent demonstration. "I think the African American community feels like—I don't know. They came out with an entire list first semester, just their requests and stupid stuff like changing the mascot because it is offensive or something." He rolls his eyes. "I don't—see, that's completely stupid for me, some of their requests." Shane's tone and demeanor give the sense that he sees the ABS demands as trivial and unnecessarily disruptive. He sounds frustrated.

Cristian, a White* student at Private, feels similarly: "There are a few organizations like ABS for example that seem to think that they're really oppressed . . . they seem to think that because of their skin color they're really more marginalized or bogged down in a way. And I've never seen that." Here he pauses and hedges a bit: "It could be a completely different story if I were walking in their shoes, but I honestly think that by making such a big deal out of it, they're perpetuating the issue. Because it creates a divide that I don't think was there before." Cristian is a continuing-generation student. Befitting his White* identity and experiences, he exemplifies here the racial-majority perspective: when diversity takes the form of social protest, challenging the status quo and its inequities, it is perceived as divisive and overblown (Anderson 2016). Wendy Moore argues that a feature of "color-blind racism" is that it "allows white students, faculty and administrators to suggest that students of color are misperceiving their own experiences" (2008, 139), just as Cristian suggests here, because color-blindness involves denying that power dynamics are embedded in race relations.

Like Cristian, ethnoracial-majority students tend to see such actions as antithetical to improving racial dynamics: they "create a divide" when, from their perspective, the path to move beyond ethnoracial injustice is for everyone just to stop talking about the problems of the past and to start getting along harmoniously with each other. Castagno argues, "Being nice encourages us to gloss over ugly, tense or otherwise hurtful things—and to do so carefully and precisely" (2014, 9). Thus, calling up racial issues and demanding that the campus community pay attention to ugly realities, as the ABS protest did, are perceived as frustratingly antithetical to niceness for students like Cristian and Shane.

Haley, the continuing-generation student at Private who told us earlier, "I just have my friends. I don't even consider what race they are," thinks that even the solicitations to get involved in campus organizations could be nicer. "I feel like they might push certain things too hard," she tells me. With characteristic niceness, she interrupts herself to clarify, "I feel bad saying it because I totally agree with what they're doing . . . these are all very real things and I support them." I ask for an example of what she is thinking of, and Haley responds: "Like sustainability, or different organizations. Reaching out, like the Women's Center or Black Lives Matter . . . I feel like sometimes I'm asked to be—pushed to be—involved in things or go to events." These invitations make Haley feel uncomfortable, similar to White students whom Warikoo interviewed at Brown who felt that multiculturalism was "shoved in their faces" (2016, 75). These efforts at inclusion seem to run counter to Haley's expectations for a "nice" campus environment.

Even when racial-majority students like Haley recognize disparity and the need for student activism to make issues known, they still expect it to be nonconflictual, "glossing over" contentious issues, and they describe it that way. Easton at Public, for example, is a continuing-generation student who identifies as "I would say White. My dad is fully Swedish. I call myself Western European." He says, "I enjoy the diversity" at Public because his hometown is "97 percent White." He comes from out of state and by the end of his second year, he has

> gotten used to California's diversity . . . There might only be a small percent African American population here, but because that's the situation, their voice—or some of them—have made their culture and voice and activism on campus is more known. It's there. It's presented to you and there might be large percent Asian American, or Asian descent here, but there's such a massive portion of it that it's—everyone roughly balances out, in a way. Some push harder than others.

Easton does not find the disproportionate representation of African Americans and Asians problematic because he believes that each group has a recognized place in the campus community. Whether a particular group had to fight for visibility on campus or whether visibility came automatically as a result of large numbers is neither here nor there for him: it has all just worked itself out. Oliver, a White* first-generation student at Private, has a similar perspective. When I ask what he thinks about the racial diversity on his campus he says, "Actually, I quite enjoy it." He adds, "Where I'm from there's a very White majority. My hometown is less than 2 percent African American. So, if it weren't for my neighbors being African American back home, I would never see anyone with a culture identity. But here on campus at least every day I see my friend Chris, who is African American and he loves—he has these t-shirts. One has Malcom X on it, and another has a quote by Nat Turner. I love how fiercely he represents his culture because it's like, 'Dude.' It's awesome. And it makes me chuckle a little bit."

Oliver uses the example of t-shirts depicting historical Black rebellion leaders as signals of his friend Chris taking pride in Black culture. The t-shirts are visible but not threatening, which we know because Oliver's response is to "chuckle a little bit." He seems amused rather than wary, perhaps because the shirts honor historical struggles over racial injustice rather than contemporary ones. It might be different for Oliver if Chris were in the habit of wearing Black Lives Matter t-shirts. Either way, this form of "fiercely" representing Black culture fits easily into the nonconfrontational expectations for racial diversity that majority students have. It's an easy, "nice" kind of diversity.

Oliver believes that ethnoracial minorities are socially accepted on campus: "I feel like they feel they are welcome here. Here, maybe not in the country with the political climate. But I feel like they feel welcome here. But I would definitely love to see more and more diversity and I definitely think there is room for improvement." Interestingly, Oliver's hometown is in central California where a substantial population of Chicanos and Latinos reside. He does not seem to be thinking of them when he describes home as a place where the only "culture identity" he sees is in one household of African American neighbors. Instead, he brings it up when I ask him how he identifies racially. He tells me "I'm half Mexican, a quarter German and a quarter French." In an earlier interview he described himself as "kind of White, kind of not." Oliver says that most people assume that he is White: "I'm White enough that people will mistake me for a tall tan guy. But I'm also dark enough that people will believe I'm Mexican."

Oliver talks at length about his uncertain and conflicted feelings over his Mexican identity, telling me at the end of his second year that now, at Private he can comfortably say, "I'm a Mexican"—but at home it is different. "It becomes less—not less important—but it becomes more casual to say that without having any kind of a response negatively. Whereas back home . . . being a Mexican in the Central Valley is very much like—you are a laborer. And my family isn't, but that's the idea. Because it is a farming community and there's a lot of laborers there." Evidently in his hometown he does not view himself as part of the community identified as Mexican. Here at Private he is not sure whether he "counts" as Mexican either, but he wants to. "Just because I am English speaking—for lack of a better term, gringo or Whitewashed. I don't know what the real term is. But the point is that I can't speak Spanish. I don't eat Mexican food every day. In that way I don't know if I count, but I would like to." Despite his desire to "count" as Mexican, I classify Oliver as White* because he shows in many ways that his lived experiences and his identity align with the ethnoracial majority; for example, when he refers to minorities as "they," not "we," and when he talked a great deal in our first interview about how delighted he was to be able to take German classes and learn for the first time about his German heritage. He joined the German Cultural Club and eagerly hoped to study abroad in Germany down the line. Interestingly, Oliver never mentions Latinx students when he answers my questions about racial diversity at Private. In all our interviews he either uses the umbrella term "minority groups" or discusses African Americans in particular. I took it as evidence of his ambivalent feelings about his own White* identity.

Oliver highlights how complicated ethnoracial identities can be. He believes that "minorities" at Private feel welcome. Perhaps it is precisely because his ethnoracial identity does not undermine his campus-community belonging that he cannot imagine that anyone else's identity might do so. He accepts and values his friend Chris's nonconfrontational (but fierce) "culture identity" as expressed through historical figures on t-shirts, and he "would like to be" counted as having an ethnic identity himself in the "nice" environment he experiences in Private's campus culture. This stands contrary to his hometown culture where he does not want his Mexican heritage to associate him with "laborer" families. Thus, Oliver's White* perspective on diversity and harmony fits neatly in the pattern I find among ethnoracial-majority students at both schools.

The Desire for Not-So-Nice Diversity

Not surprisingly, many students in my study who identify as Black, Latinx, and non-White* multiracials are not interested in "nice" diversity. Students of all races are likely to say that what we gain from a diverse student body is exposure other groups, chances to get to know each other, and opportunities to build friendships. Again, this is what Warikoo calls a "diversity frame." However, minority students of color tend to emphasize breaking down stereotypes and becoming more aware and more sensitive to others' challenges as a way to fight for social justice, what Warikoo describes as the "power analysis frame." For example, Lucia at Public says, "If we had more real diversity within the racial demographics, more people would be exposed to more cultures and be more aware of the language that they use, or the way that they're impacting other groups." Like others, Lucia thinks that admitting more students with marginalized ethnoracial identities is the a critical first step: "If we had a larger indigenous population on campus, I would maybe be more conscious of the way that I'm appropriating culture, or the way that I can support a community that's in pain, that's hurting. Because I feel like it's my responsibility. If I have the power to help a community that's not being treated right, I should do so. But what's the exposure there? How am I being asked to learn about it? So, when it comes to numbers, they're super important."

Similar to Lucia, the example that comes to mind for Serena at Private, whose dark skin "sticks out like a sore thumb" among her White sorority sisters, is that students might "think twice" before saying something hurtful:

> I think that people would just be more well-rounded and even more sensitive and understanding—because sometimes I'll hear people say things on campus. And if they had more—not necessarily minority friends—but just friends from different races or different backgrounds in general, then they would be more understanding and maybe think twice about saying some of those things.

I ask if any examples jump to mind. She replies somberly: "I've heard people use the N-word a lot. I don't use the N-word. But non-African American people use it a lot to refer to other people." I want to be sure that I understand Serena's experiences, and I find myself fumbling over how to ask: "Oh, like in that camaraderie, uh, 'Hey Bro!' kind of way? Or in that angry, derogatory—uh . . ." I trail off, unwilling to voice anything further now that I see where my own sentence is heading. Serena does not seem fazed by my lack of grammar and grace. She answers simply, "Both."

This desire for diversity to bring greater social justice sounds compatible with niceness, especially in the example of refraining from saying hurtful things. However, Serena's and Lucia's examples reveal the hypocrisy of White niceness on college campuses. Somehow it is the burden of Black students to demonstrate niceness by tolerating the N-word in communal spaces and "All lives matter" on the basketball court, as well as direct comments such as "you speak rather articulately for a Black woman," as we saw in chapter 5. Black students are expected to be nice and not remind people that such words and phrases matter because they are steeped in racist history and oppression. Instead, that ugliness should be "glossed over" because to remind people of it would cause conflict and disharmony.

Niceness and Campus-Community Belonging

Understanding the role that niceness plays in ethnoracial-majority students' view of the goals of diversity helps us recognize an important layer of tension on college campuses that undermines Black and Latinx students' access to campus-community belonging. It is not accidental that Emily at Public and Ethan at Private, whose quotes opened the previous chapter, both describe their campuses as full of "nice" people. As members of the White majority, the niceness they perceive is part of what makes them feel that they belong to the campus-community. Importantly, from their perspective, the nice, welcoming environment seems universal, offered to everyone. Thus, such students feel surprised, confused, and even annoyed when students of color do not embrace the niceness. Self-segregating in groups and centers around campus is perceived as a rejection of mainstream campus culture; it is viewed with suspicion because the expectation is that students of color should be "mixing" or "blending" into the wider campus community instead. Further, when these self-segregated groups call attention to oppression and injustice, it "creates a divide that I don't think was there before," as Cristian phrases it.

In a sympathetic light, we can understand how ethnoracial-majority students might be genuinely confused if they do not hold a power analysis frame. From their view, marginalized students seem to be intentionally creating problems that otherwise would not exist. Warikoo found the same sentiment among some students at Harvard and Brown, not just when oppression or injustice was invoked but even when race itself was acknowledged. Although Warikoo does not offer insights into how this attitude affects student belonging, it is clear that ethnoracial-majority students at Public and Private actively withhold campus-community belonging from students with marginalized ethnoracial identities. It runs counter to White sensibilities to validate and value people who do not exhibit niceness, who violate the rules, and who willfully reject nice culture.

7

Recommendations
for Campuses

● ●

I have argued throughout this book that we have been neglecting a fundamental insight about the nature of belonging: it is something that is offered by
communities, not something that individuals can willfully acquire on their
own. Thus, universities' approach to fostering belonging for students by providing smaller subcommunities on campus, such as student organizations,
athletic teams, academic clubs, and the like, is shortsighted. Although membership in such groups is well documented to be beneficial for student belonging, it is inadequate to the task, particularly for first-generation students and
minority students of color.

A critical part of meeting students' belonging needs more completely is
understanding that college belonging has multiple dimensions. Students in
my study describe their experiences of belonging in three distinct but interrelated realms: social belonging, academic belonging, and campus-
community belonging. Experiencing belonging in any one of these realms
does not automatically lead to belonging in another realm. For example,
social belonging might be offered by a favorite student organization where
a student feels at home and cared about, but that does not mean that she
feels a sense of belonging to the wider campus community, nor does it mean

that she feels that she belongs academically. Thus, to support holistic and comprehensive belonging in our students, we must pay attention to how we are fostering and offering the gift of belonging in each realm. Further, to support first-generation and minority students of color, we must recognize the attributes they bring with them, such as impressive self-reliance and familiarity with habits, tastes, and values that differ from the "nice" White, middle-class, and affluent cultural expectations that characterize most universities. We must strategize to create campus cultures and classroom dynamics that recognize and validate first-generation and students of color for who they are (Jehangir 2010; Havlik et al. 2020). In a nutshell, that is what it means to offer belonging: validating individuals for who they are, showing them that what they bring to the larger community is valued, and communicating that they are wanted and that they matter to the group. To accomplish that work of extending belonging to all of our students, I offer the following suggestions to campuses.

1. Offer Welcoming Messages

Eliminate discourse (and thinking) that encourages students to "find their place" on campus. Replace it with discourse based on the assumption that the entire campus is a place where we should strive to make students feel that they belong. Endorse slogans such as "Welcome Home: What will you explore today?" Encourage faculty, staff, and administrators alike to communicate to students through their everyday interactions that they are important. The university exists because students exist.

In addition, endorse slogans such as "This is your library, come browse your books." First-generation students are less likely to perceive campus amenities as theirs but instead as property of the institution. They do not hold the view that libraries, dining halls, classrooms, swimming pools, and dormitories are there for the sole purpose of serving students, including themselves. They do not exhibit the same sense of entitlement and ownership over resources and communal spaces that continuing-generation students do, for reasons discussed in chapter 2. Whereas continuing-generation and more affluent students see college "as theirs for the taking" (Jack 2019, 88), first-generation and lower-income students are much more hesitant (Thiele 2015; Schwartz et al. 2018). They may not walk into the Wellness Center, for example, simply because they might wonder whether they have to show an insurance card to qualify to be there. They might be inside the library, feeling confused but not feel comfortable enough to ask the librarians for information, because they want to show their respect by not bothering them with their neophyte questions (A. Yee 2016; Calarco 2018).

Promote targeted outreach with messages that remind students that the burden of figuring out how the campus works and where they belong in it does not rest on their shoulders. Bombard them with messages that communicate that librarians, wellness staff, and everyone else in the campus community wants to meet them, to share their resources, and to be part of their college experience.

2. Welcome Students with More than Words

Messages are an important start, but we must also cultivate campus environments that do in fact make students from a wide range of backgrounds feel at home. Allow campus eateries, shops, and common spaces to reflect the tastes, familiar products, and cultural habits of the full range of students who comprise your student body. Recall Javier's complaint in chapter 5 that he never sees items in campus markets that he would find in markets in Latinx neighborhoods like his own. Develop systematic ways to invite students' input for decisions on everyday details, including what items to stock on shelves, what music to play in campus coffee shops, what languages and images to include in campus murals, and anything else that students may suggest. The critical element here is to strategically listen to the voices of students whose numbers are small on campus, rather than making decisions based on what most students say they want (Moore 2008; Gusa 2010). This will extend campus-community belonging to students who are members of groups in "small numbers" by showing them that their backgrounds are valued and are proudly displayed as a visible part of the collective campus environment.

3. Put Your Money Where Your Mouth Is

Explicitly articulate to students and everyone else who is part of the campus community what your campus is all about and what you value. Bear in mind that this is only effective if your organizational structures align with what you say about yourself. If you claim that first-generation students' academic success is important, then support resources should be located in a central, visible part of campus, as discussed in chapter 2. It should also be amply funded with highly competent staff.

Draw on Samuel Museus's (2014) culturally engaging campus environments model to help you think through what assets you already have to foster stronger belonging and where you need to invest in developing more. Museus's model has nine factors—including what he calls cultural validation, collectivist cultural orientations, proactive philosophies, and holistic support—each of which has a significant effect on student belonging (Museus, Yi, and Saelua 2017).

Further, if your campus prides itself on engagement in the local community, environmental conservancy, international experiences, artistic contributions, or whatever it may be, ensure that your programs are attractive to the entire range of your student body. Let the gamut of opportunities reflect the gamut of issues, concerns, and approaches that make sense to various populations of students. For example, if you are not sure why Latinx students or first-generation students participate in your signature programs at lower rates, simply ask them. Then commit to make changes to those programs to make them more inviting, rather than trying to convince students that they should find those programs desirable as is.

In addition, ensure that programs are easily affordable for low-income students (E. Yee 2016; McClure and Ryder 2018). They are often working multiple jobs to make ends meet. When programs are only available to students who can afford them, it sends a clear message to low-income students that the university does not care whether they are a part of things. If you value low-income students, subsidize their participation fees. Show all students that their participation matters to the campus community by tailoring (at least parts of) the opportunities specifically to the different needs and sensibilities of different groups. Keep in mind that this tailoring is already being done for many continuing-generation and ethnoracial-majority students. They experience campus life as rather seamlessly catering to their cultural sensibilities and their ability to pay (Martin 2012; Jack 2019). Extend that gift beyond the majority of students, and you will extend campus-community belonging beyond the majority.

4. Be Intentional in How Your Campus Prioritizes Belonging

Understand how the relationships between social belonging, academic belonging and campus-community belonging play out on your campus. Systematically interview students, conduct focus groups, or engage in any other method that will help you learn how a wide range of students on your campus experience belonging. Identify organizational structures such as first-year student housing, general education requirements, and so on, that prioritize academic belonging over social belonging or the reverse, as discussed in chapter 2. Evaluate whether those structures and policies are furthering your goals. For example, to increase access to academic belonging, a school like Public might change its policies for entering impacted majors. Meanwhile a school like Private might make its Summer Bridge program longer than one week to increase first-generation students' access to academic belonging.

An important part of evaluating whether policies and programs meet your campus' goals is to assess whether they balance the needs of both first-generation and continuing-generation students, as well as the needs of ethnoracial-majority students, students of color, and those with all forms of marginalized identities, including religious minorities and members of the LGBTQ+ community. There is no one method or formula that works for all campuses, of course. The point is to be intentional about what you want to prioritize in your campus culture—whether it is academics as Public does, or relationships as Private does, or perhaps something else unique to your institution. Then design your housing policies, curricular programs, the physical location of relevant resources and centers, and all your offerings to align with those priorities.

5. Offer Curricula and Co-Curricular Programs that Address Inequities

Require that curricula or co-curricular programs meaningfully address issues of inequalities on campus, in the wider U.S. society, and around the world. See Natasha Warikoo's (2016) description of Brown University's educational programming through the Brown Center for Students of Color (formerly called the Third World Center). It is an example of how impactful intentional teaching and learning can be to shift students' thinking toward a power-analysis frame for understanding diversity. By providing required curricula and co-curricular programs on inequality and inequity, we can help students understand the structural forces that hinder historically oppressed and disenfranchised segments of our society while privileging other segments. This can help them disentangle previously confusing or seemingly one-sided racial dynamics. Ensure that the curriculum does not present marginalized groups through a deficit lens, but rather through one that highlights the strengths and assets of relevant groups, however marginalized they may be in U.S. society. Assess the efficacy of this curriculum in terms of both student learning and shifts in the wider campus climate over time. In particular, pay attention to expectations for "nice" diversity, including whether frustrations over students of color "huddling off" together are mitigated (see chapter 6).

Further, develop and fund curricula and co-curricular programs that target students who hold a color-blindness frame for diversity. Push their understanding of the causes and consequences of the many inequities that exist in our society. To help marginalized students navigate campus cultures, universities often offer support and programming that ignore or devalue their identities and histories. It is less common for programming to target majority students, putting the onus of responsibility on their shoulders to recognize that expecting "nice" diversity is a blind spot. Lead students to see that "integration" and "coalition" building are their jobs, not the task of underrepresented students (Reyes 2018), and that this work requires an appreciation for voicing injustice and collaborating on resolutions, all of which might very well involve conflict, confrontation, and disharmony in the process (Ahmed 2012; Castagno 2014).

When the university promotes this kind of personal growth through classroom and experiential learning, it communicates that "glossing over" the ugliness of injustice is not the goal and that color-blindness frames should be shed and replaced by power-analysis frames. In turn, this offers campus-community belonging to students who hold marginalized identities.

6. Cross-Pollinate Student Organizations

Providing centers and other spaces that are safe havens for students is critically important. Students benefit from joining organizations where they find others who share their same background or identity in some way (Cerezo and Chang 2013). If your campus does not already have a wide array of subcommunities for students, the first order of business is to streamline the process for students to establish appropriate new organizations that they dream up and to create the infrastructure for easy expansion. In addition, enable intramural athletics, campus chapters of larger national and international organizations, and partnerships with local ones. Recognize, however, that these student organizations can also be a site of tension on campus, at least in part because of the self-segregating effects such groups can have. We saw it in particular with Lati-Chi at Public and Associated Black Students at Private, where ethnoracial identities are at the heart of membership. We know that these tensions do not exist on all campuses, particularly those that are not predominately White institutions (Reyes 2018). But where they are an issue, the second order of business is to develop structured ways to mitigate those tensions. I offer a few ideas for campuses that struggle with this dynamic.

Perhaps representatives from relevant student organizations can serve on an inter-organizational board with the power to make recommendations to the administration. Perhaps the university may facilitate multi-organization events where, say, the astronomy club invites the LGBTQ+ Center for an evening of stargazing, or the salsa dancing club invites the improv theater troupe to an evening where they perform for each other and teach each other new modes of fun. Perhaps instead, the university invites and funds executive board members from various organizations to leadership workshops where students can develop skills alongside others who hold similar roles in dissimilar organizations.

The goal is to structure interaction across groups that fosters dynamics that encourage students to feel that the campus is a place where they can develop friendships with those who are similar to themselves as well as with those who are not. It is important to encourage groups with largely ethnoracial-majority membership to interact with groups largely comprised of minority students of color. The goals will be much more holistically achieved if the university also requires curricula and co-curricular programming that push students toward a power-analysis frame, as suggested in no. 5. Either way, relationships across differences are easier to initiate when people are operating from a place where they feel secure in their social belonging. Thus, representing their favorite student organization can provide the confidence students might need to branch out and get to know others from different organizations, because doing so is less risky: they already feel accepted by their own group.

When the university facilitates this kind of cross-pollination among student organizations, it sends the message that it values and respects relationships that bridge differences. This is one way that inclusive climates can be built, especially when students are simultaneously exposed to curricula that tackle patterns of injustice in the wider society. This cross-pollination is also an example of how institutions can strategically leverage the social belonging students already have to foster campus-community belonging that might be lacking.

7. Encourage Faculty to Offer Academic Belonging

Facilitate faculty development to improve their pedagogy in ways that mediate the issues that all first-year students experience as they make the transition to college academics. In particular, help faculty understand who first-generation students are, what characteristics they bring with them to their learning, and what obstacles they are likely to face because of their K–12 schooling histories (Lundberg et al. 2007; Hawk and Lyons 2008; Hurtado, Alvarado, and Guillermo-Wann 2015). Teach faculty small everyday ways to affirm the presence of first-generation and students of color in higher education in general and in their own classrooms and office hours in particular (Vetter, Schreiner, and Jaworski 2019).

I humbly recommend following the guidance in a book that came out of this same study of Public and Private titled *33 Simple Strategies for Faculty: A Week-by-Week Resource for Teaching First-Year and First-Generation Students* (Nunn 2019). The strategies and advice I offer there all came from the same interview data that drive the chapters you have been reading here. You will recognize most of the students who are highlighted. The thirty-three strategies are practical, concrete suggestions that can be accomplished in five to fifteen minutes a week. They range from facilitating brief interactions among classmates to making simple changes to the ways we, as faculty, react to students and interact with them. For example, we can share small bits of our lives, our challenges, and our failures to normalize the ups and downs students face as they adjust to college life. We can change our speech habits from: "I know most of you already know this from your AP class in high school" to "I know some of us are seeing this for the first time." The book offers a host of ways that we can validate first-generation students and all first-year students, to make them feel seen and valued.

Regardless of whether your campus motivates faculty to read a teaching guidebook such as mine, the student experiences I present in chapters 3 and 4 provide ample examples of implicit do's and don't's that faculty can practice to more systematically offer academic belonging to students. Universities can show their commitment to fostering academic belonging by structuring reward systems for faculty, including promotion requirements, around engaging in intentional efforts to offer it to students.

8. Do Not Allow Policies and Logistics to Impede Academic Belonging

Declaring a major is a critical part of experiencing academic belonging, because students envision their major as a fundamental element of who they are and the future they hope to pursue. The problem is that many students enter college unsure about their interests. They want desperately to have a spark of passion awakened in them, to discover their calling, their life purpose, their true sense of self—all of which would point them undeniably toward the major that is right for them, which in turn will prepare them for the career that will bring meaning and joy to their future selves. Not to mention money and their parents' approval. It is a tall order.

In the midst of all this uncertainty over the big picture, logistics often unnecessarily make students feel even further defeated (Schreiner and Tobolowsky 2018). Hassles in the process of registering for classes, declaring a major, changing a major, understanding the general education requirements for graduation, and the like are impediments that deny academic belonging to students, because it reinforces their sense that they do not know what they are doing. Do students who cannot figure out which classes to take and do not know what major they want to study even belong in college at all? Streamline and simplify logistics. Make academic guidance readily available and reliable. Eliminate programs that send students to unknowledgeable faculty members for advice, as happened to Sabrina at Private. Eliminate policies that unfairly bog down students who change majors, like Valentina at Public who was stuck with multiple calculus courses, even though her new major did not require more than college algebra (both Sabrina and Valentina are discussed in chapter 2).

Let your policies reflect the reality that many first-generation students do not start the process well informed and have precious few avenues through which to learn the college knowledge that would demystify these logistics and decisions. They need flexibility in the system and unsolicited advice at every turn.

9. Reach Out and Reach In

First-generation students do not know what they do not know, so they cannot be expected to come up with all the right questions to ask. It is important to reach out directly to them with invitations to participate in activities and organizations and to use resources such as tutoring or writing centers and academic advising appointments. Follow Jenny Stuber's recommendations in her 2011 book, *Inside the College Gates: How Class and Culture Matter*, and promote activities and resources through mass emails and flyers in public spaces to ensure that information dissemination does not require personal social networks. Stuber's research found that continuing-generation students have much stronger access to information about opportunities on campus via personal networks than do first-generation students.

Do not worry if ethnoracial-majority, continuing-generation students like Haley feel "pushed" by invitations that make them uncomfortable (see chapter 6). Let all students know that your campus values and promotes action toward social justice. Remind students like Haley that complacency with the status quo and the color-blindness frame are not moving your campus forward. I further recommend targeting students who identify as first-generation or hold minority-ethnoracial identities with additional outreach and invitations, because we know that they generally experience belonging at lower rates (Stebleton, Soria, and Huesman 2014; Vaccaro and Newman 2016; McClure and Ryder 2018).

In addition to reaching out, I suggest finding ways to reach in. By that I mean going beyond distributing announcements that this event is happening or that resource center is available. This book demonstrates that the belonging needs of first-generation and students of color are not met as straightforwardly as the needs of continuing-generation and ethnoracial-majority students, and this holds true in all three realms of belonging. Design ways to reach in to students' lives to ask how they are doing going and to offer mentorship and help, in much the same way that many continuing-generation students' parents do (Smith 2013; King, Griffith, and Murphy 2017; Schwartz et al. 2018; Roksa and Kinsley 2019).

Do not wait for first-generation and minority students of color to come to their RA, their TA, their professor, or the Wellness Center with their concerns. Create structures where someone knowledgeable checks in on individual students to say hello and help them problem solve. These interventions are sometimes called "nudges" and they are effective (Thaler and Sunstein 2008; Darby and Lang 2019). Consider using the SSR peer mentor system as a model or hire dedicated staff for this important work. Develop a list of students who are a priority to be checked on. Your list might include students who were assigned cross-racial roommates, as discussed in chapter 5; students who drop classes with Ws, as discussed in chapter 4; and students whose financial packages were significantly reduced at the last minute, as discussed in chapters 1 and 4.

Call these students on the phone, knock on their door, meet them for coffee outside their first class. Do whatever it takes to find a way to touch base with them that does not involve them making their way to anyone's office. Friendly and straightforward questions will likely do the job of opening the door for students to share what is going on, so that you can see where and how to intervene; for example, "I know that rooming with someone who comes from a different background can have serious ups and downs. Can you tell me one thing you are loving about your roommate right now and one thing that you find disappointing?" or "I'm proud of you for getting back in the saddle this semester on that math class you took a W in last time. On a scale from one to ten, how are you feeling in there this week? If you get stuck on your homework tonight, where will you turn for help?" or "I imagine you are pretty frustrated right now with the news about your financial package. Have you and your family been able to come up with any solutions? Can I help you write an appeal letter?"

Reach in. Ask questions. Bombard them with advice.

Concluding Thoughts

Knowing that first-generation students are incredibly self-reliant puts the responsibility on the university to ensure they are not trying to figure everything out on their own (Davis 2010; Duncheon 2018b). We must endeavor to meet students' needs, and for first-generation students that means we need to do more than sit patiently in our offices and resource centers waiting for them to come to us for help. Continuing-generation students are much more likely to know how to find us and much more likely to make their requests of us. We need to adapt policies and programs to cater to the sensibilities and strengths that first-generation students hold, just as many campuses, including Public and Private, currently cater to the sensibilities and strengths of continuing-generation students. If we want all our students to thrive on our campuses, we need to meet their belonging needs in systematic and intentional ways. This chapter's list of recommendations is woefully incomplete, but I hope it will start conversations in your institution that will lead to targeted and meaningful change.

Theoretical Appendix

● ● ● ● ● ● ● ● ● ● ● ● ● ● ● ● ● ● ● ●

Durkheim and Belonging

Emile Durkheim (1858–1917), a foundational thinker in the discipline of sociology, gave us an understanding of how communities work that allows us to see belonging in a fundamentally sociological way: belonging is something that communities provide for individuals; individuals cannot garner it for themselves. This insight about the nature of belonging is embedded in Durkheim's larger theory about social life. According to Durkheim, a healthy society integrates its members and regulates its members. He writes about these dynamics in multiple ways in various works over his career, namely in *Suicide* (1897); *Moral Education* (1925), which was published posthumously; and in *The Division of Labor in Society* (1893); (see Marks 1974; Besnard 1993; Acevedo 2005). Integration and regulation are two interrelated dynamics.

First, regarding integration, a healthy society ensures that individuals feel that they are a part of the society, that they are emotionally and functionally connected to the larger community. Durkheim calls integration "attachment to social groups" in *Moral Education*, but in his earlier work *Suicide*, he uses the term "integration" explicitly. He theorizes, "When society is strongly integrated, it holds individuals under its control" ([1897] 1951, 209). Durkheim goes on to explain that, "when belonging to a group they love," individuals are able to transcend their "private interests" and feel as if they are part of something larger than themselves, a community whose "interests they put above their own" (209–210). Durkheim is clear that attachment to a group one "loves" produces this desire in us to prioritize the well-being of the community over ourselves, and that sentiment frees us somewhat from our own suffering: "The bond that unites them with the common cause attaches them to life and the lofty goal they envisage prevents their feeling their personal troubles so deeply" (210). Thus, society holds each of us "under its control," but we benefit from that control because it gives meaning and purpose to our lives.

According to Durkheim, it is the "bond" an individual has to her community as a "common cause" that accomplishes integration, and it is that integration that rescues the individual from feeling that life is meaningless: "Life is said to be intolerable unless some reason for existing is involved, some purpose justifying life's trials. The individual alone is not a sufficient end for his activity. He is too little. . . . When, therefore, we have no other object than ourselves, we cannot avoid the thought that our efforts will finally end in nothingness, since we ourselves disappear" ([1897] 1951, 210). Durkheim is clear that it is membership in society that gives us "purpose," which is why we are inspired to put the group's interests above our own. Thus, if our community does not integrate us, we despair. We are "unable to escape the exasperating and agonizing question: to what purpose?" (212). Society is what we live for. As he writes in *Moral Education*, "It is society that we consider the most important part of ourselves" ([1925] 1973, 71).

Durkheim theorizes that these critically important social bonds are created and maintained through direct social interaction among community members: "There is, in short, in a cohesive and animated society a constant interchange of ideas and feelings from all to each and each to all, something like mutual moral support, which instead of throwing an individual on his own resources, leads him to share in the collective energy and supports his own when exhausted" ([1897] 1951, 210). Likewise, when a society fails in its function of producing and maintaining strong social bonds, Durkheim describes social life as having "currents of depression and disillusionment emanating from no particular individual but expressing society's state of disintegration"; these currents "reflect the relaxation of social bonds, a sort of collective asthenia or social malaise" and that "as these currents are collective, they have, by virtue of their origin, an authority which they impose on the individual . . . [toward a] state of moral distress directly aroused in him by the disintegration of society" (214). Thus, both individual members and the collective group benefit from members' mutual attachment. When social bonds are weakened in the collectivity, everyone suffers.

Durkheim's conception of what social bonds are and how they function is key to understanding the second feature of a healthy society: regulation. According to Durkheim, social bonds are constructed out of shared norms and values. To be a member of a particular society means to believe in that society's shared moral code, to be willing to behave in accordance with that code, and to hold others accountable to it. That is, society must "regulate" its members. In *Moral Education* Durkheim uses the phrase "the spirit of discipline" to describe regulation, and he posits that discipline is the key to maintaining the strength of social bonds. Members of society must be taught to understand what is expected of them. "All discipline has a double objective: to promote a certain regularity in people's conduct, and to provide them with determinate goals that at the same time limit their horizons. Discipline promotes a preference for the customary, and it imposes restrictions. It regularizes and it constrains" ([1925] 1973, 47). Discipline, then, is how society ensures that all members share a common morality, which includes a commitment to abide by the limits that society has set for the kinds of goals and aspirations that are considered to be morally acceptable. These shared beliefs and behaviors comprise the social bonds that bind members to the collective, and those bonds are created and maintained through social interaction: "The individual does not carry within himself the precepts of morality.... Such precepts do not emerge except through the relationships of associated individuals, as they translate and reflect the life of the relevant group or groups" (86).

The importance of the idea that society performs this function of regulation cannot be overemphasized. Durkheim sees regulation as impossible for individuals on their own to accomplish: "Men would never consent to restrict their desires ... they cannot assign themselves this law of justice. So they must receive it from an authority which they respect, to which they yield spontaneously ... society alone can play this moderating role; for it is the only moral power superior to the individual, the authority of which he accepts" ([1897] 1951, 249).

Importantly, regulation is the key to happiness in Durkheim's theory. In *Moral Education* he argues, "By means of discipline we learn the control of desire without which man could not achieve happiness" ([1925] 1973, 48). In *Suicide*, he explains further, "This relative limitation and the moderation it involves make men contented with their lot while stimulating them moderately to improve it; and this average contentment causes the feeling of calm, active happiness, and the pleasure in existing and living which characterizes health for all societies as well as for individuals" ([1897] 1951, 250). Society teaches us what is appropriate to aspire to in our lives through regulation, and society binds us to each other and to the group with social bonds that integrate us. We can do neither of these things for ourselves.

It is important for our understanding of belonging to underscore that Durkheim's theory presents society as an entity that inspires feelings in each of us, that motivates our behaviors, that teaches us what to value, and that shows us our place within the group. Society is comprised of the individuals who are members, but in its collectivity, society is something "other than a sum of individuals; it must constitute a being sui generis, which has its own special character distinct from that of its members and its own individuality different from that of its constituent individuals" ([1925] 1973, 60). Yet neither is society an entity that is entirely separate from us: "Certainly society is greater than, and goes beyond, us, for it is infinitely more vast than our individual being; but at the same time it enters into every part of us. It is outside and envelops us but it is also in us and is everywhere an aspect of our nature. We are fused with it" (71).

This brings us to a decidedly sociological understanding of what sense of belonging is and where it comes from. Durkheim's theories offer the insight that the feelings of belonging and attachment that we experience are due to the group's effect on us: "The influence of society is what has aroused in us the sentiments of sympathy and solidarity drawing us toward others; it is society which, fashioning us in its image, fills us with religious, political and moral beliefs that control our actions . . . these superior forms of human activity have a collective origin and a collective purpose . . . they are society itself incarnated and individualized in each one of us" ([1897] 1951, 211–212).

We feel that we belong to a society, community, or group because that group has "aroused in us the sentiments of sympathy and solidarity." Our emotional ties to the group that allow us to feel a sense of belonging are not forged by our own hand; instead they are bestowed on us by the group itself. That is, one person cannot simply decide that she is a member of a society or a social group; the group must extend such membership to her. The group must integrate and regulate her, which inspires a feeling of acceptance in her, a sense that she is valued and wanted, a sense that she belongs. Belonging must be given. It is a gift. It only exists when a group collectively offers it to a member.

Methodological Appendix

The Project

When I first embarked on this research, I knew that first-generation college students were an important part of the study, but I did not realize that they would end up being the primary category for my analysis. I wanted to learn more about how students' academic successes and struggles shaped their perceptions of themselves as college students and how academics contribute to a sense of belonging to their schools. As an organizations scholar, I was interested in the ways that resources such as the federal TRIO Student Support Services (SSS) program play a role in students' educational experiences and also how students make sense of those experiences in terms of their self-perceptions. Did SSS students see themselves as people who needed extra help? If so, how did they feel about that? Did students from less rigorous K–12 backgrounds find themselves in classes feeling lost or outpaced by their better-prepared classmates? If so, how did they handle it? Is it possible for students feel a sense of belonging in the campus community, even if they feel inadequate academically?

To start answering those questions, I designed a research project with the TRIO SSS program as the center point. As I explained in chapters 2 and 3 this program serves low-income, first-generation, and disabled undergraduate students. SSS targets these students because they are likely to struggle with college academics. We know that the population of students served by SSS have stronger academic success and persistence than those who do not receive those services (Department of Education, 2011, 2014). It is a program that works. Both Public and Private have generously expanded the scope of the federal SSS parameters, so I signify their centers as Students Support Resources (SSR) throughout the book.

Because budgets are limited, not all students who qualify for SSR can be enrolled in the program. In addition, not all students who qualify are interested in participating, and some of those enrolled do not make much use of these services. And what about students who are not eligible? Did they use other campus resources such as tutoring centers? If so, how did they feel about using them? The transition to college is something that all students must navigate, whether first-generation, low-income, disabled, or not, and academics are a critically important element of college life. I wanted to learn how various students' academic experiences differ to inform where to intervene and how to improve both academic outcomes and the emotional journey that is part of the transition to college.

The Samples

Working with the admissions offices and the SSR offices at both Public and Private, I was given access to a random sample of incoming first-year students. I asked that the sample be stratified into three groups: SSR-enrolled students, SSR-eligible students who were not enrolled, and students who were not eligible for SSR. I was aiming for 10 students in each group at each school, for a total of 30 at Public and another 30 at Private, for 60 students altogether. I was committed to including every student who replied to my email solicitations, regardless of how long it took them to respond, so I ended up with 31 students at Public and 36 at Private for the first interview. The samples included 14 men and 17 women at Public; 19 men, 16 women, and 1 nonbinary student at Private. Of those original 67 interviews, 29 students at Public and 34 at Private participated in the second interview, and a year later, 25 at Public and 31 at Private participated in the third interview. Thus, 56 of the original 67 students remained in the study through the final wave of data collection: they included 12 men and 13 women at Public, and 15 men, 14 women, and 1 nonbinary student at Private. All the analyses of changes in belonging over time include only these 56 who were part of the third wave of interviews at the end of their second year in college. Altogether, I conducted 186 interviews.

As the first round of interviews unfolded, I came to realize that the three groups of my stratified random sample were not yielding the distinctions that I had anticipated. I found myself writing notes in my field journal (where I recorded copious ethnographic details, as well as my own thoughts about each interview) that such-and-such interview respondent did not actually match the characteristics of their category. It seemed that the boxes students had checked on their admissions forms did not always accurately reflect my three categories as I had understood them.

There are multiple explanations for this mismatch. Identifying who counts as a first-generation college student is tricky, because there are multiple definitions. Some count students as first generation only if neither parent ever attended college at all. Others count them if neither parent ever earned a postsecondary degree, including an associate's degree from a community college (this is FAFSA's definition). Still others, researchers like me included, count students as first-generation students if neither parent ever completed a four-year bachelor's degree. In addition, it is easy for a university to end up with conflicting or missing information about any given student's first-generation status, because this information may be collected by various campus entities, each of which uses different definitions. It is also easy, as a student, to be unsure whether one should check that box.

It turned out that the most analytically important dividing line for my samples was first-generation versus continuing-generation student. The more I read and learned about first-generation students, the more this made sense. Starting in the second interview I asked each student about her parents' college histories. It turned out that, at Public, just about every student in the SSR-enrolled group and in the SSR-eligible group was a first-generation student by the definition I used. This is how my sample at Public ended up with 20 first-generation students and 11 continuing-generation students, because I had been aiming for 10 in each group at the outset. At Private, there was more variation, and I ended up with 21 continuing-generation students and 15 first-generation students.

As I discussed in chapters 5 and 6, ethnoracial majority and minority status also became an analytically important dividing line in my study. I did not systematically stratify the samples based on ethnoracial status, but there was enough variation in the samples to draw meaningful conclusions about the ethnoracial dynamics of college belonging. I made an intentional decision when writing this book (and another one that came out of the same project) to allow room for students' full descriptions of their ethnoracial identities. The words and phrases that they use carry meaning. They are rich indicators of how students perceive their place in the ethnoracial landscape of our society and of their campus homes. Their descriptions are valuable elements for understanding students' experiences, so I left them as intact as possible, hoping that readers will bear with the cumbersome grammar and sentence flow that result.

The Interviews

I decided to follow students through the end of their second years, because we know that if students are going to transfer or drop out of college, they typically do so within the first two years. For the first interview, I waited until they had at least a month of college under their belts so that they could meaningfully talk about how things were going for them. Then I followed up within the last six weeks or so of their first year so they could reflect back on their initial transition to college and also talk about how they felt things were going at that point. I waited a full year before the third interview, by which time they had nearly two years of college experience to draw on. I asked them again to reflect on their transition to college the previous year and to talk about their current circumstances as well.

The first two interviews lasted approximately an hour each, and the third was approximately forty minutes long. All but 3 of the 186 interviews were conducted face to face; those 3 were conducted over the phone, and all were with students from Private. Madison and Justine had transferred to new universities and generously agreed to catch me up on their decisions to leave Private and to answer my interview questions over the phone. Jeff did not intend to leave Private but had found himself in financial circumstances that required him to take a semester off. He still felt very connected to Private and eagerly accommodated a phone interview.

Each interview was different. The first asked several questions about their college application process and how the students made the ultimate decision of where to attend. I asked about the differences between high school and college in terms of academics. I asked several questions about their favorite and least favorite professors and courses, their study habits, and which resources, tutoring centers, office hours, and so on, they had used. I employed open-ended questions to help minimize the sense that they *should* be using such resources. For example, I started with, "When a class is hard, what do you do?" The second and third interviews shifted away from high school and college applications and focused on their college experiences, including questions that asked them to reflect back on things they struggled with as they "were getting the hang of college." In all three interviews I kept a few questions consistent, including those about belonging. Since I was interested in belonging and the holistic experience of the transition to college, I asked about friendships, roommates, joining student organizations, and keeping in touch with family. I also asked them each time to describe what a successful college student is like and then asked them how close or far away from that description of success they felt at the moment.

The Analysis

In asking explicitly about belonging in every interview, I found that students described experiences of being offered belonging or having belonging withheld from them at multiple and various moments as they discussed their range of college experiences. I coded these instances separately in my early analysis, so that I could understand the differences students expressed between the three realms of belonging, as well as the patterns within them. Then, in my final round of analysis, I coded the interviews holistically. I read through an entire interview from start to finish and categorized each based on whether it demonstrated (1) Belonging, (2) Partial belonging (including students who expressed belonging in one place or one moment but not another, who were ambivalent, or who explicitly said they belonged "kind of," "sort of," or "in some ways"), or (3) Absent belonging. I coded each interview with these categories for all three realms of belonging: social, academic, and campus-community belonging. As part of the holistic coding, I read each student's interviews back to back in chronological order and coded the set of interviews as demonstrating (1) increased belonging over time, (2) steady belonging over time, (3) steady partial belonging, (4) decreased belonging, (5) steady no belonging, or (6) up and down belonging. These holistic codes allowed me to calculate the percentages of belonging for various groups that I present throughout the chapters. Although my sample sizes are not large enough to be statistically generalizable, the descriptive data help present the overall picture of belonging that, as we know, is quite complex.

Acknowledgments

This work would not exist without the sixty-seven first-year college students who were willing to share their experiences, thoughts, feelings, and perspectives with me in interviews. Thank you. During the first year of data collection, a team of talented undergraduate research assistants helped launch many of the ideas that become foundational to the final analysis: Kaylin Bourdon, Paola Carrasco, Kayla Williams, Dalia Martin Del Campo, Jennifer Baltadano, and Cassandra Huinquez. Thank you for your intellectual energy and your college wisdom. Many colleagues and friends also helped shape this work through insightful conversations and inspiring writing sessions: Karen Teel, Jonathan Bowman, Diane Keeling, Beth O'Shea, Angela Nurse, Mike Williams, Stephanie Chan, and the entire community of the Sociology of Education Association. Of course, nothing in my life is accomplished without the love of my family. Thank you.

Notes

Introduction

1 All student names and institution names used in this book are pseudonyms. Any identifying details of people or places were altered to protect confidentiality.
2 Vaccaro and Newman found important differences in the definitions of belonging that privileged students in their study gave compared to minoritized students. Although, overall, students in my study responded similarly to students in theirs, my data do not show all the same patterns that they found; namely, in my study "safe" and "respect" were not words used exclusively by nonprivileged students.
3 Along with using the pseudonyms Public University and Private University I also altered the identifying details of each school.
4 Student participants in this research were drawn from stratified random samples of incoming first-year students in the fall 2015 cohort. A total of 67 participants across the two universities participated in the first wave of interviews, and 56 remained in the study through three waves of interviews.
5 There is little consensus on how to define first-generation college students. For example, a recent National Center for Education Statistics (NCES) study only counted students whose parents never attended college. By that measure, 24% of today's college students are first-generation (Redford and Hoyer 2017). Many scholars who study the dynamics of students' lived experiences in college follow the definition I use: neither parent holds a four-year degree. Still other entities, such as Free Application for Federal Student Aid (FAFSA) use an intermediary definition: neither parent has earned any postsecondary degree (including an associate's degree). There is also debate over the use of the term more broadly (Nguyen and Nguyen 2018).
6 In fact, Grayson is one of the nine students I categorize as White*. Please see chapter 6 for further explanation and discussion.

Chapter 1   Social Belonging versus Campus-Community Belonging

1 The statistics here (and throughout this chapter and the next) showing percentages of the sample who experienced or did not experience belonging at a particular moment represent all the cases; however, statistics that show how belonging shifts over time only include the 56 cases who were part of the study across the two years, so that changes over time could be wholly accounted for.

2 I categorized students' descriptions of social belonging, academic belonging, and campus-community belonging separately for each of their interviews. The categories were (1) Having belonging, (2) Partial belonging (including mixed experiences where it was present here but not there), and (3) Absent belonging. See "Methodological Appendix" for more details.

3 Summer Bridge is a program that brings qualified students (a combination of low-income, first-generation, and disabled students) to campus to live and learn together during the summer before their first year begins. It is intended to help familiarize students with the expectations of college academics and to introduce them to the supports and resources available on campus. Summer Bridge is run through the federal TRIO's Student Support Services, and at both Public and Private, the federal funding for it has been supplemented by university funds so that the program can serve a much larger number of eligible students.

4 AVID, or Advancement via Individual Determination, is a program in which many public schools participate. It offers training for teachers and special elective classes with resources for students who have the academic potential to succeed (based on their GPA) and who want to attend college but need extra support to achieve that goal.

Chapter 6   "Nice" Diversity

1 Latino and Hispanic are designations that are sometimes considered "ethnicity" and, other times, "race." However this distinction is not widely understood among everyday Americans, and it is not unilaterally valued by those who do understand it. Thus, throughout the book I used the term "ethnoracial" to describe identities or discussions of groups that include people who identify as Latinx as parallel to individuals who identify as White, Asian, or Black. Here, the discussion of "multiracial" students includes those who consider themselves both Latinx and White, or Latinx and Black, even though I am not altering the term to something like multi-ethnoracial.

2 Johnston-Guerrero and Renn offer an explanation that resonates with my analysis. They write that that we need to clarify how race is operationalized in university programs "before moving forward in designing practices to meet the needs of multiracial students since some students might fit the multiracial ancestry category but not claim a multiracial identity" (e.g., a student who has some Native American ancestry but lives her life as a White person), while others claim a multiracial identity but might not get counted as "'two or more races'" based on what boxes they may have checked at the time of admissions (e.g., a biracial Black-Asian American student who worries about higher standards for Asian American applicants and so checks only "'Black' on the admissions form" (2016, 143).

References

Acevedo, Gabriel A. 2005. "Turning Anomie on Its Head: Fatalism as Durkheim's Concealed and Multidimensional Alienation Theory." *Sociological Theory* 23 (1): 75–85.

Ahmed, Sara. 2012. *On Being Included: Racism and Diversity in Institutional Life.* Durham NC: Duke University Press.

Allen, Jeff, and Steven B. Robbins. 2008. "Prediction of College Major Persistence Based on Vocational Interests, Academic Preparation, and First-Year Academic Performance." *Research in Higher Education* 49 (1): 62–79.

Anaya, Guadalupe, and Darnell. G. Cole. 2001. "Latina/o Sudent Achievement: Exploring the Influence of Student-Faculty Interactions on College Grades." *Journal of College Student Development* 42 (1): 3–14.

Anderson, Carol. 2016. *White Rage: The Unspoken Truth of Our Racial Divide.* New York: Bloomsbury.

Anderson, Elijah. 2015. "'The White Space.'" *Sociology of Race and Ethnicity* 1 (1): 10–21.

Antonio, Anthony Lising. 2004. "The Influence of Friendship Groups on Intellectual Self-Confidence and Educational Aspirations in College." *Journal of Higher Education* 75 (4): 446–471.

Apple, Michael. 1979. *Ideology and Curriculum.* London: Routledge & Kegan Paul.

Armstrong, Elizabeth A., and Laura Hamilton. 2013. *Paying for the Party: How College Maintains Inequality.* Cambridge, MA: Harvard University Press.

Aroujo, Alice, and Andreas Anastasiou. 2009. "The Role of Generational Status, Program Affiliation, and Cultural Background in the Performance of College Students." In *The Invisibility Factor: Administrators and Faculty Reach Out to First-Generation College Students*, edited by Teresa Heinz Housel and Vickie L. Harvey, 47–58. Boca Raton, FL: BrownWalker Press.

Arum, Richard, and Josipa Roksa. 2011. *Academically Adrift: Limited Learning on College Campuses.* Chicago: University of Chicago Press.

Azmitia, Margarita, Grace Sumabat-Estrada, Yeram Cheong, and Rebecca Covarrubias. 2018. "'Dropping Out Is Not an Option': How Educationally Resilient First-Generation Students See the Future." *New Directions for Child and Adolescent Development 2018* 160: 89–100.

Bastedo, Michael N., and Ozan Jaquette. 2011. "Running in Place: Low-Income Students and the Dynamics of Higher Education Stratification." *Sociology of Education* 33: 318–339.

Beattie, Irenee R. 2018. "Sociological Perspectives on First Generation College Students." In *Handbook of the Sociology of Education in the 21st Century*, edited by Barbara Schneider and Guan Saw, 171–192. New York: Springer.

Beattie, Irenee R., and Megan Thiele. 2016. "Connecting in Class? College Class Size and Inequality in Academic Social Capital." *Journal of Higher Education* 87 (3): 332–362.

Berrey, Ellen. 2015. *The Enigma of Diversity: The Language of Race and the Limits of Racial Justice*. Chicago: University of Chicago Press.

Besnard, Philippe. 1993. "Anomie and Fatalism in Durkheim's Theory of Regulation." In *Emile Durkheim: Sociologist and Moralist*, edited by Stephen P. Turner, 163–183. London: Routledge.

Binder, Amy. 2007. "For Love and Money: Organizations' Creative Responses to Multiple Environmental Logics." *Theory and Society* 36 (6): 547–571.

Binder, Amy, Daniel B. Davis, and Nick Bloom. 2016. "Career Funneling: How Elite Students Learn to Define and Desire 'Prestigious' Jobs." *Sociology of Education* 89 (1): 20–39.

Binder, Amy, and Kate Wood. 2013. *Becoming Right: How Campuses Shape Young Conservatives*. Princeton: Princeton University Press.

Bonilla-Silva, Eduardo. 2002. "We Are All Americans! The Latin Americanization of Racial Stratification in the USA." *Race and Society* 5 (1): 3–16.

———. 2018. *Racism without Racists: Color-Blind Racism and the Persistence of Racial Inequality in America*. 5th ed. Lanham, MD: Rowman & Littlefield.

Bourdieu, Pierre. 1977. "Cultural Reproduction and Social Reproduction." In *Power and Ideology in Education*, edited by Jerome Karabel and A. H. Halsey, 487–511. New York: Oxford University Press.

Bourdieu, Pierre, and Jean-Claude Passeron. 1977. *Reproduction in Education, Society and Culture*. London: Sage.

Brint, Steven. 2011. "Focus on the Classroom: Movements to Reform College Teaching, 1980–2008." In *The American Academic Profession: Transformation in Contemporary Higher Education*, edited by Joseph C. Hermanowicz, 44–91. Baltimore: Johns Hopkins University Press.

Brower, Aaron M. 1992. "The 'Second Half' of Student Integration: The Effects of Life Task Predominance on Student Persistence." *Journal of Higher Education* 63 (4): 441–462.

Brown, Brené. 2010. *The Gifts of Imperfection: Let Go of Who You Think You're Supposed to Be and Embrace Who You Are*. Center City, MN: Hazelden Publishing.

Bryan, Elizabeth, and Leigh Ann Simmons. 2009. "Family Involvement: Impacts on Post-Secondary Educational Success for First-Generation Appalachian College Students." *Journal of College Student Development* 50 (4): 391–406.

Buchmann, Claudia, Dennis J. Condron, and Vincent J. Roscigno. 2010. "Shadow Education, American Style: Test Preparation, the SAT and College Enrollment." *Social Forces* 89 (2): 435–461.

Bui, Khanh Van T. 2002. "First-Generation College Students at a Four-Year University: Background Characteristics, Reasons for Pursuing Higher Education, and First-Year Experiences." *College Student Journal* 36 (1): 3–12.

Burnett, Bill, and Dave Evans. 2016. *Designing Your Life: How to Build a Well-Lived, Joyful Life*. New York: Knopf.

Byrd, W. Carson. 2017. *Poison in the Ivy: Race Relations and the Reproduction of Inequality on Elite College Campuses*. New Brunswick, NJ: Rutgers University Press.

Cairns, James. 2017. *The Myth of the Age of Entitlement*. Toronto: University of Toronto Press.

Calarco, Jessica McCrory. 2018. *Negotiating Opportunities: How the Middle Class Secures Advantages in School*. Oxford: Oxford University Press.

Carter, Prudence L. 2012. *Stubborn Roots: Race, Culture, and Inequality in U.S. and South African Schools*. New York: Oxford University Press.

Castagno, Angelina E. 2014. *Educated in Whiteness: Good Intentions and Diversity in Schools*. Minneapolis: University of Minnesota Press.

Cerezo, Alison, and Tai Chang. 2013. "Latina/o Achievement and Predominately White Universities: The Importance of Culture and Ethnic Community." *Journal of Hispanic Higher Education* 12 (1): 72–85.

Chambliss, Daniel F., and Christopher G. Takacs. 2014. *How College Works*. Cambridge, MA: Harvard University Press.

Chory, Rebecca M., and Evan H. Offstein. 2017. "'Your Professor Will Know You as a Person': Evaluating and Rethinking the Relational Boundaries between Faculty and Students." *Journal of Management Education* 41 (1): 9–38.

Clark, Kallie. 2017. *Decoding College: Stories, Strategies, and Struggles of First-Generation College Students*. Molena, GA: Rowe Publishing.

Clydesdale, Tim. 2015. *The Purposeful Graduate: Why Colleges Must Talk to Students about Vocation*. Chicago: University of Chicago Press.

Collier, Peter J., and David L. Morgan. 2008. "'Is That Paper Really Due Today?' Differences in First-Generation and Traditional College Students' Understandings of Faculty Expectations." *Higher Education* 55 (4): 425–446.

Collins, Patricia Hill. 2009. *Another Kind of Public Education: Race, Schools, the Media, and Democratic Possibilities*. Boston: Beacon Press.

Conefrey, Theresa. 2018. "Supporting First-Generation Students' Adjustment to College with High-Impact Practices." *Journal of College Student Retention: Research, Theory & Practice*. https://doi.org/https://doi.org/10.1177/1521025118807402.

Covarrubias, Rebecca, Ronald Gallimore, and Lynn Okagaki. 2018. "'I Know That I Should Be Here': Lessons Learned from the First-Year Performance of Borderline University Applicants." *Journal of College Student Retention: Research, Theory & Practice* 20 (1): 92–115.

Covarrubias, Rebecca, Ibette Valle, Giselle Laiduc, and Margarita Azmitia. 2019. "'You Never Become Fully Independent': Family Roles and Independence in First-Generation College Students." *Journal of Adolescent Research* 34 (4): 381–410.

Cuevas, Adolfo G., Beverly Araujo Dawson, and David R. Williams. 2016. "Race and Skin Color in Latino Health: An Analytic Review." *American Journal of Public Health* 106 (12): 2131–2136.

Dachner, Alison M., and Brian M. Saxton. 2015. "'If You Don't Care, Then Why Should I?' The Influence of Instructor Commitment on Student Satisfaction and Commitment." *Journal of Management Education* 39 (5): 5549–5571.

Damon, William. 2008. *The Path to Purpose: How Young People Find Their Calling in Life*. New York: Free Press.

Darby, Flower, and James M. Lang. 2019. *Small Teaching Online: Applying Learning Science in Online Classes*. San Francisco: Jossey-Bass.

Davis, Jeff. 2010. *The First-Generation Student Experience: Implications for Campus Practice, and Strategies for Improving Persistence and Success*. Sterling, VA: ACPA College Student Educators International.

Delgado-Guerrero, Maria, Mayra A. Cherniak, and Alberta M. Gloria. 2014. "Family away from Home: Factors Influencing Undergraduate Women of Color's Decisions to Join a Cultural-Specific Sorority." *Journal of Diversity in Higher Education* 7 (1): 45–57.

Dennis, Jessica M., Jean S. Phinney, and Lizette Ivy Chuateco. 2005. "The Role of Motivation, Parental Support, and Peer Support in the Academic Success of Ethnic Minority First-Generation College Students." *Journal of College Student Development* 46 (3): 223–236.

Department of Education. 2011. *TRIO Student Support Services (SSS) Performance and Efficiency Measure Results: 2009–10*. Washington, DC: Department of Education.

———. 2014. *Student Support Services Program Performance and Efficiency Measure Results for 2012–13*. http://www2.ed.gov/programs/triostudsupp/sss-efficiency2012 -13.doc.

DeRosa, Erin, and Nadine Dolby. 2014. "'I Don't Think the University Knows Me': Institutional Culture and Lower-Income, First-Generation College Students." *Interactions: UCLA Journal of Education and Information Studies* 10 (2): 1–18.

DiAngelo, Robin. 2018. *White Fragility: Why It's So Hard for White People to Talk about Racism*. Boston: Beacon Press.

Dixon, Angela R., and Edward E. Telles. 2017. "Skin Color and Colorism: Global Research, Concepts, and Measurement." *Annual Review of Sociology* 43: 405–424.

Duncan, Greg J., and Richard J. Murnane. 2014. *Restoring Opportunity: The Crisis of Inequality and the Challenge for American Education*. Cambridge, MA: Harvard Education Press.

Duncheon, Julia C. 2018a. "Making Sense of College Readiness in a Low-Performing Urban High School: Perspectives of High-Achieving First Generation Youth." *Urban Education 2018*. (online first).

———. 2018b. "'You Have To Be Able To Adjust Your Own Self': Latinx Students' Transitions into College from a Low-Performing Urban High School." *Journal of Latinos and Education* 17 (4): 358–373.

Durkheim, Emile. [1897] 1951. *Suicide: A Study in Sociology*. Translated by John A. Spaulding and George Simpson, edited by George Simpson. New York: Free Press.

———. [1925] 1973. *Moral Education: A Study in the Theory and Application of the Sociology of Education*. Translated by Everett K. Wilson and Herman Schnurer. New York: Free Press.

———. [1893] 1984. *The Division of Labor in Society*. Translated by W. D. Halls. New York: Free Press. 1893.

Dwyer, Rachel E., Laura McCloud, and Randy Hodson. 2012. "Debt and Graduation from American Universities." *Social Forces* 90 (4): 1133–1155.

Einarson, Marne K., and Marne E. Clarkberg. 2004. *Understanding Faculty Out-of-Class Interaction with Undergraduate Students at a Research University.* CHERI Working Paper No. 57. Cornell University Higher Education Research Institute. http://digitalcommons.ilr.cornell.edu/cheri/20.

Elliott, Gregory, Suzanne Kao, and Ann-Marie Grant. 2004. "Mattering: Empirical Validation of a Social-Psychological Concept." *Self and Identity* 3 (4): 339–354.

Engberg, Mark, and Gregory C. Woiniak. 2013. "College Student Pathways to the STEM Disciplines." *Teachers College Record* 115 (1): 1–27.

Engle, Jennifer, and Vincent Tinto. 2008. *Moving beyond Access: College Success for Low-Income, First-Generation Students.* Washington, DC: Pell Institute for the Study of Opportunity in Higher Education.

Espinosa, Lorelle. 2011. "Pipelines and Pathways: Women of Color in Undergraduate STEM Majors and the College Experiences that Contribute to Persistence." *Harvard Educational Review* 81 (2): 209–241.

Everitt, Judson G. 2012. "Teacher Careers and Inhabited Institutions: Sense Making and Arsenals of Teaching Practice in Educational Institutions." *Symbolic Interaction* 35 (2): 203–220.

———. 2017. *Lesson Plans: The Institutional Demands of Becoming a Teacher.* New Brunswick, NY: Rutgers University Press.

Feagin, Joe R. 2013. *The White Racial Frame: Centuries of Racial Framing and Counter-Framing.* 2nd ed. New York: Routledge.

———. 2014. *Racist America: Roots, Current Realities, and Future Reparations.* 3rd ed. New York: Routledge.

Feagin, Joe R., Hernán Vera, and Pinar Batur. 2001. *White Racism: The Basics.* 2nd ed. New York: Routledge.

Feagin, Joe R., Hernán Vera, and Nikitah Imani. 1996. *The Agony of Education: Black Students at White Colleges and Universities.* New York: Routledge.

Fletcher, Jason, and Marta Tienda. 2010. "Race and Ethnic Differences in College Achievement: Does High School Attended Matter?" *Annals of the American Academy of Political and Social Science* 627 (1): 144–166.

Flores, Angel D. 2014. *50 Things I Wish Someone Would Have Told Me about College: Straight Talk for First-Generation Students FROM First-Generation Graduates.* CreateSpace Independent Publishing Platform.

Franklin Jeremy, D., William A. Smith, and Man Hung. 2014. "Racial Battle Fatigue for Latina/o Students: A Quantitative Perspective." *Journal of Hispanic Higher Education* 13 (4): 303–322.

Freeman, Tierra M., Lynley H. Anderman, and Jane M. Jensen. 2007. "Sense of Belonging in College Freshman at the Classroom and Campus Levels." *Journal of Experimental Education* 75 (3): 203–220.

Furquim, Fernando, Kristen M. Glasener, Meghan Oster, Brian P. McCall, and Stephen L. DesJardins. 2017. "Navigating the Financial Aid Process: Borrowing Outcomes among First-Generation and Non-First-Generation Students." *Annals of the American Academy of Political and Social Sciences* 671 (1): 69–91.

Garcia, John A., Gabriel R. Sanchez, Shannon Sanchez-Youngman, and Edward D. Vargas. 2015. "Race as Lived Experience: The Impact of Multi-Dimensional

Measures of Race/Ethnicity on the Self-Reported Health Status of Latinos." *Du Bois Review: Social Science Research on Race* 12 (2): 349–373.

Gin, Kevin J., Ana M. Martinez-Aleman, Heather T. Rowan-Kenyon, and Derek Hottell. 2017. "Racialized Aggressions and Social Media on Campus." *Journal of College Student Development* 58 (2): 159–174.

Givens, Jarvis R. 2015. "The Invisible Tax: Exploring Black Student Engagement at Historically White Institutions." *Berkeley Review of Education* 6 (1): 55–78.

Glenn, Evelyn Nakano. 2008. "Yearning for Lightness: Transnational Circuits in the Marketing and Consumption of Skin Lighteners." *Gender and Society* 22 (3): 281–302.

Gofen, Anat. 2009. "Family Capital: How First-Generation Higher Education Students Break the Intergenerational Cycle." *Family Relations* 58 (1): 104–120.

Grigsby, Mary. 2009. *College Life through the Eyes of Students.* New York: SUNY Press.

Gusa, Diane Lynn. 2010. "White Institutional Presence: The Impact of Whiteness on Campus Climate." *Harvard Educational Review* 80 (4): 464–490.

Haedicke, Michael A. 2016. *Organizing Organic: Conflict and Compromise in an Emerging Market.* Stanford: Stanford University Press.

Haedicke, Michael A., and Tim Hallett. 2015. "How to Look Two Ways at Once: Research Strategies for Inhabited Institutionalism." In *Handbook of Qualitative Organizational Research: Innovative Pathways and Methods*, edited by Kimberly D. Elsbach and Roderick M. Kramer, 99–111. New York: Routledge.

Halawah, Ibtesam. 2006. "The Impact of Student-Faculty Informal Interpersonal Relationships on Intellectual and Personal Development." *College Student Journal* 40 (3): 670–679.

Hallett, Tim. 2010. "The Myth Incarnate: Recoupling Processes, Turmoil, and Inhabited Institutions in an Urban Elementary School." *American Sociological Review* 75 (1): 52–74.

Hamilton, Darrick, Arthur H. Goldsmith, and William Darity Jr. 2009. "'Shedding Light on Marriage': The Influence of Skin Shade on Marriage for Black Females." *Journal of Economic Behavior & Organization* 72 (1): 30–50.

Hamilton, Laura. 2013. "More Is More or More Is Less? Parental Financial Investments during College." *American Sociological Review* 78 (1): 70–95.

———. 2016. *Parenting to a Degree: How Family Matters for College Women's Success.* Chicago: University of Chicago Press.

Hamilton, Laura, Josipa Roksa, and Kelly Nielsen. 2018. "Providing a 'Leg Up': Parental Involvement and Opportunity Hoarding in College." *Sociology of Education* 91 (2): 111–131.

Hand, Christie, and Emily Miller Payne. 2008. "First-Generation College Students: A Study of Appalachian Student Success." *Journal of Developmental Education* 32 (1): 4–6, 8, 10, 12, 14–15.

Hannon, Lance, Robert DeFina, and Sarah Bruch. 2013. "The Relationship between Skin Tone and School Suspension for African Americans." *Race and Social Problems* 5 (4): 281–295.

Harper, Casandra Elena. 2014. "Pre-College and College Predictors of Longitudinal Changes in Multiracial College Students' Self-Reported Race." *Race, Ethnicity and Education* 19 (5): 927–949.

Harper, Shaun R. 2013. "Am I My Brother's Teacher? Black Undergraduates, Racial Socialization, and Peer Pedagogies in Predominately White Postsecondary Contexts." *Review of Research in Education* 37: 183–211.

Harper, Shaun R., and Sylvia Hurtado. 2007. "Nine Themes in Campus Racial Climates and Implications for Institutional Transformation." *New Directions for Student Services* 120 (Winter): 7–24.

Harwood, Stacy A., Margaret Browne Huntt, Ruby Mendenhall, and Jioni A. Lewis. 2012. "Racial Microaggressions in the Residence Halls: Experiences of Students of Color at a Predominately White University." *Journal of Diversity in Higher Education* 5 (3): 159–173.

Hausmann, Leslie R., Janet Ward Schofield, and Rochelle L. Woods. 2007. "Sense of Belonging as a Predictor of Intentions to Persist among African American and White First-Year College Students." *Research in Higher Education* 48 (7): 803–839.

Havlik, Stacey, Nicole Pulliam, Krista Malott, and Sam Steen. 2020. "Strengths and Struggles: First-Generation College-Goers Persisting at One Predominantly White Institution." *Journal of College Student Retention: Research, Theory & Practice* 22 (1): 118–140.

Hawk, Thomas F., and Paul R. Lyons. 2008. "Please Don't Give up on Me: When Faculty Fail to Care." *Journal of Management Education* 32 (3): 316–338.

Haynes, Christina S. 2019. "There's No Place like Home? African American Women in the Residence Halls of a Predominately White Midwestern University." *Gender and Education* 31 (4): 525–542.

Hill, Jane H. 2008. *The Everyday Language of White Racism*. Malden, MA: Wiley-Blackwell.

Hoffman, Elin Meyers. 2014. "Faculty and Student Relationships: Context Matters." *College Teaching* 62 (1): 13–19.

Holland, Megan. 2018. *Divergent Paths to College: Race, Class and Inequality in High Schools*. New Brunswick, NJ: Rutgers University Press.

Horvat, Erin McNamara, and Anthony Lising Antonio. 1999. "'Hey, Those Shoes Are out of Uniform': African American Girls in an Elite High School and the Importance of Habitus." *Anthropology and Education* 30 (3): 317–342.

Houle, Jason N. 2014. "A Generation Indebted: Young Adult Debt across Three Cohorts." *Social Problems* 61 (3): 448–465.

Hunt, Judith. 2008. "Make Room for Daddy . . . and Mommy: Helicopter Parents are Here." *Journal of Academic Administration in Higher Education* 4 (1): 9–11.

Hunter, Margaret. 2005. *Race, Gender, and the Politics of Skin Tone*. New York: Routledge.

———. 2007. "The Persistent Problem of Colorism: Skin Tone, Status, and Inequality." *Sociology Compass* 1 (1): 237–254.

———. 2016. "Colorism in the Classroom: How Skin Tone Stratifies African American and Latina/o Students." *Theory into Practice* 55 (1): 54–61.

Hurtado, Sylvia, Adriana Ruiz Alvarado, and Chelsea Guillermo-Wann. 2015. "Creating Inclusive Environments: The Mediating Effect of Faculty and Staff Validation on the Relationship of Discrimination/Bias to Students' Sense of Belonging." *Journal Committed to Social Change on Race and Ethnicity* 1 (1): 60–80.

Hurtado, Sylvia, and Deborah Faye Carter. 1997. "Effects of College Transition and Perceptions of the Campus Racial Climate on Latino College Students' Sense of Belonging." *Sociology of Education* 70 (4): 324–345.

Ispa-Landa, Simone, and Jordan Conwell. 2015. "'Once You Got to a White School, You Kind of Adapt': Black Adolescents and the Racial Classification of Schools." *Sociology of Education* 88 (1): 1–19.

Jack, Anthony Abraham. 2016. "(No) Harm in Asking: Class, Acquired Cultural Capital, and Academic Engagement at an Elite University." *Sociology of Education* 89 (1): 1–19.

———. 2019. *The Privileged Poor: How Elite Colleges Are Failing Disadvantaged Students*. Cambridge, MA: Harvard University Press.

Jehangir, Rashné Rustom. 2010. *Higher Education and First-Generation Students: Cultivating Community, Voice, and Place for the New Majority*. New York: Palgrave Macmillan.

Johnson, Allan G. 2017. *Power, Privilege and Difference*. 3rd ed. Boston: McGraw-Hill Education.

Johnston, Marc P., C. Casey Ozaki, Jane Elizabeth Pizzolato, and Prema Chaudhari. 2014. "Which Box(es) Do I Check? Investigating College Students' Meanings behind Racial Identification." *Journal of Student Affairs Research and Practice* 51 (1): 56–68.

Johnston-Guerrero, Marc P. 2017. "The (Mis)Uses of Race in Research on College Students: A Systematic Review." *Journal Committed to Social Change on Race and Ethnicity* 3 (1): 6–41.

Johnston-Guerrero, Marc P., and Kristen A. Renn. 2016. "Multiracial Americans in College." In *Race Policy and Multiracial Americans*, edited by Kathleen Odell Korgen, 139–154. Bristol: Policy Press.

Jury, Mickaël, Cristina Aelenei, Chen Chen, Céline Darnon, and Andrew J. Elliot. 2019. "Examining the Role of Perceived Prestige in the Link between Students' Subjective Socioeconomic Status and Sense of Belonging." *Group Processes & Intergroup Relations* 22 (3): 356–370.

Katrevich, Alina V., and Mara S. Aruguete. 2017. "Recognizing Challenges and Predicting Success in First-Generation University Students." *Journal of STEM Education: Innovations & Research* 18 (2): 40–44.

Kerby, Molly B. 2015. "Toward a New Model of Student Retention in Higher Education: An Application of Classical Sociological Theory." *Journal of College Student Retention: Research, Theory & Practice* 17 (2): 138–161.

Khan, Shamus Rahman. 2010. *Privilege: The Making of an Adolescent Elite at St. Paul's School*. Princeton: Princeton University Press.

Kim, Young K., and Linda J. Sax. 2009. "Student–Faculty Interaction in Research Universities: Differences by Student Gender, Race, Social Class, and First-Generation Status." *Research in Higher Education* 50 (5): 437–459.

———. 2017. "The Impact of College Students' Interactions with Faculty: A Review of General and Conditional Effects." In *Higher Education: Handbook of Theory and Research*, edited by Michael B. Paulsen, 85–139. New York: Springer.

King, Colby R., Jakari Griffith, and Meghan Murphy. 2017. "Story Sharing for First-Generation College Students Attending a Regional Comprehensive University: Campus Outreach to Validate Students and Develop Forms of Capital." *Teacher-Scholar: The Journal of the State Comprehensive University* 8 (1): 3–23.

Kozol, Jonathan. 2005. *The Shame of the Nation: The Restoration of Apartheid Schooling in America*. New York: Crown Publishers.

Kuh, George D., Jillian Kinzie, John H. Schuh, Elizabeth J. Whitt, and Associates. 2010. *Student Success in College: Creating Conditions that Matter*. San Francisco: Jossey-Bass.

Langhout, Regina Day, Peter Drake, and Francine Rosselli. 2009. "Classism in the University Setting: Examining Student Antecedents and Outcomes." *Journal of Diversity in Higher Education* 2 (3): 166–181.

Lareau, Annette. 2003. *Unequal Childhoods: Class, Race, and Family Life*. Berkeley: University of California Press.

Lareau, Annette, and Kimberly Goyette, eds. 2014. *Choosing Homes, Choosing Schools*. New York: Russell Sage Foundation.

Leibel, Esther, Tim Hallett, and Beth A. Bechky. 2018. "Meaning at the Source: The Dynamics of Field Formation in Institutional Research." *Academy of Management* 121 (1): 154–177.

LeMoyne, Terri, and Tom Buchanan. 2011. "Does "Hovering" Matter? Helicopter Parenting and Its Effect on Well-Being." *Sociological Spectrum* 31 (4): 399–418.

Lerma, Veronica, Laura Hamilton, and Kelly Nielsen. 2019. "Racialized Equity Labor, University Appropriation and Student Resistance." *Social Problems*, 1–18. https://doi.org/10.1093/socpro/spz011.

Levett-Jones, Tracy, and Judith Lathlean. 2008. "Belongingness: A Prerequisite for Nursing Students' Clinical Learning." *Nurse Education in Practice* 8 (3): 103–111.

Lewis, Amanda E., and John B. Diamond. 2015. *Despite the Best Intentions: How Racial Inequality Thrives in Good Schools*. New York: Oxford University Press.

Lewis-McCoy, and R. L'Heureux. 2014. *Inequality in the Promised Land: Race, Resources, and Suburban Schooling*. Stanford: Stanford University Press.

Lipka, Sara. 2007. "Helicopter Parents Help Students, Survey Finds." *Chronicle of Higher Education* 54 (11): A1.

Lipson, Daniel M. 2007. "Embracing Diversity: The Institutionalization of Affirmative Action as Diversity Management at UC-Berkeley, UT-Austin, and UW-Madison." *Law and Social Inquiry* 32 (4): 985–1026.

Lowe, Katie, and Aryn M. Dotterer. 2018. "Parental Involvement during the College Transition: A Review and Suggestion for Its Conceptual Definition." *Adolescent Research Review* 3 (1): 29–42.

Lundberg, Carol A., Laurie A. Schreiner, Kristin Hovaguimian, and Sharyn Slavin Miller. 2007. "First-Generation Status and Student Race/Ethnicity as Distinct Predictors of Student Involvement and Learning." *Journal of Student Affairs Research and Practice* 44 (1): 57–83.

Maestas, Ricardo, Gloria S. Vaquera, and Linda Muños Zehr. 2007. "Factors Impacting Sense of Belonging at a Hispanic-Serving Institution." *Journal of Hispanic Higher Education* 6 (5): 237–256.

Malgwi, Charles A., Martha A. Howe, and Priscilla A. Burnaby. 2005. "Influences on Students' Choice of College Major." *Journal of Education for Business* 80 (5): 275–282.

Marine Nin, Orlantha F., and Rebecca Gutierrez Keeton. 2019. "Challenges and Realizations of First-Generation Students Who Navigated through Transfer Momentum Points." *Community College Journal of Research and Practice*. DOI: 10.1080/10668926.2019.1585303.

Marks, Stephen R. 1974. "Durkheim's Theory of Anomie." *American Journal of Sociology* 80 (2): 329–363.

Martin, Nathan D. 2012. "The Privilege of Ease: Social Class and Campus Life at Highly Selective, Private Universities." *Research in Higher Education* 53 (4): 426–452.

Martinez, Julia A., Kenneth J. Sher, Jennifer K. Krull, and Phillip K. Wood. 2009. "Blue-Collar Scholars? Mediators and Moderators of University Attrition in First-Generation College Students." *Journal of College Student Development* 50 (1): 87–103.

McCabe, Janice M. 2009. "Racial and Gender Microaggressions on a Predominately-White Campus: Experiences of Black, Latina/o and White Undergraduates." *Race, Gender & Class* 16 (1/2): 133–151.

———. 2016. *Connecting in College: How Friendship Networks Matter for Academic and Social Success*. Chicago: University of Chicago Press.

McCabe, Janice M., and Brandon A. Jackson. 2016. "Pathways to Financing College: Race and Class in Students' Narratives of Paying for School." *Social Currents* 3 (4): 367–385.

McCarron, Graziella Pagliarulo, and Karen Kurotsuchi Inkelas. 2006. "The Gap between Educational Aspirations and Attainment for First-Generation College Students and the Role of Parental Involvement." *Journal of College Student Development* 47 (5): 534–549.

McClure, Kevin, and Andrew J. Ryder. 2018. "The Costs of Belonging: How Spending Money Influences Social Relationships in College." *Journal of Student Affairs Research and Practice* 55 (2): 196–209.

McDermott, Monica, and Frank L. Samson. 2005. "White Racial and Ethnic Identity in the United States." *Annual Review of Sociology* 31: 245–261.

McDonough, Patricia M. 1997. *Choosing Colleges: How Social Class and Schools Structure Opportunity*. Albany: SUNY Press.

Means, Darris R., and Kimberly B. Pyne. 2017. "Finding My Way: Perceptions of Institutional Support and Belonging in Low-Income, First-Generation, First-Year College Students." *Journal of College Student Development* 58 (6): 907–924.

Mehta, Sanjay S., John J. Newbold, and Matthew A. O'Rourke. 2011. "Why Do First-Generation Students Fail?" *College Student Journal* 45 (1): 20–36.

Meyerhoff, Eli. 2019. *Beyond Education: Radical Studying for Another World*. Minneapolis: University of Minnesota Press.

Micari, Marina, and Pilar Pazos. 2012. "Connecting to the Professor: Impact of the Student–Faculty Relationship in a Highly Challenging Course." *College Teaching* 60 (2): 41–47.

Miller, Claire Cain, and Jonah Engel Bromwich. 2019. "How Parents Are Robbing Their Children of Adulthood: Today's 'Snowplow Parents' Keep Their Children's Futures Obstacle-free—Even When It Means Crossing Ethical and Legal Boundaries." *New York Times*, March 16.

Miller, Ryan A., Tonia Guida, Stella Smith, S. Kiersten Ferguson, and Elizabeth Medina. 2018. "Free Speech Tensions: Responding to Bias on College and University Campuses." *Journal of Student Affairs Research and Practice* 55 (1): 27–39.

Monk Jr., Ellis P. 2014. "Skin Tone Stratification among Black Americans, 2001–2003." *Social Forces* 92 (4): 1313–1337.

———. 2015. "The Cost of Color: Skin Color, Discrimination, and Health among African-Americans." *American Journal of Sociology* 121 (2): 396–444.

Monroe, Carla R., ed. 2017. *Race and Colorism in Education*. New York: Routledge.

Moore, Wendy Leo. 2008. *Reproducing Racism: White Space, Elite Law Schools, and Racial Equality*. Lanham, MD: Rowman & Littlefield.

Moore, Wendy Leo, and Joyce M. Bell. 2017. "The Right to be Racist in College: Racist Speech, White Institutional Space, and the First Amendment." *Law and Policy* 39 (2): 99–120.

Morales, Erik E. 2014. "Learning from Success: How Original Research on Academic Resilience Informs What College Faculty Can Do to Increase the Retention of Low Socioeconomic Status Students." *International Journal of Higher Education* 3 (3): 92–102.

Morrow, Jennifer Ann, and Margot E. Ackermann. 2012. "Intention to Persist and Retention of First-Year Students: The Importance of Motivation and Sense of Belonging." *College Student Journal* 46 (3): 483–491.

Moschetti, Roxanne Venus, and Cynthia Hudley. 2015. "Social Capital and Academic Motivation among First-Generation Community College Students." *Community College Journal of Research and Practice* 39 (3): 235–251.

Mullen, Ann. 2010. *Degrees of Inequality: Culture, Class, and Gender in American Higher Education*. Baltimore: Johns Hopkins University Press.

Museus, Samuel D. 2008. "The Role of Ethnic Student Organizations in Fostering African American and Asian American Students' Cultural Adjustment and Membership at Predominately White Institutions." *Journal of College Student Development* 49 (6): 568–586.

———. 2014. "The Culturally Engaging Campus Environments (CECE) Model: A New Theory of College Success among Racially Diverse Student Populations." In *Higher Education: Handbook of Theory and Research*, edited by Michael B. Paulsen, 189–227. New York: Springer.

Museus, Samuel D., Varaxy Yi, and Natasha Saelua. 2017. "The Impact of Culturally Engaging Campus Environments on Sense of Belonging." *Review of Higher Education* 40 (2): 187–215.

Nathan, Rebekah. 2005. *My Freshman Year: What a Professor Learned by Becoming a Student*. New York: Penguin Books.

Nguyen, Thai-Huy, and Bach Mai Dolly Nguyen. 2018. "Is the 'First-Generation Student' Term Useful for Understanding Inequality? The Role of Intersectionality in Illuminating the Implications of an Accepted—yet Unchallenged—Term." *Review of Research in Education* 42 (1): 146–176.

Noddings, Nel. 1984. *Caring: A Feminine Approach to Ethics and Moral Education*. Berkeley: University of California Press.

Nuñez, Anne-Marie. 2009. "Latino Students' Transitions to College: A Social and Intercultural Capital Perspective." *Harvard Educational Review* 79 (1): 22–48.

Nunn, Lisa M. 2014. *Defining Student Success: The Role of School and Culture*. New Brunswick, NJ: Rutgers University Press.

———. 2019a. *33 Simple Strategies for Faculty: A Week-by-Week Resource for Teaching First-Year or First-Generation Students*. New Brunswick, NJ: Rutgers University Press.

———. 2019b. "First-Generation College Students." In *Education and Society: An Introduction to Key Issues in the Sociology of Education*, edited by Thurston Domina, Benjamin G. Gibbs, Lisa Nunn, and Andrew Penner, 110–128. Berkeley: University of California Press.

Ochoa, Gilda L. 2013. *Academic Profiling: Latinos, Asian Americans, and the Achievement Gap.* Minneapolis: University of Minnesota Press.

Odenweller, Kelly G., Melanie Booth-Butterfield, and Keith Weber. 2014. "Investigating Helicopter Parenting, Family Environments, and Relational Outcomes for Millennials." *Communication Studies* 65 (4): 407–425.

O'Keeffe, Patrick. 2013. "A Sense of Belonging: Improving Student Retention." *College Student Journal* 47 (4): 605–613.

Oldfield, Kenneth. 2009. "Humble and Hopeful: Welcoming First-Generation Poor and Working-Class Students to College." In *The Invisibility Factor*, edited by Teresa Heinz Housel and Vickie L. Harvey, 59–73. Boca Raton, FL: BrownWalker Press.

Ostrove, Joan M., and Susan M. Long. 2007. "Social Class and Belonging: Implications for College Adjustment." *Review of Higher Education* 30 (4): 363–389.

Owens, Ann. 2017. "Income Segregation between School Districts and Inequality in Students' Achievement." *Sociology of Education* 91 (1): 1–27.

Ozaki, C. Casey, and Marc Johnston. 2008. "The Space in Between: Issues for Multiracial Student Organizations and Advising." In *Biracial and Multiracial Students: New Directions for Student Services*, edited by Kristen A. Renn and Paul Shang, 53–72. San Francisco: Jossey-Bass.

Padgett, Ryan D., Megan P. Johnson, and Ernest T. Pascarella. 2012. "First-Generation Undergraduate Students and the Impacts of the First Year of College: Additional Evidence." *Journal of College Student Development* 53 (2): 243–266.

Panzar, Javier. 2015. "It's Official: Latinos Now Outnumber Whites in California." *Los Angeles Times*, July 8.

Park, Julie J. 2013. *When Diversity Drops: Race, Religion, and Affirmative Action in Higher Education.* New Brunswick, NJ: Rutgers University Press.

Pascarella, Ernest T., and Patrick T. Terenzini. 2005. *How College Affects Students: A Third Decade of Research.* San Francisco: Jossey-Bass.

Pascarella, Ernest T., Patrick T. Terenzini, and Lee M. Wolfle. 1986. "Orientation to College and Freshman Year Persistence/Withdrawal Decisions." *Journal of Higher Education* 57 (2): 155–175.

Pittman, Laura D., and Adeya Richmond. 2008. "University Belonging, Friendship Quality, and Psychological Adjustment during the Transition to College." *Journal of Experimental Education* 76 (4): 343–361.

Pollock, Mica. 2004. *Colormute: Race Talk Dilemmas in an American High School.* Princeton: Princeton University Press.

Quadlin, Natasha. 2017. "Funding Sources, Family Income, and Fields of Study in College." *Social Forces* 96 (1): 91–120.

Quadlin, Natasha, and Daniel Rudel. 2015. "Responsibility or Liability? Student Loan Debt and Time Use in College." *Social Forces* 94 (2): 598–614.

Quaye, Stephen John, and Shaun R. Harper, eds. 2015. *Student Engagement in Higher Education: Theoretical and Practical Approaches for Diverse Populations.* 2nd ed. New York: Routledge.

Radford, Alexandria Walton. 2013. *Top Student, Top School? How Social Class Shapes Where Valedictorians Go to College.* Chicago: University of Chicago Press.

Rauscher, Emily. 2016. "Passing It On: Parent-to-Adult Child Financial Transfers for School and Socioeconomic Attainment." *Russell Sage Foundation Journal of the Social Sciences* 2 (6): 172–196.

Ray, Rashawn, and Jason A. Rosow. 2010. "Getting off and Getting Intimate: How Normative Institutional Arrangements Structure Black and White Fraternity Men's Approaches toward Women." *Men and Masculinities* 12 (5): 523–546.

———. 2012. "The Two Different Worlds of Black and White Fraternity Men: Visibility and Accountability as Mechanisms of Privilege." *Journal of Contemporary Ethnography* 41 (1): 66–94.

Ray, Victor. 2019. "A Theory of Racialized Organizations." *American Sociological Review* 84 (1): 26–54.

Rayle, Andrea Dixon, and Kuo-Yi Chung. 2007. "Revisiting First-Year College Students' Mattering: Social Support, Academic Stress, and the Mattering Experience." *Journal of College Student Retention: Research, Theory & Practice* 9 (1): 21–37.

Redford, Jeremy, and Kathleen Mulvaney Hoyer. 2017. *First-Generation and Continuing-Generation College Students: A Comparison of High School and Post-Secondary Experiences*. Washington, DC: National Center for Education Statistics, U.S. Department of Education.

Reed, Kayla, James M. Duncan, Mallory Lucier-Greer, Courtney Fixelle, and Anthony J. Ferraro. 2016. "Helicopter Parenting and Emerging Adult Self-Efficacy: Implications for Mental and Physical Health." *Journal of Child and Family Studies* 25 (10): 3136–3149.

Reid, M. Jeanne, and James L. Moore. 2008. "College Readiness and Academic Preparation for Postsecondary Education: Oral Histories of First-Generation Urban College Students." *Urban Education* 43 (2): 240–261.

Reyes, Daisy Verduzco. 2015. "Inhabiting Latino Politics: How Colleges Shape Students' Political Styles." *Sociology of Education* 88 (4): 302–319.

———. 2018. *Learning to Be Latino: How Colleges Shape Identity Politics*. New Brunswick, NJ: Rutgers University Press.

Roderick, Melissa, Vanessa Coca, and Jenny Nagaoka. 2011. "Potholes on the Road to College: High School Effects in Shaping Urban Students' Participation in College Application, Four-Year College Enrollment, and College Match." *Sociology of Education* 84 (3): 178–211.

Roksa, Josipa, and Peter Kinsley. 2019. "The Role of Family Support in Facilitating Academic Success of Low-Income Students." *Research in Higher Education* 60 (4): 415–436.

Rosenbaum, James E. 1976. *Making Inequality: The Hidden Curriculum of High School Tracking*. New York: Wiley.

Schlossberg, Nancy K. 1989. "Marginality and Mattering: Key Issues in Building Community." *New Directions for Student Services* 48 (Winter): 5–15.

Schreiner, Laurie A. 2018. "Thriving in the Second Year of College: Pathways to Success." *New Directions for Higher Education* 183 (Fall): 9–21.

Schreiner, Laurie A., and Barbara F. Tobolowsky. 2018. "The Role of Faculty in Sophomore Success." *New Directions for Higher Education* 183 (Fall): 59–70.

Schwartz, Sarah E. O., Stella S. Kanchewa, Jean E. Rhodes, Grace Gowdy, Abigail M. Stark, John Paul Horn, McKenna Parnes, and Renée Spencer. 2018. "'I'm Having a Little Struggle with This, Can You Help Me Out?' Examining Impacts and Processes of a Social Capital Intervention for First-Generation College Students." *American Journal of Community Psychology* 61 (1–2): 166–178.

Segrin, Chris, Alesia Woszidlo, Michelle Giverz, and Neil Montgomery. 2013. "Parent and Child Traits Associated with Overparenting." *Journal of Social and Clinical Psychology* 32 (6): 569–595.

Shook, Natalie J., and Russell H. Fazio. 2008. "Roommate Relationships: A Comparison of Interracial and Same-Race Living Situations." *Group Processes & Intergroup Relations* 11 (4): 425–437.

Silver, Blake R. 2020. *The Cost of Inclusion: How Student Conformity Leads to Inequality on College Campuses*. Chicago: University of Chicago Press.

Silver, Blake R., and Josipa Roksa. 2017. "Navigating Uncertainty and Responsibility: Understanding Inequality in the Senior-Year Transition." *Journal of Student Affairs Research and Practice* 54 (3): 248–260.

Smith, Buffy. 2013. *Mentoring At-Risk Students through the Hidden Curriculum of Higher Education*. Lanham, MD: Lexington Books.

Smith, Tovia. 2017. "As White Supremacists Push onto Campuses, Schools Wrestle with Response." *All Things Considered*, May 12.

Soria, Krista M., and Michael J. Stebleton. 2012. "First-Generation Students' Academic Engagement and Retention." *Teaching in Higher Education* 17 (6): 673–685.

———. 2013. "Social Capital, Academic Engagement, and Sense of Belonging among Working-Class College Students." *College Student Affairs* 31 (2): 139–153.

Spady, William G. 1970. "Dropouts from Higher Education: An Interdisciplinary Review and Synthesis." *Interchange* 1 (1): 64–85.

Stebleton, Michael J., Krista M. Soria, and Ronald L. Huesman Jr. 2014. "First-Generation Students' Sense of Belonging, Mental Health, and Use of Counseling Services at Public Research Universities." *Journal of College Counseling* 17 (1): 6–20.

Stevens, Mitchell L. 2009. *Creating a Class: College Admissions and the Education of Elites*. Cambridge, MA: Harvard University Press.

Strayhorn, Terrell L. 2008. "The Role of Supportive Relationships in Facilitating African American Males' Success in College." *NASPA Journal* 45 (1): 26–48.

———. 2012. *College Students' Sense of Belonging*. New York: Routledge.

Stuber, Jenny M. 2010. "Integrated, Marginal, and Resilient: Race, Class and the Diverse Experiences of White First-Generation College Students." *International Journal of Qualitative Studies in Education* 24 (1): 117–136.

———. 2011. *Inside the College Gates: How Class and Culture Matters*. Lanham, MD: Lexington Books.

———. 2015. "Pulled in or Pushed Out? How Organizational Factors Shape the Social and Extra Curricular Experiences of First-Generation Students." In *College Students' Experiences of Power and Marginality: Sharing Spaces and Negotiating Differences*, edited by Elizabeth M. Lee and Chaise LaDousa, 118–135. New York: Routledge.

Sue, Derald Wing. 2015. *Race Talk and the Conspiracy of Silence: Understanding and Facilitating Difficult Dialogues on Race*. Hoboken, NJ: John Wiley and Sons.

Tatum, Beverly Daniel. 1997. *"Why Are All the Black Kids Sitting Together in the Cafeteria?" and Other Conversations about Race*. New York: Basic Books.

Thaler, Richard H., and Cass R. Sunstein. 2008. *Nudge: Improving Decisions about Health, Wealth and Happiness*. New York: Penguin Books.

Thiele, Megan. 2015. "Resource or Obstacle? Classed Reports of Student-Faculty Relations." *Sociological Quarterly* 57 (2): 333–355.

Thiele, Megan, and Karen Jeong Robinson. 2019. "Within Elite Academic Walls: Inequity and Student Experience on Campus." In *Education and Society: An*

Introduction to Key Issues in the Sociology of Education, edited by Thurston Domina, Benjamin G. Gibbs, Lisa Nunn, and Andrew Penner, 222–236. Oakland: University of California Press.

Thomas, James M. 2018. "Diversity Regimes and Racial Inequality: A Case Study of Diversity University." *Social Currents* 5 (2): 140–156.

Tinto, Vincent. 1975. "Dropout from Higher Education: A Theoretical Synthesis of Recent Research." *Review of Educational Research* 45 (1): 89–125.

———. 1993. *Leaving College: Rethinking the Causes and Cures of Student Attrition.* 2nd ed. Chicago: University of Chicago Press.

———. 1997. "Classrooms as Communities: Exploring the Educational Character of Student Persistence." *Journal of Higher Education* 68 (6): 599–623.

———. 2012. *Completing College: Rethinking Institutional Action.* Chicago: University of Chicago Press.

———. 2017. "Through the Eyes of Students." *Journal of College Student Retention: Research, Theory & Practice* 19, (3): 254–269.

Toutkoushian, Robert K., Jennifer A. May-Trifiletti, and Ashley B. Clayton. 2019. "From 'First in Family' to 'First to Finish': Does College Graduation Vary by How First-Generation College Status Is Defined?" *Educational Policy.* doi.org/10.1177 /0895904818823753.

Vaccaro, Annemarie, and Barbara Newman. 2016. "Development of Sense of Belonging for Privileged and Minoritized Students: An Emergent Model." *Journal of College Student Development* 57 (8): 925–942.

Valenzuela, Anglea. 1999. *Subtractive Schooling: U.S.-Mexican Youth and the Politics of Caring.* Albany: SUNY Press.

Van Ryzin, Mark J., Amy A. Gravely, and Cary J. Roseth. 2009. "Autonomy, Belongingness and Engagement in School as Contributors to Adolescent Psychological Well-Being." *Journal of Youth and Adolescence* 38 (1): 1–12.

Vargas, Nicole. 2015. "Latina/o Whitening? Which Latina/os Self-Classify as White and Report Being Perceived as White by Other Americans?" *Du Bois Review: Social Science Research on Race* 12 (1): 119–136.

Vetter, Matthew, Laurie Schreiner, and Brian Jaworski. 2019. "Faculty Attitudes and Behaviors that Contribute to Thriving in First-Year Students of Color." *Journal of the First Year Experience and Students in Transition* 31 (1): 9–28.

Villalpando, Octavio. 2003. "Self-Segregation of Self-Preservation? A Critical Race Theory and Latina/o Critical Theory Analysis of a Study of Chicano/a College Students." *International Journal of Qualitative Studies in Education* 16 (5): 619–646.

Walker, Jay K., Nathan D. Martin, and Andrew Hussey. 2015. "Greek Organization Membership and Collegiate Outcomes at an Elite, Private University." *Research in Higher Education* 56 (3): 203–227.

Walton, Gregory M., and Geoffrey L. Cohen. 2011. "A Brief Social-Belonging Intervention Improves Academic and Health Outcomes of Minority Students." *Science* 331: 1447–1451.

Ward, Lee, Michael J. Siegel, and Zebulun Davenport. 2012. *First Generation College Students: Understanding and Improving the Experience from Recruitment to Commencement.* San Francisco: Jossey Bass.

Warikoo, Natasha K. 2016. *The Diversity Bargain: And Other Dilemmas of Race, Admissions, and Meritocracy at Elite Universities.* Chicago: University of Chicago Press.

Weis, Lois, Cameron McCarthy, and Greg Dimitriadis, eds. 2006. *Ideology, Curriculum, and the New Sociology of Education: Revisiting the Work of Michael Apple.* New York Routledge.

Wildhagen, Tina. 2015. "'Not Your Typical Student': The Social Construction of the 'First-Generation College Student.'" *Qualitative Sociology* 38 (3): 285–303.

Wise, Tim. 2011. *White like Me: Reflections on Race from a Privileged Son.* 3rd ed. Berkeley: Soft Skull Press.

Yee, April. 2016. "The Unwritten Rules of Student Engagement: Social Class Differences in Undergraduates' Academic Strategies." *Journal of Higher Education* 87 (6): 831–858.

Yee, Elizabeth. 2016. *Class and Campus Life: Managing and Experiencing Inequality at an Elite College.* Ithaca: Cornell University Press.

Yosso, Tara, William Smith, Miguel Ceja, and Daniel Solorzano. 2009. "Critical Race Theory, Racial Microaggressions, and Campus Racial Climate for Latina/o Undergraduates." *Harvard Educational Review* 79 (4): 659–691.

Zumbrunn, Sharon, Courtney McKim, Eric Buhs, and Leslie R. Hawley. 2014. "Support, Belonging, Motivation, and Engagement in the College Classroom: A Mixed Method Study." *Instructional Science* 42 (5): 661–684.

Index

nice, 141; as safe spaces, 11, 125–126, 163; social belonging in, 125; students running, 125–126; White students protesting, 126–128, 132

Inhabited Institutionalism theory, 64–65

Inside the College Gates (Stuber), 167

institutions, 8–9; diversity claims by, 115–116; normative institutional arrangements in, 51; as PWI, 10, 115, 122, 129, 164; students not supported by, 117–118; welcome lack by, 113–114; for White students, 117, 119. *See also* universities

integration: desire for ethnoracial, 131, 148–149, 151, 157, 163; Durkheim on, 6–9, 14, 33, 171–173; scholarship on belonging and, 2

Jack, Anthony, 3, 80–81

Johnston-Guerrero, Marc, 143, 184n2

K-12 schools: academic belonging influenced by, 74–77; of affluent students, 48, 87; of first-generation students, 52–53, 81, 165

Latinx students, 68, 125; belonging interviews of, 161–162; campus-community belonging undermined for, 157; colorism on, 123–124; as ethnicity or race, 184n1; mentors and, 54, 101; niceness required of, 150–151; for not-nice diversity, 14, 155–156; otherness and, 36; Private percentages of, 114–115; Public University and, 114–115, 118–119; on service workers, 121; students on being, 154; universities alienating, 117; visibility of, 118

Lowe, Katie, 91

low-income students: on favors, 80; as first-generation students, 74; high school and cultural capital for, 80–81; joining and belonging for, 32–33; K-12 schools of, 52, 74, 165, 175; otherness, outsiders for, 36; on professor interactions, 81; TRIO SSS for, 52–53, 175–176. *See also* finances; financial aid

majors: academic belonging and, 55–56, 68–71, 166–167; academics required by, 69–70; changing challenges on, 55–56, 71, 166; college debt influencing, 87; as competitive, 69–70, 72–73; as declared, 68–69; for Public first-year students, 50–51; Public University with impacted, 55, 70–71, 107–108, 162; rejection on, 55–56, 71

Maslow, Abraham, 3–4

mattering, 3

McCabe, Janice, 125

mentorships, 11, 40, 54, 73–74, 101, 104, 167–168

methodology, 4; analysis in, 179–180; on belonging, 179; belonging categorization in, 184n2; coding in, 72; ethnoracial majority vs. minority in, 177–178; first-generation college students in, 175; first-year students and study, 183n4; generational status in, 5; of interviews, 178–179; participants with pseudonyms, 183n1, 183n3; samples in, 176–178; statistics in, 184n1

minority faculty and staff, 120–121

minority students: belonging and, 147, 158, 183n2; as huddling off, 129, 131–132, 150, 163; mentors for, 11, 40, 54, 73–74, 101, 104, 167–168; for not-so-nice diversity, 14, 155–156; race tensions for, 126, 129, 132, 136–137, 152; on respect and safety, 1–2, 109, 113, 132, 183n2; as self-segregating, 14, 129–132; student belonging as, 144; universities and problems for, 65; universities and tastes by, 160; visibility, 117–119, 124–125, 153, 160–161

Moore, Wendy, 119–120, 127–129, 152

multiracial students, 141–143, 184n2; for not-nice diversity, 14, 155–156; White* students as, 142–144; White* students vs., 146. *See also* ethnoracial identity

Museus, Samuel, 161

Newman, Barbara, 2, 183n2

niceness: Black students for not-nice diversity in, 155–156; blending for, 151; campus-community belonging and, 157;

About the Author

LISA M. NUNN is a professor of sociology and director for the Center for Educational Excellence at University of San Diego. She is the author of *Defining Student Success: The Role of School and Culture* and *33 Simple Strategies for Faculty: A Week-by-Week Resource for Teaching First-Year and First-Generation Students.*

Printed in the United States
By Bookmasters